A STOUT PAIR OF BOOTS

I0879348

A STOUT PAIR OF BOOTS

A guide to exploring Australia's battlefields

PETER STANLEY

ALLEN&UNWIN

First published in 2008

Copyright © Peter Stanley 2008

All rights reserved. No part of this book may be reproduced or transmitted in any form or by any means, electronic or mechanical, including photocopying, recording or by any information storage and retrieval system, without prior permission in writing from the publisher. The *Australian Copyright Act* 1968 (the Act) allows a maximum of one chapter or 10 per cent of this book, whichever is the greater, to be photocopied by any educational institution for its educational purposes provided that the educational institution (or body that administers it) has given a remuneration notice to Copyright Agency Limited (CAL) under the Act.

Allen & Unwin
83 Alexander Street
Crows Nest NSW 2065
Australia
Phone: (61 2) 8425 0100
Fax: (61 2) 9906 2218
Email: info@allenandunwin.com
Web: www.allenandunwin.com

National Library of Australia
Cataloguing-in-Publication entry:

Stanley, Peter, 1956-
A stout pair of boots : a guide to exploring Australia's battlefields

Bibliography.
Includes index.
ISBN 9781741756654 (pbk.)

Battlefields--Guidebooks.
Historic sites--Guidebooks.
Australia--History, Military.
Australia--Armed Forces--History.

910.202

Set in 11/14.05 pt Garamond 3 by Bookhouse, Sydney

10 9 8 7 6 5 4 3 2 1

In memory of those in whose footsteps we walk, and with thanks to my friends and colleagues in the Australian Army History Unit, who have allowed me to do so

Contents

Foreword

In November 1974 I set off to pre-independence Papua New Guinea to undertake research for what became my first book, *Crisis of Command*. Earlier that year I had dragged my long-suffering wife to US Civil War battlefields, and in 1971 I had patrolled with chilling fascination through the Long Tan plantation in Viet Nam, but this was my first proper battlefield research.

As I was then a serving Army captain I was sponsored by the Australian Army, and while visiting Kokoda and the sites of the Buna–Gona battles on the north coast of Papua I lived with the Army survey unit at Popondetta. On my last day there, in an Army Land Rover, with driver, I arrived at the Duropa coconut plantation, where the 18th Australian Brigade, gallantly support by Australian-manned Stuart tanks, assaulted the Japanese in December 1942. Watched at a distance by surly Papuans, I leapt from my vehicle, dressed in my green Army uniform, map in one hand, notebook in the other, and began pacing around in the plantation.

Later that day I flew to Lae to continue my research. There, in the following morning's newspaper, I read about the outcome of my visit. The Papua Basena Movement, headed by a charismatic

Papuan politician, Josephine Abaijah, was seeking an independent Papua. The Duropa plantation was being run by Papuan squatters, as its Australian expatriate owner was ill and could not manage his property. Nonetheless, the owner had warned the squatters, who supported Papua Basena, that if they did not leave he would send in the Army. Then, so the story went, an Australian Army officer had recently arrived to carry out a reconnaissance for this assault. In the face of this provocation, a group of north coast Papuans had decided to take up arms, and they were marching over the Kokoda Trail to force the issue in Port Moresby. Fortunately wiser heads prevailed and they later gave up their mission.

Had I read Peter Stanley's book I might have been more ready to try to explain my mission to the squatters, notwithstanding the language difficulties. Perhaps I might also have sought a better understanding of the cultural and political environment in which I was operating. The book has, however, caused me reflect on the fact that visiting battlefields or key historical sites has been integral to my work. On a later visit to Papua New Guinea, with students from the Joint Service Staff College, I was able to bring out some important lessons of joint operations by visiting Wau, Finschhafen, Wewak, Manus Island and Rabaul. In my own research, I have commented many times that going to battlefields always gives you a new perspective—they are never quite what you imagined them to be. For my recent project, my interviews with participants in peacekeeping operations have proved to be immeasurably more productive when it becomes clear to them that I have visited the places they are talking about.

This book will be immensely valuable to both longstanding battlefield trekkers, and new researchers. But readers should be warned. Battlefield research can be addictive. Only this year my wife and I flew by light plane from Saipan to Tinian to see the installations where the atomic bombs were loaded, and the remains of the vast airfields from which the B-29 Superfortresses took off to bomb Japan. A few days later, having looked at Iwo Jima and Okinawa on the way, we were in Nagasaki to gain an understanding of what one of the bombs had done.

I hope that this book contributes to greater professionalism in the study of Australian military history, whether by academic professionals or enthusiastic amateurs. I also hope that it will lead to a deeper appreciation of Australian military history, for this book is not just for researchers. Anyone even vaguely interested in Australian military history who is contemplating an overseas holiday might profit by factoring in a visit to one of Australia's overseas battlefields. I guarantee that they will come away much wiser.

David Horner
Professor of Australian Defence History
Australian National University

Acknowledgements

Many people—too many to list individually and equitably—have walked battlefields with me. They include family, friends, colleagues, customers and helpers of various kinds. All of them have contributed to the knowledge and experience on which this book is based, and I am grateful to them individually and collectively.

Several of these trips were funded in whole or in part and made possible by the Army History Unit, headed by the energetic, effective and imaginative Roger Lee, whose research, conference and publication programs have done so much for the study of Australian military history.

I particularly appreciate Prof. David Horner's willingness to contribute a foreword, drawing upon his extensive experience of battlefield visits. I have a great admiration for David's knowledge, insight and productivity as a military historian, and especially his contribution to fostering the study of Australia's military history through his association with the Army History Unit.

For this book, I'm grateful to many friends and colleagues who generously shared their memories, ideas and reflections. They include Jean Bou, Phil Bradley, Jo and Ian Brennan, Harvey

Broadbent, Baz Clark and Claire Hoey (Manning Clark House), David Carment, Anne-Marie Condé, Graeme Davison, Craig Deayton, Peter Dowling, Brian Farrell, Andrew Faulkner, Jeff Grey, Margaret Hadfield, Ros Hearder, Tom Heath, Matthew Higgins, David Horner, Mark Johnston, Martin Kerby, Terence King, Peter Londey, Brad Manera, Michael McKernan, Mat McLachlan, Ross McMullin, Michael Molkentin, Robert Nichols, Melanie Oppenheimer, George Parsons, Rob Pascoe, Peter Pedersen, Garth Pratten, Richard Reid, Bruce Scates, Christina Spittell, Nigel Steel, Libby Stewart, Craig Tibbitts and Craig Wilcox. Many read drafts of the manuscript and made extensive comments, corrections, suggestions and contributions. I am responsible for the errors that remain.

I am grateful to Mal Booth of the Australian War Memorial and Anne-Marie Schwirtlich of the State Library of Victoria for granting me permission to use images from their collections.

I would welcome comments and reports or accounts of other battlefield researchers' methods, projects or experiences. Please feel free to contact me c/o p.stanley@nma.gov.au.

I am grateful once again to Ian Bowring of Allen & Unwin for backing an idea and to John Mapps and Angela Handley for their help in editing and producing this book. I thank Claire, Claire and Jane for tolerating me disappearing both to the Somme and to the study yet again.

INTRODUCTION

'Sniffing the ground'

I've stood on Baby 700 and watched the sun rise over the Dardanelles and tried to work out where the lost parties of Australians disappeared in the hours following the landing at Anzac. On the Borneo island of Tarakan I've pushed my way through the jungle on top of a hill that I think was the same one that the Australians of Oboe One force called 'Freda', listening to the roar of the insects of the rainforest, and tried to understand how they could possibly have worked out where their enemy was. At El Alamein I've stood in the Egyptian sun with a friend and colleague on Tel el Eisa, and worked out exactly where the Panzers came towards the 2/48th Battalion on the morning of 10 July 1942. I've strolled in the gentle French sunshine to find the spot where three Victorians died on Mont St Quentin on an afternoon in 1918. And in each case I then went off and wrote a book.

I've been lucky enough to have these experiences because for nearly 30 years I've been trying to understand and explain that bit of the human experience of the past we call 'Australian military history'. So as well as keeping up with what other people have said about war, reading documents in archives and listening to people who've experienced it, I've visited many of the places where battles occurred and looked and thought about what happened there.

Visiting places like Gallipoli, Tarakan, Alamein and Mont St Quentin, among others, has given me some of the most exciting times a military historian can have, some of the most satisfying experiences in writing history and some sobering moments of sadness and poignancy. I was fortunate to be able to do this because I made the most of the opportunities that came to me, partly because of the job I did in the service of the Australian War Memorial, Australia's national military museum and a centre of research in Australian military history. I wasn't able to visit all of the places I would have liked to. I didn't get to Beersheba or Damascus, I wasn't brave enough to visit Papua New Guinea, and I wasn't interested enough to go to Korea or Viet Nam. But I did visit a lot of battlefields—well-known places like Pozières, Crete and Balikpapan, and obscure places like Miřetín and Pinjarra. I also sought out non-Australian battlefields, in India, the United States, Britain and Europe—Gwalior, the Mule Shoe, Culloden and Waterloo.

The sorts of battlefield research I did, you could do as well. The sorts of things I learned from visiting battlefields you could too. This book offers a guide. Its title comes from a well-known (but much misquoted) remark by the British historian (and Somme veteran) Richard Tawney, who said that historians needed not more documents but 'a stout pair of boots'. It's always bemused me that as an economic historian Tawney was hardly known for his field work, and doesn't seem to have published anything that depended on investigating an event on the site (and tracking down an exact source for this seemingly apocryphal quotation took me hours by itself). Still, his advice has been a beacon for a certain sort of historian ever since. Many Australian historians—including Manning Clark, Russel Ward and Keith

Hancock—have echoed Tawney's admonition; this book represents merely its latest outing.

Military historians aren't the only people to have taken an interest in field work. But while historians of industry have also donned their stout boots (and while archaeologists have picked up trowels and toothbrushes too), among the most determined followers of Tawney's dictum have been military historians.

I once wrote an article about my explorations of the battlefields of Borneo (including the Sandakan death march route). In it I recalled how my first boss at the Memorial had been very sceptical of the value of visiting battlefields. A few weeks after he arrived, in about mid-1980, we were discussing which applications for support we should recommend under the Australian War Memorial's late and very much lamented Research Grants Scheme—perhaps the single most important element in priming what became the boom in military history in this country. We had an application from Peter Pedersen, then a captain in the Royal Australian Regiment but also one of the handful of able historians the Army produced in the 1980s. He wanted to visit the battlefields of Gallipoli and the Western Front to help him understand John Monash as a military commander—the title of what became his PhD and a book. I had recommended that we give him a grant. My boss seemed unconvinced. 'What's he going to do', he demanded, 'sniff the ground?' But he must have relented because we gave Peter a grant, and 30 years on I now know what I only suspected then: just how valuable it can be to sniff the ground. This book explains why, and how you can too.

'There are few things more interesting than a visit to an old battlefield...'

—British antiquarian William Howitt, in his *Visits to Remarkable Places*, reflecting on a visit to Culloden, exactly 90 years after the battle, in 1836

PART 1

Battle plan: Why battlefield research?

Anzac Day banners

In his book *What is History?*, a text familiar to most students of history, the British historian Edward Carr famously advised his students to 'first study the historian'. For me, that study needs to go back to Anzac Day in the late 1960s. Recent migrants to Australia, living in a booming new provincial city (Whyalla, in South Australia), my family felt no need to attend the Anzac Day march that belonged to 'old' Australians in the established part of our city. But we did watch the ABC broadcast of the Adelaide march on television. I can remember my curiosity when seeing the last Boer War veteran in the march, and the taxis carrying the few frail Great War men, just as they now carry Second World War men. And I can remember the banners.

I remember feeling a thrill at the banners carried by Anzac Day marchers. They bore not only the names of units and associations, ships and squadrons; they proclaimed the campaigns, battles and theatres in which the marchers had served. It was from them that I first learned names such as Bardia, Tobruk, Crete, Milne Bay, Shaggy Ridge, Balikpapan and Tarakan. Even now, when I've seen dozens of marches and have had the honour of commentating on ABC broadcasts of marches in Sydney and Canberra, I never fail to feel a quiver at those names and what they mean. Many of them are the names of otherwise unknown hills, villages and other features, places that would have remained obscure except that a couple of dozen or a few hundred Australians fought Turks, Germans, Japanese or some other enemy there, usually a long time ago. Some of them are now the location of cemeteries in which the bodies of Australians lie; others have fallen back into obscurity, except that they live on in our imaginations. That sense of wonder at the places named on Anzac Day banners is no less now that I know a bit about what happened in these places, and have visited many of them.

Anzac Day banners: the banner carried by the Royal Australian Corps of Signals Association, Canberra, Anzac Day 2008, showing the names of battles and campaigns that stimulate the imagination and curiosity of the battlefield researcher. (Claire Cruickshank)

That's where this book begins: with an invitation to consider understanding those places, their history and what they mean by visiting them not as trippers or passive tourists, but as active, enquiring battlefield researchers.

Australia's overseas battles have usually happened in really interesting places: France, Greece, Egypt, Borneo—places you'd want to go to anyway, for the food and wine, for ancient cultures or fascinating (if threatened) environments. But for Australians these places have more than just a cultural or ecological attraction. They are places where thousands of Australians have served and died over the past century. Many families (though no longer perhaps most) have some connection to a member of one or another of the Australian Imperial Forces in the world wars. Despite the passage of decades since more than a few hundred Australians served overseas in any one place at war, and despite great changes in Australian society (and several deeply unpopular conflicts) many Australians retain a deep and abiding interest in their nation's military history. As the turn-out on Anzac Day suggests, many families cherish those long-standing connections, even if they don't know very much to substantiate them.

Indeed, for all of this strong personal or family connection, until quite recently Australians generally did not take an active interest in their military past. On Anzac Day they acknowledged those who used to be called 'returned servicemen' (now we have adopted the American 'veteran'). Families tolerated the reminiscences of Great War and Second World War men, and were vaguely familiar with names like 'Armentières' or 'Madang', even if they weren't quite sure what happened there, or even where they were. But until about 1980, military history was very much an arcane minority interest, and it happened in places that no one expected to want to go to.

That has all changed. Two striking phenomena have occurred over the past couple of decades. One is that Australians have begun to read more about their military history—the boom in military publishing that began just about when I began work as a military historian shows no sign of ending. The other, more recent, phenomenon is that Australians seem to be increasingly willing to travel to the places where much of their nation's military history happened, particularly the battlefields of Gallipoli, the Western Front in France and Belgium, and lately the Kokoda Trail (or Track: either is correct). Sadly, other Australian battlefields, in Korea, the Middle East, Papua New Guinea and Singapore, are as neglected as ever. While some of these visitors are backpackers, most are not: they represent a cross-section of the nation—the bit identifying with old Anglo-Celtic Australia anyway. They are for the most part ordinary working Australians, with a natural bias towards the older and wealthier—people with income and leisure to at last travel to see the places where Great Uncle Jim served or died. This change in Australia's attitude to its war history is welcome, provided it results in a more knowledgeable and mature attitude towards our military past (and not simply nationalistic barracking). It deserves to be encouraged, and this book tries to do just that by providing a how-to-and-where guide to Australia's battlefields.

This book, then, is intended to provide a guide to those who might like to visit an Australian battlefield purposefully, or who might never have thought of doing so but might respond to encouragement. It is aimed not at professional military historians (who to be honest don't need any urging to get their boots dirty) but at those who share a genuine curiosity about Australia's rich, varied and too often tragic military past, and who want to go and see what it looks like.

Call to imagination: A short history of Australian battlefield visits

Today we take it for granted that you can't write about battles convincingly without visiting the places in which they happened, but in the past, when overseas travel was expensive and unusual, it was common to read books about battles based on nothing but paper sources. Then in the 1970s Australians began to travel overseas in large numbers. John Richardson, in his *History of Australian Travel and Tourism*, provides startling figures on the affordability of overseas travel. In 1945 the cheapest Sydney–London airfare cost the equivalent of 130 weeks of the average wage; in 1965 it cost 21 weeks, and by 1995 just 3.5 weeks. The year 1950 saw about 25 million international tourists in motion annually; this year the figure will probably be over 750 million. A small but growing number of these travellers were seeking out battlefields.

Australians have been visiting battlefields for just over a century. My colleague Craig Wilcox generously lent me his notes on battlefield visits by Australians in the decades before the Great War. They suggest that just as the armed struggle for their own continent was ending, with its occupation and settlement, Australians began travelling to Europe to visit the scene of the battle that ended the dream (or spectre) of a French domination of Europe. They wanted to see the field of Waterloo, the great victory that gave Britain its standing as the superpower of the nineteenth century. Colonial Australians developed a taste for battlefield visits if they were able to do so, and especially to Waterloo. Even if Wellington had beaten Napoleon only with the help of Blücher's Prussians, nineteenth-century Britons (as the Australian colonists considered themselves) saw Waterloo as the battle that had made Britain Great.

The charismatic Henry Parkes, for instance, when not advocating democracy and federation, revelled in his visit to Waterloo, in 1882. Like thousands of British travellers before him, Parkes looked over the museum established by Sergeant Major Edward Cotton, a British hussar who practically invented the idea of the battlefield tour franchise, and then gathered flowers from a field 'richly fertilised by heroic blood'. With renewed interest he turned eagerly to the poems he knew describing the great battle, having seen the site for himself. We still do exactly that today, at Fromelles or Hamel.

After Parkes a Tasmanian clergyman teaching in Britain took his family off to Brussels for a couple of winters. Edwin Bean saw the battlefield with a military historian's eye. He climbed the Lion mound—a vast conical hill topped with a monument that disfigures the battlefield—to take it in from the air, so to speak. Then he walked the field, noticing a stable 'that had evidently been used in the struggle' (the imaginative eye is an essential item in the day-pack). While exploring the roads in the rear of the French position, the Rev. Bean noticed that they were 'deeply sunken'. This, he thought 'must have made the retreat of the Young Guard a fearful havoc'. He would pass on his eye for ground and ability to craft a battle narrative to his son.

Young Charlie Bean was about nine during these visits. He remembered that his father had been 'intensely interested' in Waterloo—a passion for understanding is another item to pack with the digital camera and compass. He and his brother Jack

The author perpetuates an Australian tradition by visiting the Waterloo battlefield in Belgium. (Claire Cruikshank)

(who served as a regimental medical officer in the AIF) went with their father and caught the infection from him. In the Hotel du Musée, Sergeant Major Cotton's old establishment, they spent hours studying what Bean described as 'relics' from the battlefield. Bean recalled glass cases containing 'shakos or helmets and tunics of the Old Guard or the British infantry, some with the marks of battle on them', as well as skulls disfigured by shot holes and sabre-chips. Twenty-five years later, Charlie and Jack were on Gallipoli. When the historian saw Australians sending home souvenirs of the campaign, he assumed that 'there would almost certainly be some museum in Australia in which war relics would be presented'. Of course they still are, not just in the memorial-museum Bean founded, but in dozens of local and regional collections in the towns and cities the first Anzacs came from.

One of the most influential Australians in the decade before the Great War was William Fitchett, a Melbourne literary entrepreneur. Fitchett wrote a series of books, notably *Deeds that Won the Empire*, which expressed and conveyed the values of duty, loyalty and valour that seem to have done so much to inspire the young men who served on Gallipoli and in the trenches of Flanders and Picardy. In 1911 Fitchett also visited Waterloo. Like many before and since—including myself—he stood where Wellington had been, trying to 'call to imagination the stages of the great fight as he saw it'. Fitchett made the observation that first strikes many visitors to Waterloo today, that 'the ground . . . seems to the modern observer absurdly contracted'. Can a couple of hundred thousand men and horses have fought for a torrid afternoon on this tiny field—little bigger than the area of the Parliamentary Triangle in Canberra? And how could 40,000 bodies have littered it at dusk?

All of these visitors—Henry Parkes, Edwin Bean and his boys, and William Fitchett—were seeing Waterloo in person; they were not just reading about it. So there seems to be a tradition in Australia of visiting battlefields. But it has had a tenuous life.

Besides occasional 'pilgrimages' by returned men and women, and later their families—which are a different sort of battlefield visit—few Australians sought out battlefields between Bean's return from Gallipoli in 1919 and about 1980.

Students of war have visited battlefields for a hundred years or more. Military academies invented the idea of the 'staff ride' as a way of training future commanders when battles were directed from horseback. Officers would ride around the Shenandoah Valley of Virginia or the battlefields of eastern France, looking at where Stonewall Jackson beat the Yankees or where Moltke the Elder beat the French, and ask why and how. They knew that thinking of battles on the spot—preferably in a knowledgeable group prepared to debate and argue about them—was more informative than just reading.

American Air Force officers continue the tradition of the 'staff ride' at Little Round Top, on the battlefield of Gettysburg, Pennsylvania—even if today they get around on big, noisy tour buses. (Peter Stanley)

But it's not just soldiers who can learn from visiting battlefields. A great deal can be learned about the human experience of war by going to the places where it happened. And Australians never quite stopped visiting battlefields. Occasional articles in ex-service magazines and books aroused momentary curiosity, and books like John Laffin's accounts of his visits to Papua New Guinea and the Mediterranean battlefields in the 1950s suggest that the tradition never quite died out. A few dedicated individuals seriously investigated battlefields, such as Major Andrew Balsillie, an Australian serving in Malaysia. While his field work turned up relics (such as the 'Singapore surrender table' which the Australian government obtained for the Australian War Memorial), Balsillie unfortunately published nothing of any magnitude. But Robert O'Neill, the most distinguished scholarly soldier Australia has yet produced (after serving in Viet Nam he became a military historian and strategic analyst of international repute), visited Gallipoli and advised Peter Pedersen on his pioneering visit in 1981.

Not that only military historians feel the need to sniff the ground. Manning Clark's reflections on his career are littered with accounts of visiting evocative, symbolic or actual sites. While writing his epic *History of Australia* he visited Shark Bay (to reflect on what early Dutch explorers saw and felt), Norfolk Island (to understand its penal past), Maiden's Hotel, Menindee, and Cooper's Creek (in search of Burke and Wills), the Barcoo and Barcaldine (to do justice to the birth of the Labor Party), and many places overseas, including the Seamen's Chapel at New Bedford, Massachusetts, to ponder the work of Herman Melville and the place of good and evil in human affairs. On his trips he carried pocket notebooks so he was always able to record an observation or an idea. In his Boyer Lectures, *A Discovery of Australia*, Clark reaffirmed his belief in the worth of the historian donning boots: 'a historian must also go to the place where the events he is describing took place'.

The modern interest in Australian military history owes a great deal to Ken Inglis, who as a young lecturer in history in Adelaide in 1965 travelled to Gallipoli with a group of returned men and wrote articles about what he had witnessed. While he did not write about the detail of the actions the old men recalled (though he did effectively invent the field of memory studies), his articles showed how valuable it was for historians to pay attention to what were soon being called 'veterans'. Soon after, a young protégé of Inglis's at the Australian National University, Bill Gammage, wrote a doctoral thesis (published in 1974 as *The Broken Years*). Following the advice of Tawney (and Manning Clark), Gammage had based his work not only on the documents but also got his boots dirty visiting the Gallipoli and Western Front battlefields in 1970, where he checked that he had the details correct. Soon after *The Broken Years* appeared, Patsy Adam-Smith published the fruits of her work as a manuscripts field officer at the State Library of Victoria, *The Anzacs* of 1978, and she travelled to the battlefields too. By 1980 both scholarly and popular interest in military history had visibly quickened. The trickle of Australians visiting battlefields had never quite dried up, but in the 1980s it was to become a perennial flow.

On his return from sniffing the ground for his study of Monash, Peter Pedersen talked to the Memorial's two or three historians about the field work for his book. Soon after, the Memorial (then in an expansionist phase) published Pedersen's article, 'The Ghosts of Anzac', in its new *Journal of the Australian War Memorial*. For me Pedersen's article was a revelation. I had visited only one battlefield at that time, but when I began serious field work I had a clear model of how an historian could respond to seeing the ground on two related levels. Pedersen took an informed, intelligent, intense interest in the configuration of terrain and how it affected the thinking of commanders and the actions of their troops. But he was no mere 'general staff' analyst. He also responded emotionally to what had occurred in those places long ago. His 'Ghosts of Anzac' article defined a productive way for historians to engage with battlefields, and its spirit permeates the approaches discussed in this book.

By the early 1980s, then, the expectation had now been set: good military history needed to be based on a knowledge of the ground. Books are still published on battles—even by reputable historians—not based on field work, but this is becoming exceptional, and is regarded as reprehensible. Doing field work has become as necessary and useful a part of research as consulting archival records or interviewing survivors. So for the past couple of decades battlefield research has become a common, if not inescapable, part of writing military history in Australia. Why should we continue this tradition and what might we get out of it? We'll see.

No-man's-land: What is a battlefield?

Those unfamiliar with military history have vague ideas of what a battlefield might be like. A character in Sebastian Faulks's novel of the Great War, *Birdsong*, wonders: 'What did a "battlefield" look like? Was it a prepared area of conflict with each side's positions marked down? Wouldn't buildings and trees get in the way?'

A battlefield can take many forms, some pleasant and easily grasped, enjoyable for their own sake; others hard to read, unpleasant to visit. They range in size—Pinjarra can be taken in from one spot; Alamein needs several days and at some points a four-wheel drive; Bobdubi Ridge demands a fully equipped trekking expedition. At their most extreme, battlefields can constitute the entire North Atlantic Ocean or the skies of Western Europe. Some battlefields—if you're not careful, or if you're in the hands of a lazy guide—can seem like tourist traps rather than chances to touch the past. Gallipoli can seem to comprise half-a-dozen photo opportunities accompanied by some rehashed tragedy. The challenge with the seemingly familiar place is to approach it with fresh, new questions. That spirit of curiosity and imagination can make a visit to even the most heavily signposted battlefield a revelation.

Curiosity and imagination? Surely battlefields are places of trauma and horror: why would anyone want to spend time on them? J. Glenn Gray, in his book *The Warriors*, offers 'Reflections on Men in Battle', pondering why he was drawn to think and write about the Second World War in the decades after he gratefully returned from war service to the contemplative life of a philosopher. He was quite frank: battles were beautiful. This might seem a bizarre idea, especially coming from a man who served in the Italian, French and German campaigns, but Gray was grappling with the common feeling that organised violence has a drama that few of us entirely deny. We need to acknowledge the mixed range of emotions with which we approach battlefields. Australians especially seem to absorb reflective pride: on Gallipoli the average Australian visitor feels a mixture of revulsion, admiration, pride, curiosity, fantasy, appalled fascination. All of these feelings jostle within us when we stand in places where human beings have suffered and endured profound experiences. Some places in the world give off historical radiation. They're not all battlefields—the Tower of London, Auschwitz, the Hall of Mirrors at Versailles, the Houses of Parliament in London. You know—of course you can't 'sense' because historical radiation isn't real—but you know that vital decisions have been taken on this spot, executions ordered, wars declared, speeches delivered, and reputations made and broken.

The point is that you feel these emotions only because of the knowledge you bring to an historical site. Without knowing what happened there, the battleground of Pinjarra is just a muddy river

Many sites on battlefields radiate an emotional field, though not because of what they are, but because of what we bring to them. The author at the Windmill site at Pozières, a spot 'more densely sown with Australian sacrifice' than any other spot on earth. (Claire Cruikshank)

bank; Walker's Ridge is just a spectacular eroded gully; Pozières is just a bumpy field; Long Tan is just a rubber plantation. But once you know what happened there, your visit takes on new meaning. That's what it's about: meaning. By visiting, and looking, and reading, by taking bearings and working out what happened when and how (and to whom and at what cost) you are making meaning.

That's important, because (if we read Tolstoy's *War and Peace*, for example) we often think of battles as formless, even meaningless events. As well as being a great story of love and loyalty, *War and Peace* is a sustained argument that great men (such as Napoleon) only imagine that they control events, and that human affairs (such as battles) are the result of uncontrollable chance. Sacrifice in war is so often 'futile' that we automatically link the two words—think of the Nek, or Fromelles. Conventional military history, with its neat maps showing symbols and arrows, with columns moving in accord with generals' orders, would have us believe the opposite of Tolstoy, that war is a mechanical business of orders and objectives, ordered and orderly. As ever, the truth lies somewhere in between. Good military historians inhabit a no-man's-land between what the generals desire and the soldiers' chaos, making sense of each to understand the reality.

And there is a reality to understand, especially on a battlefield. As you'd guess, I'm an empirical historian: I believe that the past happened, that it was created and experienced by real people and—most importantly—that we can use the evidence they left to create an understanding of them and it. That evidence includes the landscape on which they moved and died. In many places, they are still a part of that landscape—most Gallipoli dead lie unidentified under the scrub, while on the Western Front one man in three is still 'missing'—their remains are one with the very soil they defended. We can understand their experience by going to the places in which they fought and died.

You could see . . . : Reading the battlefield

A battlefield is no ordinary stretch of country: it is a place where particular events have happened. We need to understand those events, otherwise it's just a stretch of country, beautiful and scenic, perhaps, but of no great significance. However, if you can look upon the battlefield with the eye of a military historian, asking questions and finding answers in the ground, you'll be able to get more out of your encounter with the past than you ever could by either just passing by or merely reading about it.

Some landscapes do not give up their secrets easily, and they are not always the ones choked by jungle or built over by later development. Anne-Marie Condé found that the site of the Cowra prisoner-of-war camp had been so thoroughly cleared that she had trouble establishing where episodes in the August 1944 'breakout' had occurred. 'Casual visitors like us', she concluded, 'have to work hard to get much out of this inscrutable landscape'. Many battlefield landscapes are 'inscrutable', but asking the right questions of the terrain will help the most mute landscape to speak across time.

Being able to read a battlefield involves using several skills that are actually not all that difficult to acquire. They amount to asking the right questions and being aware of relationships between several factors. They involve bringing to the front of your consciousness various things that a casual visitor might not recognise. In effect your task is to visualise, superimposed on the landscape you see, the historical landscape you're trying to imagine and understand. This sounds simple—obvious even—but often the changes between now and then are profound, and they impede easy imagining.

One of the most striking illustrations of the value of battlefield crawling comes from Malaya. In January 1942 a platoon of the 2/30th Battalion ambushed advancing Japanese troops from an embankment at Gemencheh, near Gemas. Australian accounts give Japanese losses as a thousand. Brian Farrell and Dan Crosswell investigated the site, and Brian discovered that

> simply walking the ground indicates right away that the claim of 1000 Japanese killed by this ambush cannot possibly be anything close to the truth...one platoon engaging with its own weapons, in a space that size, in a time that short, could not kill anything like that number; the killing zone is only long enough to fit in about one company...

Here the documentary sources alone give a misleading picture, but the very ground can help a curious historian to approach the truth.

Battlefields figure in the books I've written about war—becoming characters almost. I grew to understand, though never to love, the thick jungle of Borneo and the seemingly bare desert of Alamein, and to feel that I had come to know the acre of ground at Quinn's Post almost as well as some of the men who served there in 1915. Indeed, one of the claims that I make in the book *Quinn's Post, Anzac, Gallipoli*, was that I'd worked out where Quinn's actually was—it's not at the Quinn's Post cemetery as you might think. That conclusion is a result of spending days there, taking bearings, and thinking.

Think about it: Quinn's Post in 1915 was a warren of trenches and saps cut into a steep hillside. Where are they today? Indeed, where is the hillside today? The answer is that it has just about all been washed away after 90 years of winter rains. But what about Quinn's Post cemetery? Wasn't that built on top of the post? Many visitors will assume that—tour guides even tell them so, but it isn't true. If you take bearings from various points around Quinn's and plot them on a map you find that the cemetery was actually built on Bloody Angle, and that the terraces of Quinn's are long gone. So far so good: the problem is what to do with that knowledge. My answer is that it is important to understand the changes that have occurred, but then to try to work with what's left to learn more about what has gone. Quinn's Post's loss makes the documentary and photographic record even more precious, of course. But it also makes us work harder to understand what could have been seen from the post. For example, we can establish where supporting machine-gun fire came from on adjoining ridges. Standing in the scrub at the edge of the cliff face (or rather, squatting, to get as close as possible to the eye-level of Anzac sentries in 1915), we can glimpse something of what the Anzacs could have seen. To do this we have to imagine the scrub cut down by rifle and machine-gun fire, and the desiccated and rotting bodies, Turkish and Anzac, lying in a no-man's-land blasted by shells and underground mines. It's hard, but imagining it in the comfort of an air-conditioned library is even harder. The other conclusions visiting Quinn's Post forces upon the researcher is how small the post was, and how steep the ridge was—and is. Add to this the feeling of a scorching summer's day, and feeling the chill of a northerly wind in winter, and it is possible to recapture mentally something of the reality of Quinn's throughout 1915. Of course you can't actually hear the noise of continuous bomb explosions and the crackle of rifle fire, smell the stench of decay and excrement or feel the flies pestering your face. But at least you can imagine it all the better, and that's the point of the thing.

A landscape is not a 'given'. It has several components: the natural or physical, the human or cultural and military, and each part operates on a different timescale. Every place has a natural and a human history, stretching over many thousands of years of evolving landscape and hundred of years of human habitation or use. The Australian connection with these places is probably among the most recent and often the most fleeting in a long history of change. To us, though, the days or weeks of combat in a war are very important. Understanding the Australian presence in a landscape often entails getting to know these various local histories. For example, in preparing for the assault on Mont St Quentin in France in 1918, Australian units sheltered in 'Lost Ravine'. This, it turns out, was the unfinished excavation for the Canal du Nord, abandoned in 1914. Understanding this feature involved finding out something of the industrial history of the French canal system. When you visit the battlefield today, 'Lost Ravine' is the bed of the now finished canal.

Likewise, even the contours might have changed in tropical environments such as Tarakan. Between hasty battlefield burials in May 1945 and the time burial parties returned to search for the graves a month or two later, landslides shifted a whole hillside a hundred yards downhill.

Peter Pedersen, a veteran of many battlefield visits, is particularly eloquent in noticing the military implications of the landscape. In researching Monash's part in the battle of Passchendaele in 1917, he went looking for the German-held 'Crest Farm', a feature so minor it is 'easily overlooked on the map'. Pedersen found it on the ground:

> ...it threatened to break up the 3rd Division's attacks just as a wave breaks against an outlying rock. Each spur enfiladed the other two. You can see by going to the locations of the German pillboxes indicated on the map how devastating these fields of fire were.

'All this', Pedersen recalled, 'went into my account of the attack in *Monash*'. Again and again in Pedersen's reflections on how he goes about researching battlefields you find him insisting on the necessity of looking at the ground and asking questions about it. Why did Monash want such a strong force to attack at Hamel? 'It's the ground...An artillery observer with a phone [at the Wolfsberg, now the site of the Australian memorial] could bring down accurate fire on the Australians from the time they left their own line over a mile away...'

Two opinions in a trench: Doing military history

Battles have two sides, not just in combatants, but also in the arguments historians mount as a result of their research. There is rarely a single accepted interpretation for any battle. You can easily get into an argument over Agincourt, Crécy, Waterloo or Gettysburg: all have provoked rancour and contention. Australia's battles are just as contentious—Kokoda, Bullecourt, Kapyong: all provoke arguments. Who can discuss Gallipoli and agree on key questions? Did the landing go wrong? (Well, yes—but *why*?) Why did the August offensive go badly? Was Lone Pine necessary, and was it a success? These questions can be answered by finding and consulting the documents: people have written books about

Gallipoli without actually visiting the place. But all the documents leave questions unanswered. Above all, even the torn and stained pages of diaries and the fading pencil of message pads (not so indelible after all) don't tell you everything about what it was like. No one source does or can. Historians need to make the most of the range of sources available. And besides maps, orders and official reports, private diaries and memoirs—all of which need to be consulted—one of the most important sources for history is the places where it happened.

By the way, by 'places' I don't just mean 'the places where battles happened'. In researching *Quinn's Post*, thanks to an Army History Unit research grant, I was able to visit the places where Hugh Quinn and others killed at the post named after him had been born and grew up. I believe that the insights I gained at Charters Towers and Forest Hill in Queensland were as important in forming my understanding of the men who made up the First AIF as were those I gained with a map and a compass on Gallipoli. I have spent many happy hours poking around old barracks in several continents. But this book is specifically concerned with battlefield research, and we'll mostly stay there.

History is a very democratic discipline. There are no amateur brain surgeons or tax lawyers, for good reasons. Some fields are specialised or technical (or dangerous, or dull). History is none of those things. While historical research does demand knowledge and skill, these skills can be learned and practised at the 'amateur' level, and those 'amateurs' can contribute to the debate about what happened and why with equal validity. That doesn't mean that anyone's opinion is as worthwhile as anyone else's—everyone ought to meet standards of documentation, argument and evidence—but there's no reason why an informed amateur shouldn't make an impression, as many have.

Indeed, battlefield research is tailor-made for individuals to make contributions to understanding. Because so little field work has been done, despite the impression that Australian military history is a crowded field, there is vast scope for a researcher to ask new questions about an aspect of Australia's military past (pick a battle, almost any battle . . .) and to provide fresh understanding by asking questions about new evidence—the site where an event occurred. So few places have been thoroughly visited in this way that almost any study you can propose will—if you ask the right questions and present a coherent conclusion—deliver a new and worthwhile interpretation.

The great thing about battlefields is that they are cut-and-come-again places. Everyone who visits can make their own deductions and conclusions. At Anzac Cove one person may feel a surge of pride for the achievements of a soldier who might be a great uncle or a man from their own suburb or town. Another may feel only sadness and a sense of futility at the waste of life, on both sides. And the one person can experience both these emotions within the space of an hour.

A battlefield is an inexhaustible source of evidence about the past, and an unlimited stimulus to thinking about history. Every person who visits—provided they've done a modest amount of preparation—will gain some insight or take away some reflection.

Orders Group: Scoping the project

First, you'll have to be clear what you want to achieve. Project managers talk about 'scoping' their projects, and it's a useful bit of jargon. It would be worthwhile to define your goal (as formally as you like—I tend to write these things down). Your objective will depend upon your individual interest, on the time (and money) you can expend, and on how committed you (and your travelling companions) are to the venture. It's at this point that

Michael Molkentin's photograph of Ieper (Ypres) seen from a hot air balloon suggests the exotic possibilities of battlefield research from the air. (Michael Molkentin)

differences may arise, and it's better to get the differences out of the way before you buy the tickets.

Your aims could be to:

- Find Great Uncle Jim's grave
- Trace Great Uncle Jim's service
- Follow the route of Great Uncle Jim's battalion
- Do the Gallipoli pilgrimage
- Visit Long Tan because you met a man wounded there and wanted to see where it happened
- Write an article about commanders' decisions in a particular battle
- Visit the site of the Sandakan POW camp
- Find the mine craters at Messines
- Trace the location of the Great Sap on Gallipoli
- Write an account of the battle of Lagnicourt, or Giarabub, or Muar, or...

- Try to find the locations of Damien Parer's film of the Kokoda campaign
- Try to establish why something did or did not happen
- Question the conventional explanations of the Third Battle of Ypres

Notice how these aims escalate in complexity and in their outcome. The more complex the aim, the more it will take to complete successfully. You can find Great Uncle Jim's grave on a day-trip while the rest of the family are whooping it up at Euro Disney, and that may be satisfactory for all concerned. But if you're planning to investigate more than a company action, you might need several days on the ground, and if there is any doubt about finding or reaching a site, or questions about the weather, allow more time rather than less. The more complex aims will also obviously demand more extensive preparation.

An actual project might help to make the process clearer. My former colleagues Craig Tibbitts and Nick Fletcher are writing a history of the 56th Battalion, a run-of-the-mill AIF unit that served on the Western Front and which—curiously—has no published history, so far. Craig and Nick will fill that gap. Their list of the places they'll be visiting, among Bapaume, Bullecourt, Villers-Bretonneux and Péronne, includes Louverval, Doignies and Polygon Wood, near Ieper (as the town of Ypres is now called). At Louverval and Doignies (villages that screened the Hindenburg Line in 1917), Craig and Nick want to 'see the view from the little ridge overlooking the objectives where the battalions assembled for the attack, the open left-hand flank, the beetroot factory between the hamlets and the Louverval Chateau'. At Polygon Wood, the scene of 56th Battalion's major battle of 1917, they are interested in the Butte and Scott's Post, both of which are key features in the battalion's story. The latter was named after the battalion's CO, Lt Col Scott, when the battalion captured the blockhouse on 26 September, while the Butte was the scene of his death a few days later.

With all of these places, Craig writes, 'we'd like to try and gauge the distances involved, the views obtainable from key high points, and the lay of the land—especially where defilades and enfilades occur'. Like all of us, Craig wants to 'just stand there and try to imagine what was happening 90-odd years ago, what were the sights and smells, and try and go through what I know of the story'. Fortunately, the Army History Unit awarded Craig a research grant to get him to these places.

Most importantly, Craig and Nick know that they need to see the ground in order to say something sensible about the battle in question. It seems extraordinary that authors can venture to write books about battles without visiting the places in which they happened. Would anyone value books about lions written by authors who had never visited the veldt? Or books about butterflies based on pictures? Peter Pedersen is unequivocal: 'books about battles not based on field work often lose something in credibility'. I would be as trenchant. I would ask military history authors to justify why they do not visit the sites they write about.

The purpose of a field trip has to be clear: what are you trying to find out, and why? I've visited Mont St Quentin twice, though in fact the nature of the book changed radically between the time I first planned a field trip and the time I was able to get there. At the beginning I had envisaged another 'battle' book—a study of a vast, fast-moving battle of manoeuvre across 20 kilometres of French countryside. By the time I was ready to make the trip, the project had changed. I found that while I had a contract for a 'battle book' I now wanted to deal in detail with one platoon rather than range across a couple of divisions. I still needed to understand the operation as a whole, but I also needed to follow that platoon's route step by step. So in approaching the ground I needed to decide what use I made of the terrain.

Route march: Bushwalking the battlefield

Most battlefields can be traversed and understood best on foot. In the early 1980s, Nigel Jones did his 'war walk'—the length of the Western Front, a feat that could be replicated with profit. On battlefields in Greece and Crete, parts of the Middle East (notably Lebanon, subject to questions about safety) and especially France and Belgium, walking is a serious option. In Papua New Guinea it is virtually the only way to see important battlefields—not just Kokoda but around Wau, the Markham and Ramu valleys (including Shaggy Ridge) and much of the Aitape–Wewak campaign area.

For those seeking a physical but less extreme way of exploring the battlefields of the Great War, I've always been intrigued with the idea of walking the length of the Australian campaign of 1918. Has anyone ever walked from, say, Villers-Bretonneux to Montbrehain, following the route of a particular battalion, perhaps? Craig Deayton, a Hobart school principal writing *Decision at Dernancourt*, a history of the 47th Battalion, thought about tracing the 4th Division's epic 19-mile (30-kilometre) night march towards Albert in March 1918. He didn't, but now wishes he had.

My colleague Matthew Higgins is an expert on the history of the ACT–New South Wales high country, and has walked over much of it in the course of his research. He offers several tips on walking:

- If possible, never walk alone
- Make sure someone knows your route and date of expected arrival
- Carry adequate water and food
- Carry, and know how to use, a good map of the area and a compass or GPS

- Dress for possible changes in the weather
- Carry adequate equipment (e.g. tent, sleeping bag, stove, etc.)

Matthew recommends the general advice in John Siseman and John Browlie's *Bushwalking and Touring in the Bogong High Plains* as a useful guide to safe bushwalking, as relevant in the Baining Mountains of New Britain as the Brindabella Range in the ACT. Those contemplating walking the Papua New Guinea battlefields should first read the section 'Facts for the bushwalker' in Yvon Pérusse's *Bushwalking in Papua New Guinea*, as well as Phil Bradley's books on Shaggy Ridge and the Wau–Salamaua campaign and his contributions to the *After the Battle* series. Good luck!

A less strenuous form of long-distance historical understanding might be found in retracing the 'Snowball marches' of 1916. Enthusiastic volunteers marched from outlying towns towards Sydney, hoping to gather volunteers, in the same way as a snowball grows. The marchers adopted stirring nicknames—the Kangaroos, the Waratahs and the 'Snowy River Men' from Delegate. There have been some very successful re-enactments of these marches, notably the moving Gilgandra 'Cooees' march in 1996. A different route could be taken by those following what was said to be the longest route march in Australian history, as recorded in Joan Beaumont's *Gull Force*, when the 2/21st Battalion marched for eleven days, from Trawool to Bonegilla in September 1940. Sadly, the battalion was captured on Ambon early in 1942 and three-quarters of the men died in brutal captivity on Ambon and Hainan.

Forced march: Extreme battlefield research

Most Australian battlefields are within easy reach of comfortable accommodation and a range of transport options. Battlefields in Gallipoli, Greece, Singapore and Malayasia, even Viet Nam, can be reached by car or taxi from good hotels. The visitor to Pozières or Bullecourt may end the day in a sombre and reflective mood, but he or she will certainly enjoy a first-rate meal.

But some places can demand more stamina and dedication. On Gallipoli or Crete visitors can camp out—a journalist of my acquaintance slept out at Anzac in September, just to experience what it was like. My colleague Brad Manera, working on the German airborne assault on Crete, took a parachute jump, though not over Heraklion (and not into anti-aircraft fire either). But it helped him to understand the *Fallschirmjäger* that Australians, New Zealanders and Britons battled in 1941.

At Alamein in 2002 the Australian War Memorial–Imperial War Museum study tour group made an exciting excursion from the coast to the Qattara Depression, taking in several British, New Zealand and Indian battlefields en route. To reach the

The Guesthouse at Komiatum, near Shaggy Ridge, typical of the accommodation available in rural Papua New Guinea. (Phil Bradley)

Depression we engaged five four-wheel-drive vehicles, driven by experienced desert navigators who knew how to traverse the sandy and rocky country. (If you do plan desert travel, contact Hany Amr of Desert Adventures: desertadventures@gega.net.) The vehicle in which I travelled, driven by Hany, a qualified desert guide, had three punctures in the first couple of hours, and the whole convoy had to stop. Fortunately we carried three spare tyres, but as we had a different vehicle to the others, I wonder what would have happened if we'd had a fourth puncture. On the way, we saw country that few visitors could have seen without the logistical preparation we had done. We saw battlefields that had witnessed titanic fights by New Zealanders, Indians, Britons and, of course, Germans and Italians. Fifty kilometres inland from the coastal sector held by the 9th Australian Division, we saw a much harsher environment—but scenic and spectacular, as well as remote and rugged.

Walking the Kokoda Trail is of course the pre-eminent Australian battlefield research adventure. It needs to be said that for all the knowledge of the guides who take groups across it, relatively few trekkers go to understand the actions of 1942. Many, it seems, want to test themselves in a spirit of homage to the AIF and especially the militiamen of the 39th Battalion. Whether most actually understand what went on at Brigade Hill and Isurava when they slog past these places is a moot point. (I doubt that many have breath or energy enough to take in much of their surroundings, much less analyse the battle while on the spot. But not having had the opportunity to share the ordeal, I'm not going to criticise.) For those who seek battlefield research in other exotic places, some unusual destinations remain to be explored:

- Finding the SMS *Königsburg* in the Rufuji delta in Tanzania
- Walking the route of the retreat on Crete from Hania to Sphakia

The crossing over Eora Creek on the Kokoda Trail, is almost exactly the same as it was in 1942. (Phil Bradley)

- Following the route of 'Dunsterforce' in Central Asia
- Tracing the sites of the 1919 North Russian VCs
- Riding the rail route of the Australians who went to South Africa through Rhodesia (Zimbabwe) in 1900
- Driving the advance from Bardia to Benghazi in Libya in 1941
- Walking the route of the 1945 Sandakan death march in Malaysia
- Walking Kokoda
- Trekking the Bulldog Road or Black Cat Trail in Papua New Guinea
- Following the route of the 1941 retreat in Greece

R.A. Yates's *The Bulldog–Wau Road: A Bushwalking Guide*, though it is both rare and somewhat out of date, offers an invaluable aid to walking the route of one of the great engineering achievements of Australia's part in the Second World War. Adventurous scuba divers can also dive on Second World War wrecks in various parts of the Pacific, and especially around Papua New Guinea. But this is beyond the scope of my competence. I'd start with Bob Halstead and Tim Rock's *Diving and Snorkelling Papua New Guinea*, and seek expert advice. Likewise, those searching for the many wrecked aircraft still to be found in Papua New Guinea should start with Charles Darby's *Pacific Aircraft Wrecks and Where to Find Them*. Some of these suggestions would take you to remote and possibly hazardous places, and the cautions offered in the section 'Picquet lines: No-go areas?' on page 132 apply: take them seriously.

Perhaps the most adventurous land journey in search of Australian military history in remote places would be to follow as much of the route of Dunsterforce as current political conditions allow. In 1918 a British Empire mission under Major General Lionel Dunsterville was sent to Central Asia to organise resistance to a possible German thrust towards India, and to safeguard the oilfields of the Caspian Sea. Dunsterforce, as it was called, operated in Mesopotamia, Persia and Kurdistan and on the shores of the Caspian Sea. Sixty Australians were part of it, and it was supported by an Anzac Wireless Signal Squadron. Alan Stewart's *Persian Expedition* ably tells the story of this little-known force, but he did so from documents and photographs, without visiting any of the places to which it went. While it would not be possible to follow Dunsterforce's route exactly—it travelled through what is now Iraq from Basra—tracing its operations in what are now Iran and Azerbaijan would be feasible. Travel to the former Soviet Caucasus republics, while off the beaten track, is becoming more popular and easier, though I would study the Department of Foreign Affairs Travelsafe website (www.smartraveller.gov.au) and consult widely before committing to such a venture. The website gives cautious general advice and some specific advisory tips about hazards, country by country, warning prospective visitors against going to several countries (such as the Sudan) or counselling extreme caution in others (such as Indonesia).

Those contemplating battlefield research projects with more adventurous agendas such as these should consult as a starting point Simon Winser's comprehensive *Royal Geographical Society Expedition Handbook*. Its expert authors cover all aspects of planning and undertaking expeditions to environments of many kinds, offering detailed advice on insurance, logistics, navigation, environmental impacts and, where necessary, survival.

Prepare to mount!: Battlefield research in the saddle

It is perfectly feasible to tour battlefields by bicycle. The Villers-Bretonneux–Montbrehain route, for example, could also be done on a bike (as did I Anzac Cyclist Battalion, I suppose), even if most Australian soldiers in 1918 marched from one end of the Somme campaign to the other. I haven't done it, mind you, but I know people who have. Bicycles are the most energy-efficient form of transport available. Except that you're exposed to the weather (and other road users), a bicycle seems to be an ideal form of transport to investigate battlefields. It's small, can go almost anywhere a walker can, and is inconspicuous.

Some of the disadvantages of bicycles are that it is probably impractical (that is, expensive) to bring your own bike with you, and it can be difficult to hire a bike on the spot. Edward Hasbrouck's *The Practical Nomad: How to Travel Around the World* gives practical advice on borrowing or hiring bikes. However, the authors of the most detailed guidebook to Gallipoli, Phil Taylor and Pam Cupper, completed the field work for it over several summers on the peninsula, and in many ways Gallipoli is ideally suited to be explored by bicycle. Hallam Murray's chapter on cycling expeditions in the *Royal Geographical Society Expedition Handbook* gives many useful tips.

You could also emulate Richard Holmes—if you dare. He followed the 1914 retreat from Mons on horseback, a feat recorded in his admirable *Riding the Retreat*. The care he took—over his preliminary reading, his route, his writing and not least his mounts—shows why Richard Holmes is so esteemed. Battlefield research from the saddle is surely possible—after all, it grew out of the 'staff ride'—but it is a specialised pursuit beyond my experience.

James Greenwood's chapter, 'Travelling by Horse', also in the *Expedition Handbook*, is a good place to begin. He rode around the world, a project that took the best part of a decade at an average rate of about 10 kilometres a day.

Digging in: Battlefield archaeology

One of the pieces of equipment that this book doesn't recommend is a shovel or a metal detector. Since archaeology, and especially battlefield archaeology, has become popular recently, especially on television, you might think that battlefield researchers use—or should use—archaeology. In fact, they don't, and here's why.

People have been collecting stuff from battlefields for centuries—even the Romans carried off chariot-loads of 'trophies' from conquered peoples. For many years items collected from battlefields have been displayed in museums—as we saw, musket ball-pierced breast-plates gathered from Waterloo impressed the young Charles Bean when he holidayed in Belgium a century ago. (It's likely that Bean may not have had the idea of founding an Australian war memorial museum if he hadn't seen the treasures at Waterloo.)

What can battlefield archaeology tell us about Australian battles? Unfortunately for viewers of *Two Men in a Trench*, the answer seems to be 'not very much, actually'. It might help to confirm or corroborate a location recorded in the documents, but it very rarely suggests a significant difference to existing interpretation. I once trawled an entire volume of reports about battlefield archaeology undertaken on American Civil War sites and found that the best that archaeology could do was to alter the position of a Union line in an obscure action a few metres off—not an impressive result for all the soil those poor students shifted. That's not to say that archaeology isn't useful for an understanding of broader questions, especially if the battle took place before written sources were abundant or reliable, but in the modern era, and especially in particular battles, the likelihood is pretty poor. And, yes, I know about Richard Fox's famous Battle of the Little Big Horn study in which Fox reconstructed the action by analysing hundreds of cartridges and bullets, but it's the exception. It was based on one small, short action on an otherwise undisturbed area: you can't do that sort of bullet-by-bullet analysis for Gallipoli or the Somme.

In any case, you won't be allowed to dig stuff up. This is a serious warning. In Turkey they'll arrest you. In France they'll talk sternly to you. Do you think the people from *Time Team* just turn up and start digging? 'Fraid not—any archaeological venture takes as long in applying for permits as in actual excavation time. Don't even think about it.

You won't get away with digging covertly. You need to assume that you're conspicuous when you arrive in any non-European country. So few Western visitors arrive in places like Tarakan and Alamein that word of your arrival will get around very swiftly. Not to mention the fact that in some countries surveillance is one of the pillars of the regime. Indonesia has a very effective local neighbourhood watch organisation down to block level, while in

Egypt surveillance posts dot the main coast road—the only surfaced road—every few kilometres. They know where you are and, if they want to, they can find you. If you were so foolish as to dig something up, you can be sure that someone will notice. Don't try it.

John Laffin's *Digging Up the Diggers' War* was one of the most mischievous of the 110 or thereabouts books he wrote. 'Few military historians practise battlefield archaeology in any systematic way,' he wrote—and he was no exception. Laffin was a souvenir hunter with a shovel, and it behoves no one to follow his example. Still, his book contains the results of decades of research and a deep knowledge of the Western Front, those who fought there and those who remain in cemeteries. It is worth reading, provided you remain immune from the desire to dig.

If there is value in battlefield archaeology—and it is a new field—we will see it in projects that have largely not come to fruition. Michael Molkentin, a young Australian historian of the Great War, has contributed several times to archaeological projects on the Western Front, and he thinks that the approach has merit. Molkentin argues that archaeology has the potential literally to unearth new understandings—and he quotes back at me how Charles Bean used the artefacts he found on Gallipoli in 1919 to establish what happened to the lost parties after the landing. Not the least worthwhile aspect of archaeology on battlefields is that it obliges researchers to visit and look closely at battlefields, and that's never a bad thing.

Several researchers have become involved in archaeology-based projects, so many that it would be fatuous to argue that such projects are worthless. Craig Wilcox's article, 'A different type of digger' (describing a dig that uncovered the British military settlement of Fort Dundas in northern Australia, 1824–27), shows how archaeology can inform when other evidence is scanty. Michael Molkentin shows in his article, 'The Westhoek five', how archaeology can illuminate individual experience. Nigel Steel, another Great

War specialist, argues that the recent projects uncovering dug-outs near Ypres have revealed much about troops' lives that even the most detailed documents do not record. The debate continues.

Souvenirs: Relics as symbols

What does that leave us with? Are battlefield souvenirs important? It would be a hard-hearted historian who would remain unmoved by the things you do encounter on a battlefield. On my study shelf I have a collection of objects that reflect the books and articles I've written about historical places I've visited:

- A strand of barbed wire from Alamein
- Japanese bullets from Tarakan and Italian bullets from Alamein
- A corroded steel helmet from the Somme
- A metal spike from the Burma–Thailand railway

These objects have powerful ju-ju: just handling them takes you back to a patch of desert scrub or a jungle thicket. So why do we want to collect? It's not that these items have any value as evidence, no matter what the battlefield archaeology lobby will tell you. But there's a voodoo about them. Someone fired this bullet at an Australian sheltering in a trench near here; a prisoner of war held this peg while another hit it with a hammer—perhaps on the day each of them died. That's a powerful connection, but it's a magical one. It's more akin to medieval pilgrims than 21st-century researchers, perhaps—except that I've never heard of any 21st-century military historian who is immune to its lure, including me. But, as I suggest later, don't walk the battlefield with your eyes on the ground! Does this advice condone souveniring? I hope not: be selective and bring home one item that represents the emotion of the journey.

For each of us: Battlefield research or battlefield tourism?

Lots of people visit Australia's battlefields, at least on the Gallipoli–Western Front route. But *research*? (Or, as seems to be inevitable these days of Americanised pronunciation, *re*-search?) Isn't that the sort of thing only trained historians can do? Not at all: you can do it too, whoever you are.

Research is about making meaning: for you, not necessarily for anyone else. As long as you approach the places you visit in a spirit of enquiry, prepared to form your own conclusions, you can justifiably see yourself as conducting research. It's more effort than sitting in a tour bus listening to a guide's agreeable anecdotes and well-honed jokes, but it's also more rewarding.

It's better because you'll be asking your own questions, forming your own conclusions and creating your own interpretations. At bottom, that's what the study of history is about. Battlefield research allows you to make up your own mind about events that are important to you. As Tony Wright observes, in the final line of his *Turn Right at Istanbul*, the range above Anzac Cove 'can mean, for each of us, whatever we want it to mean'. Historians need to observe the rules of evidence; we can't impose a meaning independently of the evidence—including the evidence of the ground itself—but Wright's observation is essentially true. It reminds us of the glory of the Western liberal tradition of scholarship—a tradition all historians are heir to—in which we revel in the freedom to make up our own minds within the constraints imposed by our regard for the evidence.

Battlefield research might seem to be a manifestation of what John Lennon and Malcolm Foley call, in their book of that name, 'Dark Tourism', where they dissect the 'attraction of death and disaster'. Besides battlefields, they argue that dark tourism encompasses murder sites, cemeteries, mausoleums, the homes of dead celebrities, Holocaust camps and, we now need to add (their book appeared in 2000), 'Ground Zero' in New York. There is no denying the appeal of sites as varied as Changi Gaol (when it was open to visitors) or the Texas Book Depository in Dallas (and I have to confess that I have visited both). Indeed, each year nearly a million people visit Dachau, and over half a million tour the Anne Frank House in Amsterdam. Tens of thousands of Australians visit Gallipoli, the Western Front and Normandy, though many fewer seek out any other theatre of war.

Is battlefield research an aspect of this not-altogether-wholesome-seeming enterprise? Perhaps. I would like to think that battlefield researchers are drawn by a desire to understand and a wish to acknowledge the experiences of those they study.

The wonderful thing about battlefield research is that you have to do it in interesting places, and it's largely up to you. Even on well-travelled battlefields, littered with interpretative signs and memorials (such as Gettysburg, Waterloo or, indeed, Gallipoli) you can use those markers, monuments and panels as the springboard to frame your own questions and reach your own interpretations.

For example, think of the Australian battlefield most visited and most familiar, recorded and preserved in thousands of photograph albums every year—the stretch of Anzac Cove near Beach Cemetery. You can get a lot out of visiting Anzac Cove. Stand there and listen to your guide, probably someone who has read a great deal about the campaign, rarely someone who has actually written much about it. One of the problems with guides is that visitors—out of common politeness at least—tend to look at the guide, not the country. As a result they will probably remember the guide and his or her stories rather than what it was he or she was guiding you about.

The problem with many guides is that they do the same trip so often that they get into a pattern of repeating the same things over and over. They know the nuggets that work and those that don't. The result is that you get a highly polished version, one that will seem to satisfy but does not nourish. If you're not careful, you'll be consuming the military historical equivalent of fast food.

For the casual visitor that may be enough, just as a Big Mac will do if you're on the highway and in a hurry. But how often will you go to Anzac Cove? Just by reading this book you've already marked yourself off from most visitors to a battlefield. Your interest may not be that of the military historian who will walk away with enough photographs and notes for a book, but you want more than the Big Mac of Gallipoli. Fortunately you are able to make up your own mind.

Let me show you: Making the most of the guided tour

Many research projects come out of encounters with battlefield tours, indirectly if not directly. And many more people will encounter Australia's battlefields as part of an organised tour than as independent researchers. So let's make the most of these opportunities. Equipped with a more independent frame of mind, let's think about what you do when you step out of the bus at Anzac Cove. Look around. What do you see?

You take in the scene: the Aegean a few metres away; the steep bank down to what's left of the beach; the road. Looking up, you see a steep hillside clothed in low scrub. The temptation is to look at the guide as he or she launches into a spiel they've delivered many times. The group tourist obediently gathers around the guide and sees Anzac Cove through that person's eyes. The challenge is to see it through your own. If the tourist has a question (and guides' spiels generally convey more information than casual visitors need, effectively discouraging questions), the answer will be the guide's.

Don't get me wrong; I'm not opposed to guided tours. On the contrary, I've led tours; some of my best friends lead tours. But I'm conscious of the variable standard of guided tours, and want to help you get the most out of what is probably an expensive and rare opportunity. First, choose your tour carefully. If you have a choice, ask about the leaders' skills and qualifications. (Having led fifteen tours to Gallipoli is not by itself a reliable indication; tours are single-shot purchases—you rarely buy again, whether the guide is personable or execrable.)

Be especially wary of day tours on Gallipoli. Even though some groups are led by knowledgeable guides, there is a danger of being fed too much information on a standard itinerary, and being fed Turkish historical propaganda. If you go to Gallipoli in the market for an impromptu day tour, investigate the excellent virtual tours produced by Richard Reid, former principal historian at the Department of Veterans' Affairs. (Start with www.anzacsite.gov.au for the 'Anzac Walk'.) Glenn Wahlert's recent *Exploring Gallipoli* includes a CD with recorded 'stands' you can download onto your iPod.

If you're choosing from the array of Australian-based tour outfits, be equally choosy—it's your money. Don't necessarily fall for the reputation of the tour operator: the critical link in the chain is the relationship you'll form with the tour guide. Ask who they are and what justifies your investment in them. Have they published books? Are they suitably qualified? Call them and get a feel for their personality. Are they approachable or patronising? Are they there to listen to what you're interested in or do you get the feeling that you're there to listen to them? The best guides are like the best teachers. Peter Pedersen—a tour leader as well as a writer—measures the success of his tours by 'the vigour of the discussion it engenders over dinner and at the bar afterwards'.

The thoughts of two well-known Australian battlefield tour guides corroborate Pedersen's attitude. Michael McKernan leads tours to Gallipoli, North Africa and the Western Front, and Peter Dowling to Gallipoli, Greece and North Africa. I found that both structured their tours not so much according to what happened in history, as by what was best for their groups. Experienced guides built into their program the interests and experiences of their groups' members. They gave their groups time to take in and explore the landscape individually, and encouraged dialogue rather than simply assuming an omniscient role. They differed in emphasis. On Gallipoli, Peter Dowling, leader of the popular National Trust ACT groups, emphasises giving visitors the words of the men of 1915 on the spot. Asking visitors to read a diary or a letter is a powerful way to engage them on the spot. He skilfully structures his tours around individuals, establishing before departure the personal links visitors bring. Michael McKernan, a natural teacher, encourages people to talk, even to disagree, in a friendly spirit. Recognising that the terrain, so familiar to military historians, is absolutely new to most visitors, he builds in 'reprise time' so that his groups can connect with what is probably 'new knowledge'. As the author of *The Australian People and the Great War* and *The Strength of a Nation*, he is also especially attuned to the emotional impact of the visit.

Both Michael McKernan and Peter Dowling make their tours memorable because, like the best historians, their work arises from their individual personalities and their engagement with the people and the events they are interpreting. Both offer much practical advice: 'avoid Gallipoli on the weekend, when it is overrun with Turkish tour buses', 'in Turkey the entrees are better than the main courses', 'drink bottled water' and 'anytime you find a toilet use it'. They advise against going to Gallipoli for Anzac Day—the crowds and hoo-ha have destroyed the quiet remembrance that visitors to the peninsula used to value so highly. Indeed, I'd advise against going to Gallipoli on Anzac Day if you want to do any serious battlefield research.

You might be unwary or unlucky—paying a fortune on an unending lecture tour by a grand-standing know-all. Or you might choose a tour guide who enlarges your knowledge and encourages you to ask the questions that are the essence of historical study. You might find that a group tour excites your interest enough to return on your own as a battlefield researcher. I very much hope so.

'Passed staff college': Military and historical knowledge

A little knowledge, Alexander Pope warned, can be a dangerous thing. This is true in military historical research as much as in any other endeavour. Both the 'military' and the 'historical' are worth pondering.

Sometimes would-be battlefield researchers will either be reluctant to venture an opinion because they don't have any military training, or will want to take someone along who has, on the grounds that he (it's invariably a he) will know more of war by virtue of his training. In fact, military training is a mixed blessing in battlefield research.

It makes sense to take Viet Nam veterans along to investigate the battlefields of that war (and the post-1945 conflicts generally). While those who served in Viet Nam bring with them many assumptions and emotions—and may not be open to views that challenge their memories and their shared interpretations—they also carry their memories with them. Looking at the battlefields of, say, Binh Ba or Coral in the company of men who served there would be a privilege. If you do go to Viet Nam, do try to go with a veteran, and basically shut up and let them speak, asking enough questions to keep them going.

But whether a Viet Nam veteran brings any special knowledge to the study of, say, Gallipoli, the Western Front or the Second

World War, especially in the Mediterranean, is a moot point. Military training is highly specific, and the training of men in the 1950s and 1960s was very different to that of the men who fought in the Great War. The commanders who led formations on Gallipoli had been born in the 1860s, and had trained in the 1880s. Understanding low intensity counter-insurgency operations in South-East Asia 40-odd years ago doesn't necessarily equip anyone to look into the minds of commanders in 1915, or even 1941. A colleague commented that 'it always annoys and worries me when I hear ex-military men talking about the Western Front using Viet Nam-era jargon'. But I have to admit that some historians I respect don't agree. It would indeed be arrogant to decline the insights of a companion with 'psc' ('passed staff college', always in lower case) after their name. My point is that we need to recognise that military experience changes over time.

Peter Pedersen, who walked his first battlefield (the demanding Black Cat Trail in New Guinea) as a cadet at the Royal Military College, Duntroon, argues convincingly that his training as a military officer helps him understand the battlefields he visits. His training gives him real insight into, for example, whether enough time had been allowed for a move or for orders to be disseminated. This is undeniably true. The point where our arguments converge is that Pedersen, trained as an historian as well as an infantry and staff officer, does not read Gallipoli, Normandy or Dien Bien Phu in terms of the doctrine he learned twenty-odd years ago. He brings to the battlefield both his military knowledge and his knowledge of the historical sources.

In order to make up this ground, battlefield researchers need to understand what the commanders of the time brought to the battlefield in terms of military doctrine. What is useful is getting your head around the successive editions of the *Field Service Regulations* that governed the thought of British Empire officers up to the Second World War. After about 1941 a rapidly changing war forced a change in doctrine; it was still laid down but in other forms. For the Australian Military Forces doctrine was laid down in various pamphlets, papers and booklets, all preserved in the series AWM 54 at the Australian War Memorial. This means that if you want to understand why commanders made decisions on Gallipoli or on the Somme, and fought the Japanese in jungle warfare differently, then you need a nodding acquaintance with the relevant manuals.

The same sort of argument applies to historical skill. Historians are among the least stuffy of all academics about their sense of belonging to an exclusive guild. But historical expertise entails more than specialist knowledge. However expert you may become on any aspect of the human past, your training as an historian will be incomplete unless you master and practise what is sometimes grandly called the 'historical method'. Historians will (naturally) disagree with what this covers, but most would agree that it involves thinking about the ways we can understand and interpret the past. Their professional training (if that idea can be applied to the informal way most of us gained our skills) revolves around asking questions about the sources we find and create, the ways we can and can't employ the evidence, the ways we express arguments about those interpretations. An historian's training ought to be unending, because we can always learn more about how we understand the past from each encounter with a topic or a student, or indeed, with new sources, such as an unexplored battlefield.

In preparing for a project, it's not a question of having a checklist of historical skills to be ticked off, only an attitude of questioning and openness regarding where your project may lead.

The material: Sources for battlefield research

A successful field trip depends upon good preparation. A trip cannot be regarded as successful just because you reach the battlefield in question, take in the views, record your impressions, tour the cemetery and chat to a few locals. That method has been employed by more than one best-selling author professing to write military history, but it's bogus. For a battlefield research trip to be a success, you must arrive on the battlefield with enough knowledge to ask the right questions of the ground, and be equipped with enough knowledge to be able to interrogate the present in order to understand the past.

Anne-Marie Condé, now a curator at the National Museum of Australia (and the author of an insightful article on the battlefield of the Cowra prisoner-of-war camp), emphasises the folly of simply arriving to soak up some general impressions. (She would never have been accused of encouraging researchers to merely 'sniff the ground'.) She urges researchers to thoroughly understand the archival sources before embarking on field work. Field work, she warns, 'sounds sexier, more fun, more Indiana Jones-like', but unless it's backed by a solid grounding in what happened where you're going, you may well miss what you most need to find.

A successful battlefield research trip will depend upon you getting hold of the sources you need for the trip you're making, well in advance. They will inform the questions you pose and the ideas that your visit will test. You will understand the ground all the more because you will arrive with a good idea of what happened and where. Note that a successful trip doesn't depend upon getting hold of as much source material as possible—plenty of research projects, from simple articles for Military Historical Society journals to theses and books have foundered on the mistaken conviction that a researcher has to read everything before he or she can say anything. Wrong: but what's right?

Your research should be proportional to your project and its product. If you're just looking for Uncle Jim's grave, then your preparation will be less ambitious than if you're planning to produce a new book on the Malayan campaign. But if you're planning to do much more than follow the familiar route to the cemetery, then you need to go prepared. There are several crucial sources you should consider consulting.

Primary sources are:

- The unit or formation war diary
- Official records
- Private records
- Photographs
- 'Stuff'—artefacts as sources

Secondary sources are:

- The official histories
- Unit histories
- 'The literature'

Let's consider these sources individually.

Primary sources

Getting your hands on archival documents is—and believe me, remains—one of the most exciting and rewarding parts of researching and writing history. Even when sources today are so often digitised, there is still a thrill about reading a document written under fire on Gallipoli or marked by the humidity of Kokoda. What are some of these sources?

THE UNIT OR FORMATION WAR DIARY

This is the day-to-day record maintained by the unit (battalion or equivalent) or formation (brigade or above). A war diary (often given capital letters—War Diary—as if it has a special status) is the fundamental source for detailed military history. Officers (usually the unit's adjutant or the intelligence officer) filled in a narrative from hour to hour in action, and afterwards filed reports or even the originals of messages received, and maps often marked to show what happened where. Higher formation diaries are similar, but because they include orders given before battle and reports afterwards, they often provide a clearer view of what happened. Because it's closest to the action, a battalion war diary gives an immediate feel, but can also often seem confusing.

The originals of war diaries were sent back to Australia, eventually reaching the National Archives, but all war diaries are actually held by the Research Centre at the Australian War Memorial. All the Great War diaries are available on microfilm (copies of which are held by most state libraries), but digital copies are becoming available on the War Memorial's website, notably the most useful to battlefield researchers, those of headquarters and infantry battalions. The Second World War diaries are also gradually being digitised—check the War Memorial's website. These diaries include many maps, often made on the spot and at the time, the starting point for many battlefield research projects.

Details of the equivalent of war diaries and other operational sources for the Boer War can be found in Craig Wilcox's *Australia's Boer War*. For the world wars, thousands of diaries are part of the National Archives/War Memorial series (AWM 4 for the Great War and AWM 52 for the Second World War). They are organised by unit and month, so once you know which units and which period you need, you're likely to need to consult only a few diaries for particular periods. For Malaya, Viet Nam and the confrontation with Indonesia, the Army essentially followed the same system, though the unit record was renamed the 'Commander's Diary'. All of the diaries for these conflicts are held in the Australian War Memorial, and many are now available online, so you can take with you digital copies of crucial documents.

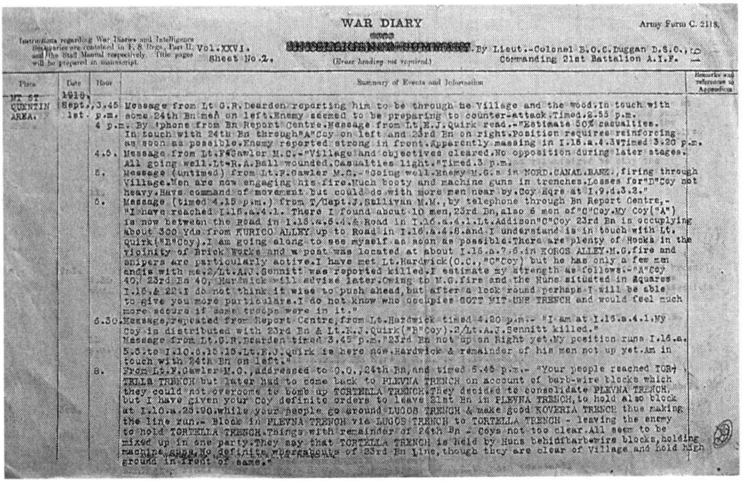

WAR DIARY

~~INTELLIGENCE SUMMARY~~

Army Form C. 2118.

Instructions regarding War Diaries and Intelligence Summaries are contained in F. S. Regs., Part II. and the Staff Manual respectively. Title pages will be prepared in manuscript.

Vol. XXVI. Sheet No. 2.

(Erase heading not required.)

By Lieut.-Colonel B.O.C. Duggan D.S.O., Commanding 21st Battalion A.I.F.

Place	Date	Hour	Summary of Events and Information	Remarks and references to Appendices
MT ST QUENTIN AREA.	1918. Sept. 1st.	3.45 p.m.	Message from Lt G.R. Dearden reporting him to be through he Village and the wood. In touch with some 24th Bn men on left. Enemy seemed to be preparing to counter-attack. Timed. 2.55 p.m.	
		4 p.m.	By 'phone from Bn Report Centre. Message from Lt E.J. Quirk read.-"Estimate 50% casualties. In touch with 24th Bn through "A" Coy on left and 23rd Bn on right. Position requires reinforcing as soon as possible. Enemy reported strong in front. Apparently massing in I.18.a.4.3" Timed 3.20 p.m.	
		4.5.	Message from Lt. F. Gawler M.C.-"Village and objectives cleared. No opposition during later stages. All going well. Lt. R.A. Ball wounded. Casualties light." Timed. 3 p.m.	
		5.	Message (untimed) from Lt. F. Gawler M.C.-"Going well. Enemy M.G.s in NORD. CANAL. BANK., firing through Village. Men are now engaging his fire. Much booty and machine guns in trenches. Losses for "D" Coy not heavy. Have command of movement but could do with more men near by. Coy Hqrs at I.9.d.3.2."	
		6.	Message (timed 4.15 p.m.) from T/Capt. J. Sullivan M.M., by telephone through Bn Report Centre,- "I have reached I.16.a.4.1. There I found about 10 men, 23rd Bn, also 6 men of "C" Coy. My Coy ("A") is now between the Road in I.15.a.6.4. & Road in I.16.a.4.1. Lt. Addison "C" Coy 23rd Bn is occupying about 300 Yds from KURICO ALLEY up to Road in I.16.a.4.8. and I understand is in touch with Lt. Quirk ("B" Coy). I am going along to see myself as soon as possible. There are plenty of Hocks in the vicinity of Brick Works and a post was located at about I.15.a.7.6. in KOROS ALLEY. M.G. fire and snipers are particularly active. I have met Lt. Hardwick (O.C., "C" Coy) but he has only a few men and is with me. 2/Lt. A.J. Sennitt was reported killed. I estimate my strength as follows.-"A" Coy 40, 23rd Bn 40, Hardwick will advise later. Owing to M.G. fire and the Huns situated in Squares I.16 & 22. I do not think it wise to push ahead, but after a look round perhaps I will be able to give you more particulars. I do not know who occupies GOTT MIT UNS TRENCH and would feel much more secure if some troops were in it."	
		6.30.	Message, repeated from Report Centre, from Lt. Hardwick timed 4.20 p.m.- "I am at I.15.a.4.1. My Coy is distributed with 23rd Bn & Lt. E.J. Quirk ("B" Coy). 2/Lt. A.J. Sennitt killed." Message from Lt. G.R. Dearden timed 3.45 p.m. "23rd Bn not up on Right yet. My position runs I.16.a. 5.5. to I.10.c.15.15. Lt. E.J. Quirk is here now. Hardwick & remainder of his men not up yet. Am in touch with 24th Bn on left."	
		8.	From Lt. F. Gawler M.C., addressed to C.O., 24th Bn, and timed 5.45 p.m.- "Your people reached TORTELLA TRENCH but later had to come back to PLEVNA TRENCH on account of barb-wire blocks which they could not overcome to bomb up TORTELLA TRENCH. They decided to consolidate PLEVNA TRENCH, but I have given your Coy definite orders to leave 21st Bn in PLEVNA TRENCH, to hold also block at I.10.a.25.90. while your people go around LUGOS TRENCH & make good KOVERIA TRENCH thus making the line run.- Block in PLEVNA TRENCH via LUGOS TRENCH to TORTELLA TRENCH - leaving the enemy to hold TORTELLA TRENCH. Things with remainder of 24th Bn - Coys not too clear. All seem to be mixed up in one party. They say that TORTELLA TRENCH is held by Huns behind barbwire blocks, holding machine guns. No definite whereabouts of 23rd Bn line, though they are clear of Village and hold high ground in front of same."	

The unit war diary of the 21st Battalion from September 1918 from the series AWM 4. This is the 'narrative' or 'chronicle' part of the diary, giving a summary of operations day by day. 'Appendices' following this part detail the unit's doings for the month. (Australian War Memorial; Peter Stanley)

Of course in practice it's not as simple as I've implied. For Gallipoli and a lot of the fighting on the Western Front, the diaries are pretty sketchy. And you may need to consult the diaries of flanking or support units, and that gets you into some murky waters, mostly in identifying which units you need. For the Great War, versions of some war diaries ended up in the National Archives in Britain, and you may need to consult them, at least if you're thinking of a serious or detailed study. And often Australian units were part of larger British Empire (or for later wars American) forces, so my books *Quinn's Post* and *Alamein* also needed British records, and for *Tarakan* American records. (Looking into the 'enemy' side of the line often demands special help. For *Alamein* my co-author Mark Johnston had German, but for *Quinn's Post*, in the absence of Ottoman language and records, all I could do was acknowledge the Turkish experience in general terms.)

Not that records in English are necessarily easy to read or use. Craig Tibbitts, who has both curated these records and is using them for his forthcoming history of the 56th Battalion, warns that because they are based on much shared knowledge it can be hard for outsiders to crack the code. He recommends moving from the published unit history to the higher formation diaries and then lastly to the more detailed unit diary. 'By the time you get to the battalion war diary', he writes, 'you'll be much better placed to understand its detail'.

On the ground, you may want to carry with you copies of reports from the diaries, and they will be the source of some of the most useful maps, and especially of sketch maps (made by patrols, for example) that only appear in unit war diaries.

OFFICIAL RECORDS

'Official records' is a catch-all term, but it isn't as vague as it seems. As often happens in military historical research, someone has been there before you and has asked similar questions, and you benefit from their work. The people who wrote the official histories were confronted with vast amounts of 'official records' of the world wars, much of it routine and transient, some of it unique and important. They essentially culled the records, and the resultant series, AWM 25 and AWM 26 for the Great War and AWM 54 for the Second World War, include records on just about every aspect of the Army's war service. These series also include reports on particular military operations and aspects of them, again, often including both orders and maps. Some of this duplicates the war diaries, but because it was compiled at a higher level, often later on, it's frequently more comprehensible. All were both indexed and cross-indexed by the official historians' 'literary assistants'. You can find your way around these series using the National Archives of Australia's excellent 'Recordsearch' database (www.naa.gov.au), entering likely terms in the search box and limiting the search to the relevant series. There are comparable records for the post-1945 conflicts, and the War Memorial's Research Centre staff are best placed to advise.

PRIVATE RECORDS

This term covers the most diverse range of sources, one that is often of most value to the historian, and also the most elusive: the records created by individuals. It certainly encompasses the classic 'letters and diaries', of the kind first used en masse by Bill Gammage in his ground-breaking *The Broken Years*. Bill showed the massive potential of the private records collected by the Australian War Memorial over the previous 50 years but hardly used by any authors until then. Even Charles Bean—to whom Bill dedicated his book—barely used the records he knew of, presumably because he was overwhelmed by the mass of official records available to him. Gammage showed us the way, and set an approach to military history we now take for granted.

Personal sources may comprise the papers of senior officers such as Monash or Blamey, to the diaries or letters of privates and gunners. Officers' papers can often shed light on dispositions and decisions—though a lieutenant's perspective on Pozières may be as murky as his men's. A private's memoir of his corner of the war may not illuminate the orders of the Great Captains, but may well tell you a great deal about what that bit of the war was like for him, in that spot, at that moment. Both can be of great value, and that value should not be underestimated.

One way to maximise the value of these personal sources is to find and use as many as you can. You can read them 'against each other', looking for hints in one for how you can understand another. Sometimes these sources give up 'hard' details of what happened, where and why. Others give atmospheric impressions of what it may have been like in general. When he reached Quinn's Post, the historian of Anzac pilgrimages, Bruce Scates, read a

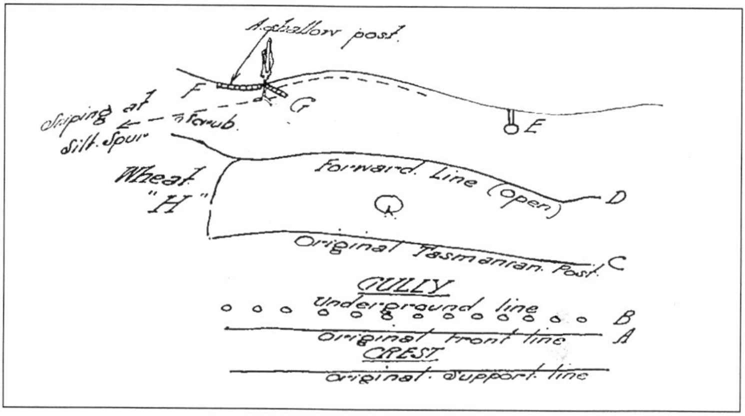

Charles Bean's diaries and notebooks contain a wealth of detail—more even than he included in the official history. The books contain many diagrams and sketch maps that trace the positions of sub-units and even individuals. This sketch details Tasmania Post, on the southern extremity of the Anzac position on Gallipoli. (Australian War Memorial; Peter Stanley)

diary kept by his grandfather on Gallipoli as a member of the Royal Naval Division. It didn't especially help his understanding of the fighting, but it certainly helped to forge an imaginative connection between the historian and the men of 1915.

The documents you can use to connect with place will reflect your interest and personality. I sang a verse or two of the 1933 musical film *Forty-second Street* while explaining the action of that name on Crete; the engaging British historian Stephen Badsey, an expert on the Boer War, has been known to recite Banjo Paterson's verse on British Army 'staff rides' in South Africa. At Klip Drift he gave them the entire poem of 'With French to Kimberley'. They're certain to remember the occasion, at least!

Often private records carry a weight disproportionate to their quantity. While the battalion war diary might provide the framework of events (including the messages to and from headquarters that reveal the drama moment-to-moment), it is

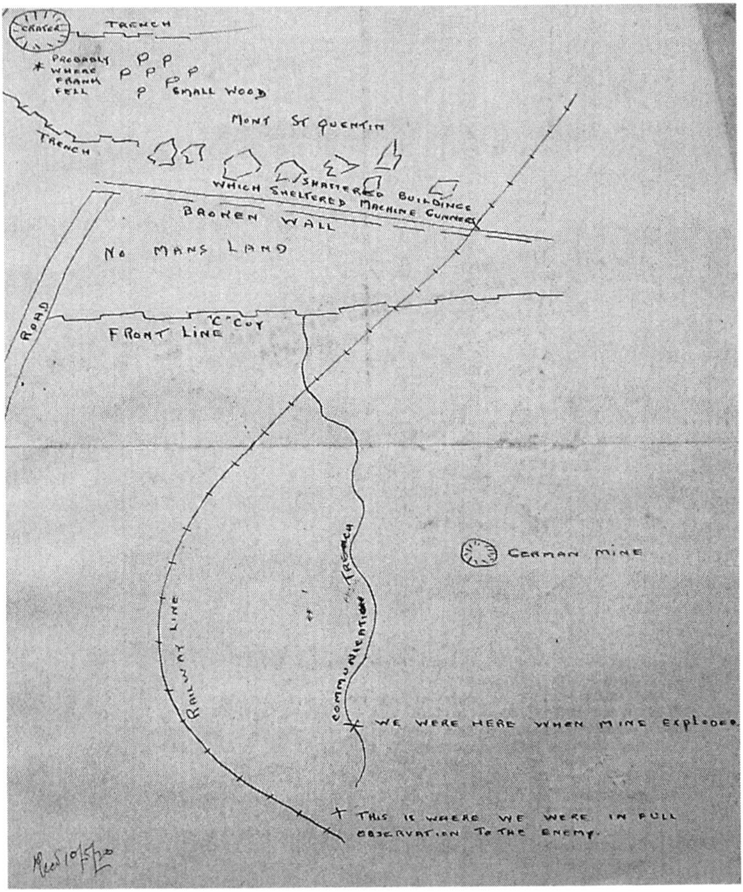

A sketch map, probably by Sergeant Vic Edwards, 21st Battalion, showing the route followed by Nine Platoon, C Company, in the fighting at Mont St Quentin on 1 September 1918. (J.G. Roberts papers, Ms 8508, State Library of Victoria; Peter Stanley)

often the personal record, a diary scribbled by a soldier by candlelight or a letter home, that reveals more of men's feelings and fears. Private records can also mislead and betray the unwary. Just this week, by comparing a corporal's private diary (actually rewritten after the war, I think) and his battalion war diary, I found that he had largely fabricated and certainly exaggerated his experience.

But without personal sources, military history is often dry stuff. For *Quinn's Post*, I consulted a great many personal sources between my first and my second visit to that scrubby ridge. I found myself on my second visit recalling descriptions and incidents. For instance, on the night of 9 May men of the 15th Battalion made a raid on the Turkish trenches opposite Quinn's. Hutton Armstrong led an assault party a couple of dozen men strong into the trenches at the head of Mule Gully. Their report recorded that they penetrated a couple of hundred yards into the Turkish lines, cutting telephone wires, smashing kit and shooting or bayoneting every Turk they found. Could they have made it so far into the Turkish lines, I wondered? I pored over the maps showing the Turkish trenches and examined the scrub-covered ground, now virtually devoid of any sign of trenches. Two hundred yards seemed a long way. I decided that as there was no suggestion that they had exaggerated the distance I would trust the eyewitness accounts.

Private records could also include memoirs and oral history written or gathered years after the events in question. Memoirs, published or not, are also an important source, though one complicated by the vagaries of memory and reputation. However, the result often repays the effort of studying them. For *Quinn's Post*, it was the diaries of engineer officers that alerted me to the dark war fought beneath the trenches, largely neglected in official records. And the abundance of frank and informative New Zealand personal sources (the New Zealanders held Quinn's through the summer) enabled me both to write a detailed and candid interpretation and to produce a truly Anzac history of this vital spot. Visiting Quinn's again after reading these sources helped me to see it through the eyes of the men who created it.

PHOTOGRAPHS

It's impossible to overestimate the value of photographs to the battlefield researcher. Fundamentally, he or she is trying to re-create a long-vanished place before establishing what happened there. If you can't locate exactly where an event happened, it will be even harder to understand or describe it. It was this lack of specific detail that led to my disillusionment with my Gallipoli project about Distinguished Conduct Medal winners: in many cases, I had vague descriptions of 'deeds' to work with, often with no indication of where they had been performed. So the physical appearance of a site is often a useful starting point.

Nigel Steel, a Gallipoli and Western Front (and lately Korean) expert, uses photographs as the initial reference point, once he reaches the locations he's investigating. Photographs often provide that starting point in a tangible, easily transported form. While vegetation and buildings often disappear or change over the decades, streams, roads, railways, bridges and horizons usually remain as they were for longer. As ever, looking up and around helps to locate what is no longer physically present. The horizon can be matched long after the trenches have gone. For the seemingly 'featureless' landscapes, such as the deserts of North Africa and the Middle East, photographs can unfortunately be a less productive source.

The best historical photographs should provide what is known in the trade as 'provenance'. Ideally a date and other details, such as who took the photograph, and why, can help a researcher to judge the value of a photograph. Even without provenance, photographs have value as evidence. Recently Andrew Faulkner, the biographer of Arthur Blackburn VC, found a stash of Gallipoli photographs in Blackburn's papers. Almost all were uncaptioned, a major disappointment, except that Andrew was often able to work from the known to the unknown. He knew where Blackburn's unit had mostly served, and was able to decide on approximate

Then and now. The entrance to the Bellicourt tunnel in France, captured by Australian troops in the attacks on the Hindenburg Line in September 1918, as depicted by war artist Arthur Streeton (top) and as seen in September 2007. (Australian War Memorial: Arthur Streeton, *Bellicourt: entrance to St Quentin Tunnel, 1918*, watercolour over pencil 37.2 × 55.4 cm, ART03517; Peter Stanley)

locations and even dates for many photographs. These photographs included shots of parts of the Anzac line rarely represented in photographs, as well as an extraordinary shot taken looking up through a collapsible periscope.

The opposite principle applies to those using photographs as prompts for a search. Peter Burness, author of *The Nek* and the most authoritative Australian guide on the Western Front, has spent many hours searching for particular places, often using a contemporary photograph as a starting point. For example, he has now traced and visited many of the chateaux in which Australian commanders and staff officers lived and worked on the Western Front, and has used contemporary photographs to establish what happened where. (Historians' jargon is the opposite to interior decorators': to decorators, 'contemporary' means 'now'; to historians, 'contemporary' means 'then'.)

'STUFF': ARTEFACTS AS SOURCES

A couple of decades ago, military history was largely a matter of veterans and military history buffs—invariably men—gathering facts about what happened in battle. Informed by twenty years of books and new approaches developed both overseas and in Australia, military history today is a much more varied and sophisticated activity. Informed by what we might call the 'war and society' school, military historians of all persuasions are much less likely to simply want to describe where a particular battalion went and chronicle what it did, and more inclined to deal with how the men involved felt about it and remembered it.

But for all this sophistication, the core of operational military history remains stubbornly intractable. For all of our concern for the way war has affected individuals and their societies, for its broader impacts and the ways it has been commemorated, understanding war on the battlefield involves understanding military organisation, weapons and tactics. You need to know how big a platoon, company or battalion was supposed to be (and whether the one you're interested in was seriously or merely ordinarily under-strength). You need to know who was in charge and what they were supposed to do, and who they took orders from. You need to know how they got those orders, and what they did to fulfil them (that is, 'tactics'). You need to know what kit they carried, what weapons they used. You need to know a bit about how their enemies were organised, equipped and armed too.

If you're not already a military buff, you'll need to acquire some of the knowledge that these people carry about with them. For Australia in the Second World War, Mark Johnston has written a series of books detailing the organisation, equipment and operations of Australian divisions; books on the 7th and 9th Divisions have already been published, and a book on the 6th is to come. (Here, I have to admit, it helps to have been a teenager in the days when they messed about with plastic models rather than Xboxes: I still use esoteric knowledge about weapons and vehicles that I acquired as a model-making nerd in the early 1970s, as do a sizeable number of my colleagues. If you lack this kind of upbringing, you'll need to find ways of acquiring this knowledge.)

One of the best sources for learning about the physical details of weapons and kit is a military museum. Just as Charlie and Jack Bean learned about Waterloo by gazing into cabinets displaying the relics of the Old Guard and the Foot Guards, so we need to do the same to understand the paraphernalia of Australia's wars. The biggest and best military museum in Australia is, of course, the Australian War Memorial, in Canberra. Its galleries display just about every weapon and piece of gear used by Australian soldiers—infantry at least—in every significant conflict or campaign from the New South Wales contingent in the Sudan in 1885 to peacekeepers in the Sudan in 2008. For the Great War, the Pacific War and several post-1945 conflicts, display cases contain

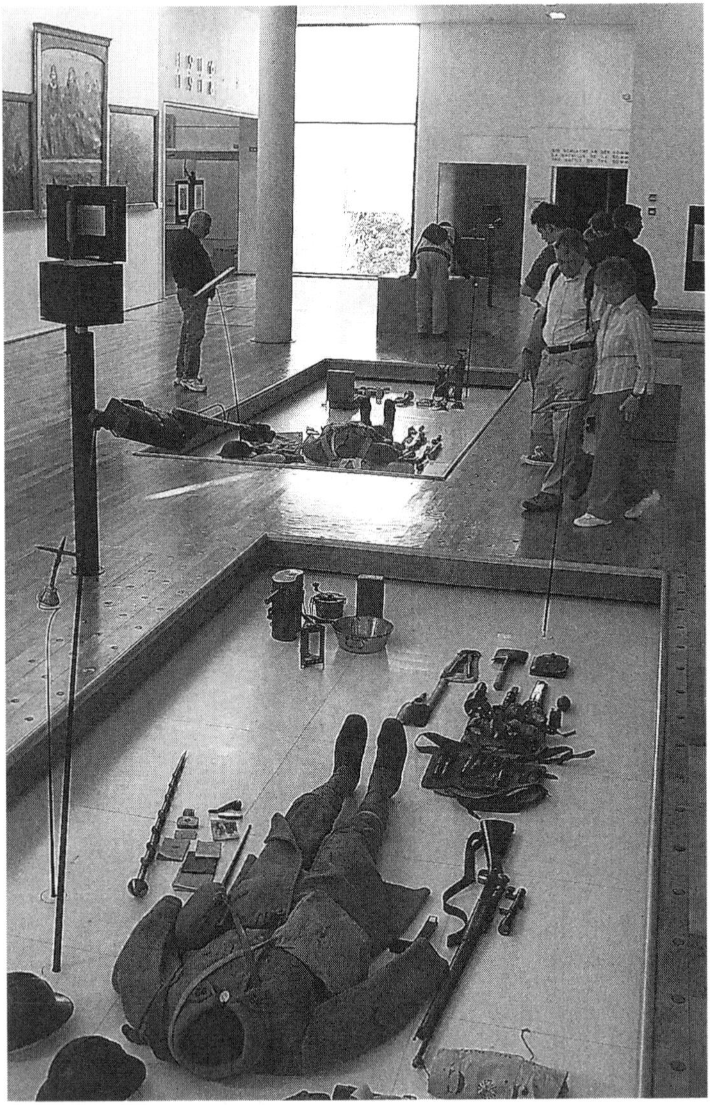

Museums are excellent places in which to get an understanding of the uniform, weapons and kit worn, used or carried by participants in the events we study. This display is in the Historial de la Grande Guerre in Péronne, France, itself a battlefield in September 1918. (Peter Stanley)

the stuff worn or carried by representative individual men—the legendary Private Giles of 1918 and the extraordinary commando Lieutenant Mick Sheehan of 1943. Many of these items can also now be seen on the War Memorial's vast but easy-to-use website (www.awm.gov.au). This means that time spent visiting either online or in person can equip you with a good basic idea of what the people you're interested in wore, carried or used.

There's an equally useful if unduly neglected resource available through the Army History Unit's Army Museums Network. The Army maintains some 27 museums, in all states, documenting the service of both particular corps and of military units generally with a connection to a particular state. The Army's museums give you the opportunity to look at (and if you ask nicely even handle) the weapons or equipment that you're particularly interested in. It is absolutely essential that you try to get a good idea of the physicality of the gear your bloke used. For example, I had no idea of the weight of a Lewis gun until I was fortunate to be able to hold one, and I tried to recall that weight on Mont St Quentin. Carrying that memory with you helps to make the past real.

Secondary sources

Historians sometimes quibble over the distinction between primary and secondary sources. Is a newspaper, published at the time but written by someone who did not witness the event, a secondary or a primary source? Is a unit history written by an eyewitness but published twenty years later really a secondary source? The distinction is fluid and flexible; the real point is to oblige us to think about who is writing or recording what about the events in question, and why. Even if the difference is strictly arbitrary, it alerts us to think about the weight and value we place on such sources. Conventionally, secondary sources come in several varieties worth distinguishing.

OFFICIAL HISTORIES

Like the United States, and Britain and other Commonwealth nations, Australia has enthusiastically embraced the idea of publishing 'official histories' of its wars. The war correspondent Charles Bean's Great War history (twelve volumes published between 1921 and 1942) was inspired by a combination of William Kinglake's history of the Crimean War and the 'staff' histories that developed in European armies in the late nineteenth century. Bean based the six volumes he wrote (dealing with the AIF on Gallipoli and on the Western Front) on his own detailed diaries and the official records and war diaries he helped to create. Six other authors wrote further volumes on other aspects of Australia's war. Bean's history, though criticised as being too parochial and focusing too closely on the men in the trenches, has endured as a lasting achievement (it is still heavily used nearly 90 years after it first appeared; this book won't be).

The 22-volume Second World War project includes the Army (six volumes), Navy (two), Air (four), Medical (four) and Civil (six) series. The official historian (like Bean, a journalist), Gavin Long, wrote three volumes in the Army series. Two volumes of the Korean War history were written by Robert O'Neill (the first professional historian), and there's Peter Edwards's yet-to-be-finished South-East Asian conflicts series, and the new official history of peacekeeping operations, edited by David Horner. As David Horner has often explained, what makes histories like his 'official' is merely that their authors are granted access to high-level official records in advance of their release. While their authors are usually knowledgeable and skilful historians, they have no special mandate and their work has been and will be open to revision as further research proceeds and records become available.

Still, Australia's official histories are among the great achievements of Australian historical scholarship, and form an invaluable starting point for battlefield research. They can be relied upon to set the scene of virtually any action you care to investigate and provide essential details to explain what was happening, to whom and why. Note, though, that they are a starting point. Bean's history in particular is so comprehensive that it can give the impression that everything that can be said has been. It has paradoxically deterred historians from attempting to add to or challenge it, and its reputation for accuracy paralysed at least one of his successors.

However, as an author of an official history, Jeff Grey, has pointed out, official histories are merely a first look, not the last word. The world wars in particular were so eventful that despite their bulk the official histories cannot possibly document, deal with or even mention everything. This fact will come home to you as soon as you look up 'your' battle or the incident you want to research in the relevant volume. At present I am writing a book about an incident in the taking of Mont St Quentin that Bean mentions in passing in one paragraph in Volume VI. At that rate there are several thousand books still to be written.

Most volumes of both Bean's Great War and Long's Second World War official histories can be picked up for between 50 and 100 dollars from second-hand bookshops or internet booksellers. However, both series can be obtained free from the Australian War Memorial's website, www.awm.gov.au. The text and index are searchable, which means that you can locate specific pages and take them with you (though you should resist the temptation to look too closely at your patch of battlefield—read the surrounding chapters to understand the bigger picture). Craig Tibbitts recommends downloading digital versions of official records, histories and maps onto your laptop to take with you. This may work for you, though the weight (and worry) of a laptop may be as great as lugging a wodge of paper with you. Please yourself.

UNIT HISTORIES

Many units, especially in the combatant arms—infantry, artillery, light horse and armour, and often engineers—wanted to record their own histories, and often published a history soon after their war ended. (It's never an 'official history', even if it was authorised or published by a unit association, but is simply a history.) Some either published nothing or published a superficial history, and some have been lucky enough to have had histories written and published as part of the boom in Australian military history, often decades after the incidents took place.

These 'unit histories', as they are known in Australia, are another invaluable starting point for battlefield research. They are often written by members of the unit (a mixed blessing—it makes them knowledgeable but also sensitive to criticism) and are in many cases based on both unit war diaries and private records, some now otherwise lost.

The unit history can often provide a departure point for a battlefield research project. For example, Cecil Lock's 1936 history of the 10th Battalion (*The Fighting 10th*) includes a detailed account of the capture of the village of Merris early in 1918. Presumably based on the battalion's war diary, the book has always struck me as being conducive to following the operation. As part of a forthcoming study of 'peaceful penetration' Michael Molkentin crawled about the hedgerows of Flanders, learning how peaceful penetration worked on the ground. The 10th Battalion history gives detailed map references, and now the battalion war diary is available on the internet through the War Memorial's website.

'THE LITERATURE'

This brings us to what historians call 'the literature'—the potentially vast field of secondary sources written by historians generally. If you're serious about understanding a battle, you'll need to look at what has been written about it. This needn't be burdensome. The more you read the more you'll get a feel for what is worth persevering with and what can be skipped or omitted.

With the exceptions of Gallipoli and Kokoda, not so much has been published on any one action to make reading the secondary literature a difficult task. For example, the battles of Bullecourt were two of the most dramatic engagements of 1917, but there's almost nothing available on them. The published material includes Bean's Volume IV on the AIF 'in France' in 1917, some out-of-print battalion histories, Jonathan Walker's *The Blood Tub* (a British study), and Eric Andrews and Bede Jordan's 1989 article, 'Second Bullecourt revisited' (although it's worth noticing that Eric and Bede did not actually 'revisit' the battlefield; they worked off maps and documents). As this book went to press, the Army History Unit announced that it had awarded a research grant to the experienced military historian David Coombes, and the grant would help him walk the ground at Bullecourt.

Likewise, if you're interested in the Ramu–Markham campaign in New Guinea, Phil Bradley's *On Shaggy Ridge*, some unit histories, David Horner's study of 'Bloody George' Vasey and David Dexter's *The New Guinea Offensives* just about cover the field. So there's ample opportunity to develop your own study of aspects of this campaign. (Some years ago, although I could not visit the place, I published an article on the commandos' seizure of Kaiapit, a highly comprehensible small action in New Guinea in September 1943. Phil Bradley has written about it after visiting: guess whose work is more informed?) Other opportunities abound in New Guinea especially. We await Karl James's book on Bougainville (the island, unfortunately, was a 'no-go' area when he wrote it.) No one has written about the New Britain campaign, an island that is crying out for studies of Arty Hill, say, based on field work.

Despite some fine works mentioned in this book, the period after 1945 is still almost an open field. The essential reference

Phil Bradley, with Wau Valley and its airfield in the distance, while on a field trip for his 2008 book *The Battle for Wau*. (Phil Bradley)

for any trip relating to peacekeepers, for example, is Peter Londey's pioneering *Other People's Wars*, the first history of Australian peacekeeping operations since 1947. It presages David Horner's official history of Australian peacekeeping, five volumes of which will be out, knowing David Horner, on time over the next few years. Many of the chapters written by his historians (including Peter Londey) are based on field work in uncomfortable and sometimes unstable places. In the meantime, articles, such as Peter Londey's 'Fifty years watch', about Cyprus—part of a series based on visits to peacekeeping missions or locales—have appeared in the War Memorial's useful *Wartime* magazine.

In approaching this literature, the first thing is to develop a working bibliography. Reading the most recent book on a subject will give an idea of what else has been written, and whether it is worth reading. Reviews of books in newspapers, journals such as the *Journal of the Australian War Memorial*, *Wartime* and *Sabretache*, or various forums online will also give you an informed perspective, though of course you should make up your own mind.

Remember, what you read will depend upon your project. For one project, a book may be vital, while for another, it may be useless; it will depend on the questions you pose. While it helps to develop a broad understanding of the context of your project, the narrower your enquiry is, the less widely you'll need to read. Don't think you need to read everything. Be discriminating: books based on solid research should trump potboilers.

There are different ways of approaching what has been published. The traditional approach would have you master the secondary sources before moving on to the primary sources. To the extent that it helps to work from the known to the unknown, that makes sense, and you may want to do that. But however disciplined I am as a scholar, I can't help dipping into the primary sources at the same time as I read secondary ones. Sometimes I feel lost in the records, because I don't fully understand who's who or what's important, but the thrill of reading archival sources and the stimulus they offer is a powerful compensation. I find that reading both primary and secondary sources at the same time is to bounce the imagination back and forth between the two.

Finally, it's hard to think of any project that wouldn't be helped by John Coates's detailed and authoritative *Atlas of Australia's Wars*, which maps Australian military history from Botany Bay to East Timor in detail. It doesn't have topographical maps, and you certainly don't want it in your suitcase, but you do want to use it to get a synoptic picture of what happened and where.

Establish what you need to read closely, what you need to be familiar with, and what you can safely pass over. Remember, for the battlefield researcher the most significant source is, in fact, the ground itself, and it's to the battlefields, where they are and what they might tell us, that we must now turn.

PART 2

Intelligence briefing: Where to go and why

Where in the world? Australian battlefields

When I began work as a military historian 30 years ago, Peter Firkins published a book called *The Australians in Nine Wars*. Since then, regrettably but not surprisingly, further conflicts have occurred, while others, previously not recognised as conflicts, have been accepted as having taken place. What do I mean by that? Well, we know that since 1975 Australia has got involved in conflicts in the Middle East, in Afghanistan and Iraq, but we have also since accepted that British settlers fought against the Aboriginal inhabitants of our continent. We now recognise that Australia has fought in at least fourteen wars:

- Wars of settlement, 1788–c. 1880 (or beyond: please yourselves)
- New Zealand wars, c. 1845–70
- Sudan, 1885
- Boer War, 1899–1902
- 'Boxer' Rebellion, 1900–01
- Great War, 1914–18 (or 1919 if you include the Russian intervention)

- Second World War, 1939–45
- Korea, 1950–53
- Malayan Emergency, 1948–60
- Confrontation with Indonesia, 1963–66
- Viet Nam, 1962–72 (or 1975 according to some)
- First Iraq War, 1990–91
- Afghanistan, 2001–
- Second Iraq War, 2003–

While war regrettably remains a part of our lives (in Afghanistan and Iraq), Australia has taken an outstanding part in trying to stop wars and conflicts, by taking part in over 50 peacekeeping missions. The Australian Defence Force has participated in operations in about 40 countries since 1947, notably in Cambodia, Indonesia, Kashmir, Egypt, Somalia, Rwanda, East Timor and Bougainville, while the Australian Federal Police has kept the peace in Cyprus since 1964.

This record of getting involved in wars and, lately, trying to stop or limit them, means that Australians can travel to most parts of the world and find some place where Australians have served. For example, as we'll see in this book, Australians fought in both northern and southern Africa, and there are rewards in visiting Egypt, Libya and South Africa. But elsewhere in Africa Australians have seen active service too. In the Great War the RAN chased the German raider *Königsberg* into the Rufuji River delta in what is now Tanzania. Troopships called into Liberia in the Great War, and both warships and troopships operated in the Red Sea in the Second World War. (That explains why there are Australians buried in Liberia's capital, Freetown.) Australian airmen trained under the Empire Air Training Scheme in what is now Zimbabwe, and flew in operations not only over Egypt and Libya but Morocco, Algeria and Tunisia. There is even an Australian nursing sister buried in a Commonwealth War Graves

Commission cemetery in Eritrea. With the possible exception of the extraordinary saga of HMAS *Pioneer* in the Rufuji delta, few of these sites are worth a visit in themselves unless you have compelling individual motives.

Australians are buried in war cemeteries in no fewer than 75 countries. There are few places in the world besides South America where you won't encounter reminders of our nation's warlike past. Individual graves and sites in out-of-the-way places are intriguing, and you should visit them if you can. But the greatest interest for Australians lies in battlefields.

For the armchair traveller—or those seriously contemplating getting out of the chair, donning a stout pair of boots and exploring some Australian battlefields—the best single place to begin is Garrie Hutchinson's *Pilgrimage: A Traveller's Guide to Australia's Battlefields*, published in 2006. It takes readers on a journey across Australian battlefields in the Middle East, Europe, North Africa, the Mediterranean, South-East Asia, New Guinea, Korea and Viet Nam. Its focus is actually more on cemeteries and memorials rather than the battlefields themselves, but Hutchinson has visited most of the places he writes about. While he often errs on the sentimental side, he also offers sensible, practical advice.

How can it be both sentimental and practical? Let me give two examples of each. He defies anyone not to cry after reading the Atatürk inscription at Anzac Cove—the one beginning 'Those heroes . . .'. I didn't cry, and don't. Its syrupy sentiment is just plain bad history—the Turks have *never* cared for Anzac graves, and between 1915 and 1919 they looted and desecrated them. For reasons unexplained, his description of New Guinea concentrates only on 1942 and he calls it the 'Battle for Australia'. While this is an emotional rather than a historical point, he concedes in the very first sentence that the Japanese did not plan to invade Australia. But practical? I'll say. He advises travellers heading to battlefields in Israel to be careful what stamps they let immigration officials put in their passports—they understand the complexities of Middle East travel and are usually happy to give you a loose-leaf visa stamp. He shows that travel to places perceived as risky—such as Libya and Lebanon—can be rewarding and enjoyable. The fact that Garrie has visited just about everywhere he writes about makes his advice trustworthy.

Pilgrimage will give even seasoned battlefield crawlers useful tips and ideas for future projects. It's not a book to take with you, but it is a book to inspire and guide, and it comes highly recommended. A spin-off from *Pilgrimage*, Hutchinson's pocket-sized guide for Gallipoli 'pilgrims', while equally mawkish over Atatürk and curiously gullible over Turkish myths, is also a good brief guide for casual visitors to the peninsula.

As Garrie Hutchinson shows, there are many places to go and battlefields to see, all with their own intellectual, physical and logistic challenges. This Part offers a survey of where to go and what to do, aimed at active battlefield researchers rather than people who only visit cemeteries and memorials.

Battlefields in Australia and New Zealand

Most Australians think of their wars happening overseas—in France, Gallipoli or Papua New Guinea. If prompted for battles within Australia, they may vaguely remember that the Japanese attacked Darwin, and weren't there Japanese submarines in Sydney Harbour? But there are many battlefields in Australia.

Battles of invasion and occupation

Over the past 30 years or so, historians, and Australians generally, have accepted that a conflict was fought across much of Australia, a war for the possession of this continent, a war between its

Aboriginal inhabitants and the British settlers who, from the defenders' point of view, came to invade and dispossess them. It's ironic that many Australian battlefield tourists leave from Sydney airport, the site of the earliest encounter between British soldiers (in this case Marines) and the Eora people of Sydney. In December 1790 Watkin Tench led a Marine patrol to capture or kill 'Indians' who had killed one of Governor Phillips's game-keepers. Tench's expedition got lost on the swampy margins of Botany Bay—the land now occupied by Kingsford Smith airport. That 'battlefield' is lost, swallowed up by the development of Sydney. But if the site of Watkin Tench's humiliation is lost forever, other sites are not.

Various specialised works deal with the battlefields of the conquest of Aboriginal Australia. One of the most intriguing cases is the site of the massacre on 26 January 1838 of Kamilaroi people by Major George Nunn's party of Mounted Police. In *Waterloo Creek*, based on extensive field research, Roger Milliss locates the site of the massacre on Waterloo Creek, south of Moree, New South Wales. For my 1986 book, *The Remote Garrison*, I used the same evidence (and my own field research—my first) to locate the site on Slaughterhouse Creek, east of Moree. I suspect that Milliss's more substantive research is probably correct, but the two accounts reinforce the relationship between archival and field research. Here, perhaps, there is a need for further research, including walking the ground.

Another instance is Pinjarra, on the Murray River an hour or so by car south of Perth. At about nine on the morning of 28 October 1834, sixteen British soldiers and eight civilians led by Governor James Stirling attacked an encampment of Nyungars on the banks of the Murray River at Pinjarra. The clash at Pinjarra, symbolic of how the settlement of the Australian continent entailed the destruction of entire Aboriginal communities, is tragic but also compelling. It is also a perfect example of how in history interpretation differs depending upon questions posed, sources consulted and assumptions made. Was it a 'battle' or rather a 'massacre', as the disparate casualty tolls suggest (two wounded soldiers, one of whom died, compared with at least twenty dead Nyungars). Did Stirling come upon the Aboriginals by chance, or did he plan to attack by surprise and from several points? Where exactly did the Europeans appear, and where were the Nyungars first fired upon?

These and many other questions fuel numerous existing and other possible studies of the event. Existing accounts include those in Geoff Blackburn's *Conquest and Settlement*, a history of the 21st (Royal North British) Fusiliers in Western Australia, Neville Green's *Broken Spears*, and Al Grassby and Marji Hill's *Six Australian Battlefields*. Peter Harries's unpublished thesis on 'the so-called battle' contains references to many useful maps (which depict the site and the events of that morning very differently). An afternoon in the Battye Library in Perth turned up a couple of dozen primary and secondary sources too numerous to list here, but including several contemporary sources that repaid study on the 'battlefield'.

Current versions of the encounter come to widely differing conclusions. While most writers on the 'battle' have visited the site, not all have used it as a source to determine what happened and why. I was able to spend only an hour on the ground, on a wet Sunday morning in June. The Murray was at a very different depth and while it was intriguing to visit the site, I wouldn't want to pontificate on the basis of a hasty visit. But a skilful battlefield researcher—such as Brad Manera or Chris Clark, say—using the various versions and sources available, could combine them with their experience of reading the ground and probably illuminate and deepen our understanding of this emblematic clash.

Chris Clark's invaluable reference, *The Encyclopaedia of Australia's Battles*, lists no fewer than 50 sites at which Aboriginals and Europeans clashed. It is also a good starting point to survey the dozens of Australian battles and actions that have not yet attracted a book or even an article-length study. (If you remain unconvinced that these encounters constituted a war, read Jeff Grey's *A Military History of Australia* or John Connor's *The Australian Frontier Wars*.)

Eureka

The idea of battlefield tourism in Australia virtually began on Bakery Hill in Ballarat, when on 4 December 1854 British troops and colonial police stormed the miners' stockade and suppressed by force the most significant political rebellion in Australian history. The site became a popular place to visit as a curiosity in late colonial Victoria. As at Botany Bay, though, modern Ballarat now covers the site of the Eureka stockade. Except to consider how the rebellion is commemorated and interpreted, there is no physical way to do field work at Eureka. This makes it one of the very few sites in Australian military history to be of no value to visit.

New Zealand

Australia's first experience of war overseas occurred in New Zealand. In 1860 the colony of Victoria sent its warship, HMCS *Victoria*, to support British forces fighting the Maoris in the second Anglo-Maori war. In the mid-1860s thousands of Australian volunteers embarked for New Zealand to serve in the Waikato Militia. Mark Whitmore's *Wartime* article, 'A Waikato tour', gives a good initial survey of the various 'Australian' sites in the Waikato region of New Zealand's North Island, notably Te Ranga, where a major action took place. Nigel Prickett's *Landscapes of Conflict* lives up to its sub-title, *A Field Guide to the New Zealand Wars*, with many maps, photographs and suggestions for further reading.

Darwin and the north

Early in 1942 the Japanese, victors of a swift and savage conquest of South-East Asia, seemed likely to invade mainland Australia. They didn't—they decided not to and never had a chance to change their minds. But they did attack Darwin and targets in Australia's north, and launched a submarine raid on warships in Sydney Harbour. (Neither was related to a possible invasion—the attacks on northern bases were made to counter Allied resistance to their Asian conquests, while the Sydney raid was a clumsy and unsuccessful attempt to divert American naval strength from the decisive battle that happened at Midway a few weeks later.) All of these raids were dramatic, and they suggest possibilities for battlefield research in both remote settlements and in the cities of Sydney and Darwin. There are literally hundreds of sites of military significance in northern Australia. Not all saw 'battle' in the strict sense, but these sites make up an important but largely unexplored part of Australia's military heritage.

Unfortunately, the sites of the Darwin and Sydney raids exemplify the difficulties of tracing air and sea battles on the surface. It's always worthwhile sitting on a Manly ferry to reflect on the Sydney Harbour attack, or on the wharf at Darwin to ponder the events of 19 February 1942. Feeling the heat and humidity of February in Darwin is salutary, but doing so doesn't give you a great insight into the historical events. Perhaps I'm asking the wrong questions, or am not using my imagination effectively.

The remains of the military history of 1942 lies all over Australia if only the researcher is informed enough to find it. For example, Richard Brown found tank traps at Belmont, near Newcastle, from the massive effort of fortification dating from the crisis of 1942. David Carment, the doyen of heritage studies in the Northern Territory, recommends Howard Pearce and Bob Alford's *A Wartime Journey: Stuart Highway Heritage Guide*, a detailed guide to military sites on and off 'the track'.

Battlefields in Western Europe

More Australians have fought and died on the battlefields of north-west Europe than in any other region, and quite small areas of northern France and Belgium provide vast scope for detailed field work.

The Western Front

The trench lines of Picardy and Flanders were on Germany's west, hence 'Western Front'. The main AIF operations on the Western Front can be summed up in the names that used to be familiar from Anzac Day banners.

1916:

- Fromelles (July)
- Pozières and Mouquet Farm (July–September)
- Somme winter (November–April)

1917:

- The advance to the Hindenburg Line (April)
- Bullecourt (first battle, April, and second battle, May)
- Messines (June)

- Third Ypres
- Menin Road (September)
- Polygon Wood (September)
- Broodseinde (October)
- Poelcappelle (October)
- Passchendaele (October)

1918:

- Villers-Bretonneux (April, May)
- Hazebrouck (April)
- Hamel (July)
- Amiens (August)
- Mont St Quentin/Peronne (August–September)
- Hindenburg Line (September)
- Montbrehain (October)

Each of these major operations saw intense and sometimes prolonged fighting, staggering losses and unimaginable individual suffering. Each could justify battlefield tramping for a week or more. Within and between these actions, however, are dozens of smaller operations, each of which offer compelling investigations. For example, except for biographers Ross McMullin (*Pompey Elliott*) and Peter Sadler (*The Paladin*), no one since Bean has written much about the 'outpost villages' in the advance to the Hindenburg Line (Doignies, Noreuil, Boursies, Hermies and Lagnicourt), each a small-scale fight. Trench raids, such as Stormy Trench or Celtic Wood, and dozens more with dates rather than names, could each be studied in greater or lesser detail, depending on the available sources. (Tony Spagnoli and Ted Smith, for example, wrote an entire book on 'the anatomy of a raid', on Celtic Wood in 1917.) Many battalions counted as their most notable engagements actions which today are just names. All of these operations justify both preparatory research and field work on the spot. Every battalion history suggests incidents and sites worth exploring in greater detail.

While Charles Bean's volumes of the official history remain the unavoidable source of detailed narrative, for the Western Front as a whole, no one has bettered Bill Gammage's book *The Broken Years* for a short, accessible overview. (It's worth noting that Bill tramped the battlefields of France and Belgium in 1970, when he checked the ground against the passages in the manuscript of his book.) If you read only one book to fuel your imagination, *The Broken Years* should be it, and it is handy enough to carry with you. A less portable but more recent book is Peter Pedersen's *The Anzacs*, the best one-volume account of Australia on the Western Front, also based on both solid archival research and thorough field work.

There are several useful guidebooks to the Australian part of the Western Front. Though it is dated, John Laffin's 1992 *Guide to Australian Battlefields of the Western Front* remains useful because of Laffin's extraordinarily detailed knowledge. He and his first wife Hazelle literally crawled around the cemeteries, recording inscriptions on individual headstones, a moving aspect of the book and, indeed, any visit to Commonwealth War Graves Commission (CWGC) cemeteries. Laffin's book is an essential preparation for any visitor, including serious researchers. Laffin was a life-long student of the Great War (and indeed, of every conflict going), and his book is full of throw-away observations, many based on his conversations with soldiers and civilians who lived through the Great War. Allan Box's 1996 *Footsteps of the Diggers* is a more selective guide to the Somme. It includes useful details on the memorials and cemeteries around Villers-Bretonneux, Pozières, Péronne and Bullecourt, with a good glossary and bibliography. But though Box is an expert, his book is essentially directed at visitors seeking particular graves, not battlefield researchers.

The way of the future may well be the website www.ww1westernfront.gov.au, produced by Richard Reid, the energetic former Principal Historian at the Department of Veterans' Affairs. This site offers descriptions, summaries, maps and directions to the major Australian sites in France and Belgium. Though aimed at casual tourists, it is also a useful guide for purposeful visitors (for example, it tells you the times of sunrise and sunset for any given point). The website has many links to other sites and is being developed with new maps and graphics, making it of increasing value and constant relevance.

It is very easy to find your way on the Western Front. It is one of the most thoroughly mapped areas of all Australian battlefields. The Michelin 1:20,000 and the Institut Géographique National 'Série Bleue' 1:25,000 include all CWGC cemeteries, as well as showing a vast range of geographic and topographic detail. Naturally, these modern maps need to be compared with 1916–18 maps, available from the Australian War Memorial's excellent Research Centre, either in person or through its website, www.awm.gov.au.

Besides the official history volumes of Charles Bean—all published between 65 and 75 years ago—it is striking just how little has been published on Australia's Western Front ordeal that has been based on sound field work. Biographies have been a strong strand—outstanding examples include Peter Pedersen's *Monash as Military Commander* and Ross McMullin's *Pompey Elliott*. There are relatively few studies of individual battles. The late Peter Charlton's *Pozières* is a popular account, but it has not yet been superseded. Fromelles has attracted some good work (Robin Corfield's *Don't Forget Me, Cobber*), as well as some overblown propaganda. Astonishingly, the only book on the Bullecourt battles is a British one, *The Blood Tub*, a good one. But what else is there? Robin Prior and Trevor Wilson, two military historians based in Australia, have published a string of major studies (of Rawlinson,

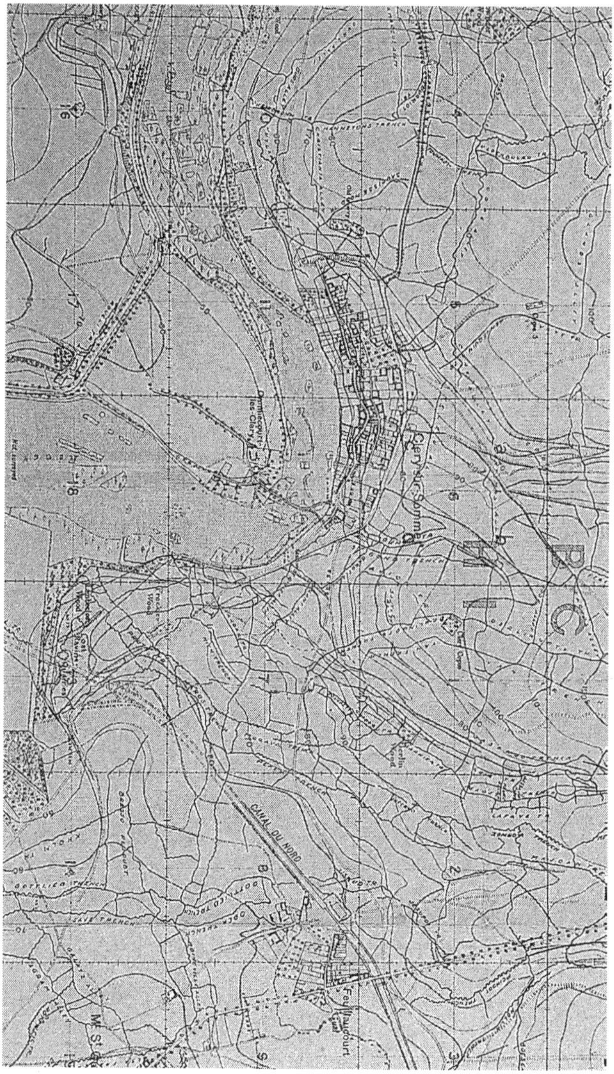

This 1918 1:20,000 trench map—which helped the author to identify where Charles Bean watched the taking of Mont St Quentin—shows the typical features of the maps found in hundreds of Great War unit war diaries. Note the shaded letters and numbered squares, the key to the map reference system used by the AIF. (Australian War Memorial; Peter Stanley)

Aaron Pegram's photograph of the battlefield of Fromelles suggests why it was such a killing ground for the 5th Australian Division on the night of 19–20 July 1916. Visitors often comment that seeing the ground helps them to understand why the attack was so costly. (Aaron Pegram)

Ypres and most recently *The Somme*), but they have written about the Western Front as a whole, without any special interest in the AIF. There is still no detailed Australian study of the breaking of the Hindenburg Line, the AIF's climactic achievement. The field is still wide open for new books about particular battles or aspects of the campaign as a whole. My own forthcoming book on the battle of Mont St Quentin is based on detailed field work, but it is *very* specific—the book deals with the experience of just *one* twelve-man platoon on one day of battle.

The most recent guide to the Western Front is Mat McLachlan's *Walking with the Anzacs*, which gives short summaries and useful modern sketch maps of all the important (and many minor) Australian sites between 1916 and 1918, along with much practical advice about routes, accommodation and further sources. He offers an excellent guide for those who want to get a good overview of Australia's Western Front battles, and the book comes highly recommended by those who have used it (including me). Those wanting to delve deeper will need to bring their own dossier of maps and documents, and walk with the Anzacs themselves.

The Second World War

Australian troops fought on the continent of Europe only twice during the Second World War, in the brief Greek campaign of April 1941, and then in the even shorter fight for Crete a month later. The Greek campaign has been extraordinarily neglected by Australian historians. Gavin Long's official history *Greece, Crete and Syria*, published in 1953, gives a solid and useful account, and various minor books and articles appeared, but not until 2008 did another Australian book appear on the campaigns, in Peter Ewer's *Forgotten Anzacs*. (For once, the adjective 'forgotten', so often overused in Australian military historical titles, was justified.) Ewer's book provides a multinational perspective on the campaigns, taking in not only the New Zealanders but also the Germans, Greeks and Britons. However, his account did not draw on field work. Brad Manera's study of the fight for Rethymnon (aka Retimo), on Crete, is eagerly anticipated.

Researching the Greek and Crete campaigns on the ground is both practicable and highly enjoyable. Greece is easy to get to and fun to get around (Crete is made for field work by scooter). It has good maps and the sources are abundant. Having investigated the Cretan battlefields around Maleme, Hania, Sfakia, Rethymnon and Iraklion (both alone and as part of a British–Australian study tour), I can emphatically assert that there is great scope for further work. Studying the terrain at Forty-second Street made clear the events of that confusing fight, in which Maoris and Victorians briefly stopped advancing German airborne troops by charging them in an olive grove.

Britain and beyond

You can find Australian battlefields in the unlikeliest places, even in the British Isles. A few Australian troops on leave in Dublin even took part in the 1916 Easter uprising—in suppressing it, as it happened. It would be possible to locate and trace their experience, adding a dimension to the standard Guinness-and-Riverdance-with-a-dash-of-Yeats tour that so many Australian visitors will take in Dublin. Jeff Kildea's *Wartime* article 'Easter Rising' offers a start-line for this journey.

The air war over the Atlantic and Europe saw Australians in action over virtually every European country and several seas. It is hard to fix air battles to any spot. The air war left Australian airmen in graves across the continent and beyond. There are Australian graves in village churchyards all over Britain, and across Europe. If you are lucky enough to visit Reykjavik in Iceland, you'll be able to track down the airfield from where Australian airmen flew Very Long Range Liberators in search of U-boats in the battle of the Atlantic. And even in Reykjavik there are Australian war graves.

The Australians who served in the war in Europe included the 10,000 or so who were members of the Royal Air Force, based in Britain, many flying in Bomber Command. It's hard today to recapture their experience at 10,000 feet over Hamburg, but those interested in the air war over Europe are able to visit some of the RAF stations from which they flew. Roger Freeman's *Bases of Bomber Command Then and Now* (an After the Battle publication) is an essential companion in this endeavour. Peter Pedersen has visited many of the British and American bomber bases scattered across the 'bomber country' of eastern England. He challenges us to 'go to any of them at winter twilight, when the drizzly mist starts to blanket everything . . . what a contrast to Australia for the airmen', he writes. This may not exactly be battlefield research (though some of the dead of the air battle lie in nearby cemeteries, and the great memorial to the missing is at Runnymede on the Thames), but visiting these bases is in a sense the starting point to investigating one of the longest Australian battles of the war.

Australian POWs

There are also Australian stories all over what was Nazi Germany and occupied Europe, most the experiences of Australian prisoners of the Germans and Italians. Some have been published in memoirs, books and articles, and some have strong geographical dimensions. Roger Absalom's accounts of Australians who escaped to fight with Italian partisans, for example, are often related to particular mountains, valleys or villages. Other stories can and perhaps will be recovered through memoirs and primary sources, both official and private. Prisoners of the Germans and Italians have been so neglected that the recovery of these stories awaits a new generation of diligent researchers.

In 2006 I was fortunate to be asked to investigate the extraordinary life and death of one Australian prisoner of war, Lawrence Saywell, a Sydney student, whose story took me to the mountains of Moravia in the Czech Republic. Saywell, a member of the Australian Army Service Corps, was captured in Greece and made several unsuccessful attempts to escape from camps in Europe. Eventually he escaped and spent the winter of 1944–45 with Czech partisans. On the very last day of the European war a German soldier fleeing from the advancing Red Army shot him in the village of Miřetín in circumstances that had never been adequately investigated.

The author on the site where Private Lawrence Saywell was killed in the Czech village of Miřetín on 8 May 1945, the last day of the European war. (Peter Stanley)

Thanks to the assistance of the Saywell family, Australian and Czech diplomats, the Czech Army Museum and not least some helpful older residents of the village of Miřetín, I was able to stand on the spot where Lawrence was shot, and visit the memorial Czech villagers erected to him, and his grave in Prague. I collected even more conflicting accounts of his death but was able to form a better understanding of what probably occurred. It was not enough just to read Saywell's story: to understand what had happened that day, a visit was necessary, and in the end seeing the site of his death made some versions of the story untenable, while others made sense. I was able to offer a brief account of this field work in the article, 'Death on the last day'.

Confronted with about a quarter of a million Allied prisoners of war, not all of whom were content to sit out the war, the

Germans created a prison camp they believed would be escape proof: Stalag IVc, at Colditz. Located in a castle on a granite bluff high above the River Mulde, Colditz is surrounded by the forests of Saxony. As Jack Champ and Colin Burgess describe in their book, *The Diggers of Colditz*, Australians, soldiers and airmen, were among Colditz's inmates.

The fortress, a mixture of medieval and nineteenth-century architecture, sits high above the town of Colditz. Freshly painted (the castle is being restored as a hostel and music conservatorium) on a bright September day, it looks much less forbidding than it appears in memoirs and wartime photographs—it is not only battlefields that oblige us to exercise our imaginations. But inside the walls, with the help of an excellent museum, which displays escape gear the German guards confiscated, the Colditz of legend becomes clearer. The prisoners' courtyard, for example, though sunny and warm, is very small and completely cut off from the outside world: what if this was all the space that prisoners could have seen for months? Inside the barrack blocks, some of which can be seen, you can feel the chill that a couple of metres of solid stone wall imparts: and then you wonder what winter must be like. Colditz is able to give up hints of what it might have been like as a prison.

Battlefields in the Middle East

Gallipoli

The Middle East has been the site of armed conflict for thousands of years, not least at Gallipoli, which is located on one of the invasion routes of the ancient world. A research project of the University of Melbourne's Centre for Classics and Archaeology and Department of Geomatics is underway, aiming to create an historical and archaeological map of the peninsula since the Hellenistic period. It will locate and record all remnants of the 1915 battlefield (including trenches, tunnels and paths), using ground-penetrating radar and magnetometry to analyse underground features such as graves and tunnels.

Amazingly, despite the explosion of interest in Gallipoli, the best Australian guidebook to the battlefields of the peninsula is still out of print: Phil Taylor and Pam Cupper's *Gallipoli: A Battlefield Guide*. Australians Phil and Pam researched and wrote their guide while they were teachers in London. They cycled around the peninsula in the good/bad-old-days. It was still largely a restricted military area, and they had to talk their way past sentries and gendarmerie posts, but apart from them, they had the place pretty much to themselves. The roads were either unsealed or pot-holed, but they were able to cycle just about anywhere. While the practicalities of travel on and around the peninsula have changed, the history is much as it was, and Phil and Pam's guide is packed with interesting and useful information. Whenever I've been to Gallipoli, I've carried it with me, and I've lent my increasingly dog-eared copy to others.

Gallipoli: A Battlefield Guide was first published by Kangaroo Press in 1989 and reprinted in 2000. I hope someone else picks it up and releases a new version soon. Besides that book, there are now several new Australian guide books. For a British view, Nigel Steel's *Battlefields of Gallipoli* is well worth consulting. For a New Zealand perspective on Gallipoli, Ian McGibbon's *Gallipoli: A Guide to New Zealand Battlefields and Memorials*, published in 2004, is the best choice.

One test of a guidebook is whether it swallows myth or not. For example, there are several fibreglass statues on Gallipoli. One commemorates a local firefighter who died in a bushfire on the peninsula; another purports to show a 'Mehmet'—a Turkish soldier—carrying a wounded Australian towards his own lines.

The plaque on the latter statue claims that the act was witnessed by Richard Casey, later Australia's governor-general, who was then a lieutenant on the staff of the Australian Division. The story is bunkum: Casey's Gallipoli diary contains no such account, as a little research in the Casey Papers in the National Library discloses. The moral is to maintain the questioning attitude of the historian when confronted by such stories. Even Garrie Hutchinson, author of excellent guides to Australian battlefields and to Gallipoli itself, commits the error of taking these stories at face value, as do thousands of visitors each year. Glenn Wahlert's recent *Exploring Gallipoli* is the best short guide for visitors to Gallipoli. It offers short descriptions of most of the 1915 locations, and is not restricted to the Anzac area.

The Turkish Peace Park authority produces a very detailed map-cum-guide, the *Gallipoli Peninsula Historical National Park Guidemap*, available for about 5 lire at the counter at the sorry-looking Kaba Tepe Museum, but apart from that there's little of practical value for the visitor. Indeed, it is prudent to be wary of almost all Turkish historical writing on Gallipoli (and the Great War as a whole). As the founding national epic, with the national hero Mustafa Kemal Atatürk as the central figure, the story is often exaggerated and unreliable. A country that has made criticism of Atatürk actually illegal (and which refuses to accept that the genocide of the Armenians even occurred) is hardly likely to produce dispassionate and accurate history about the campaign in which the nation's 'father' played a part.

Even though thousands of Australians, New Zealanders, Britons and, not least, Turks swarm over the peninsula, plenty of opportunities remain for field work on Gallipoli. Surveying the front from right to left, as Charles Bean often did in his notes, there are many possibilities. For example, no one has traced in detail the Anzac line running south from Lone Pine. The patrol and raiding war fought on the ridges and valleys at the southernmost extremity of the Anzac line suggests studies, as would the locations of the Turkish batteries that made such a nuisance on the beachhead. (James Hurst has written about the May Gaba Tepe raid, based on field work, a good example of what can be done.) The Lone Pine site itself might seem to have been spoiled for research by the presence of the imposing memorial to the missing there. Far from throwing up his hands in despair, Rhys Crawley (the author of an excellent but unfortunately unpublished thesis on the Lone Pine fight) became enthusiastic. He thought that while the memorial might take away from the historical feeling of the forward area (it has obliterated trenches, saps and bomb pits), there was much to be gained from studying the terrain on both Turkish and Australian sides. Rhys thought that getting a feel for 'The Cup', the Turkish reserve area, would still be possible. He argues that the memorial might have preserved a feeling for the terrain, which, he points out, had not occurred at Quinn's—and that hadn't stopped me from writing a book about Quinn's.

Other posts on the Anzac line could justify studies to add to the story of Quinn's Post. They may challenge or add other aspects to the story Quinn's tells. For example, artillery fire was much more a factor at Courtney's Post; underground warfare was even more important on Walker's Ridge. There are other battalions' stories to tell, and other individuals' contributions and fates to trace. The entire rear area of Anzac, the location of the medical, supply and engineering services, remains to be studied in detail. The remnants of Bully Beef Sap, running up the inland side of Walker's Ridge, can just be traced. Researching it would require tenacious searching both in the records and on the ground. Peter Burness's book, *The Nek*, on the charge at the Nek offers a reminder of what can be done with individual events. Rhys Crawley, the up-and-coming Australian scholar of Anzac, has well worked-out plans to walk the attack and supply routes for the August offensive, but the action during the autumn on the ridges north of Anzac remains virtually ignored since Bean's second volume appeared in 1922, except for Brad Manera's unfortunately unpublished work on the battle for Hill 60. Add to this the potential of writing new battalion histories of Anzac (again, James Hurst's excellent and detailed book on the 11th Battalion is a stimulating example) and you can see how open to new work the Anzac battlefield is. All of these studies demand not just the stamina to work through records in Canberra and elsewhere, but a stout pair of boots.

Visitors to Gallipoli are now able to draw on digital guides, such as the series of guides created by Richard Reid. His *Wartime* article, 'The virtual Anzac walk', describes his downloadable hand-held guide (details are available at www.anzacsite.gov.au). While expert and suited to visitors attuned to digital technology, this guide is not intended for researchers. Still, it might prompt a backpacker to read some serious history.

Israel and Palestine

Compared with Anzac, the battlefields elsewhere in the Middle East are a much more difficult proposition. Gallipoli, though rugged, is blessed by roads, paths, easily identifiable features and comfortable hotels an easy scooter ride away. By contrast, the Light Horse battlefields of Romani, Gaza, Beersheba, the Jordan Valley and the advance to Damascus, present logistical, political, geographical and practical problems. It would be discouraging to list all the problems confronting the researcher on all the battlefields. While Romani is accessible, the dynamic nature of the sand has changed the landscape beyond recognition. The battlefield of Gaza where the Light Horse fought is now submerged under one of the largest and most volatile refugee settlements in the world—which is sadly still a battleground. Many sites of the Light Horse's Palestine campaign have disappeared under new Israeli settlements and expanding Palestinian towns. The hillsides of Jordan around Es Salt and the route to Damascus, though significantly developed, can probably be traced sufficiently to make the campaign intelligible. Even so, problems of access and local sensitivity to foreigners with maps and cameras would make field work difficult, though still possible with diplomatic assistance.

Given its place in the mythology of Australia's wars, the relative neglect of the Light Horse is perplexing. With the exception of Alec Hill's *Chauvel of the Light Horse* (although political turmoil deterred field work, Alec knew the country as a subaltern in the Second AIF) and Ian Jones's devoted work, the Light Horse has been poorly served. Only recently, with Jean Bou's doctoral thesis has a new full-scale study been completed.

Jean Bou's impressions of the battlefields of Israel in 2007 make fascinating reading. He offers practical travel advice: expect long security-related delays at the airport, be wary of allowing immigration officials to stamp your passport, and anticipate that most things shut down for Shabbat. But despite the difficulties, he found visiting the sites of the Light Horse's operations a valuable experience and found new evidence on many battlefields.

Jean was able to look out on the approaches to Semakh station, which the 11th Light Horse took in a dawn attack on 25 September 1918, locate Chauvel's headquarters near Tel Megiddo, and visit the site of where the Shellal mosaic was before it was carefully and respectfully looted and carried off to Australia, where it can be seen at the Australian War Memorial. At Be'er Sheva (as 'Beersheba' is now called) he was able to orientate himself by reference to the Ottoman railway buildings and mosque that feature in contemporary accounts of the 1917 attack. To the town's south-east, Jean traced the scene of the 4th Light Horse Brigade's charge. He found a good vantage point from an elevated shopping centre car park!

One of the important conclusions Jean drew was to confirm his scepticism of the alleged photograph of the charge at Beersheba.

'Anyone who thinks that the "Beersheba charge photo" is really a photo taken at Beersheba once they have seen the place has a more vivid imagination than I do,' he reported. Here is a first-class example of the value and necessity of battlefield research. This photograph aroused acrimonious debate twenty-odd years ago between those who claimed it as genuine and those who argued it depicted a re-enactment of the charge soon after (in a different place). If battlefield evidence had been deployed, perhaps the argument might have ended sooner.

In his report of his visit, Jean refers repeatedly to the difficulties of gaining entry to sites. Some sites of military historical significance to Australians are out of bounds because they are also archaeological sites, because land uses have changed, because of development generally and, of course, because of security concerns endemic to a country embroiled in an unending crisis. He also refers often to vegetation changes (including the planting of eucalypts—'it looks just like some parts of Australia'), but Jean found many places where the scene was little changed since the Great War. Entrée to Great War sites in Egypt might be eased by making contact with Israel's Society for the Heritage of World War One.

Lebanon and Syria

The Australian part in the Anglo-French invasion of Vichy-held mandate territories in the Levant in 1941 has been relatively poorly covered since the publication in 1953 of Gavin Long's official history, *Greece, Crete and Syria,* a misleading title because it implies that the campaign was fought in Syria, whereas almost all the Australian operations occurred in Lebanon. Though battalion histories and a general account by two veterans, *Largely a Gamble*, have added to the story, no one has been game enough to write about the campaign by conducting field work in a region seen as dangerous for visitors over the past 40 years.

Iraq and Afghanistan

Since 1975 Australia has fought three conflicts, joining US-led coalitions to fight Iraq twice and in Afghanistan once. In 1990–91 Australian warships helped to reverse an Iraqi invasion of Kuwait, a commitment completed at the cost of no Australian deaths. From 2003 it joined a US coalition to invade and depose Iraq's dictator, Saddam Hussein, based on the mistaken belief that Hussein had fostered Al Qaida terrorists and possessed 'weapons of mass destruction'. In 2001 Australia joined a US and NATO coalition to defeat the Taliban regime in Afghanistan as part of the so-called 'war on terror'. Neither the Afghanistan conflict nor the Second Iraq War shows any sign of ending, a necessary pre-condition for civilian battlefield research.

Battlefields in Africa

The Sudan

In 1885 men volunteering for a New South Wales force became the first Australian *soldiers* to serve overseas. (The first *Australians* to fight overseas were the Victorian sailors who served in New Zealand waters in 1860.) Some 770 men—an infantry battalion, an artillery battery, field ambulance and headquarters—left Sydney for the Sudan in March 1885 amid rapturous scenes. The contingent was to take part in the suppression of a fundamentalist Islamic rebellion against British rule, but the campaign was called off soon after the troops' arrival. The contingent spent seven weeks around the port of Suakin, but achieved very little, especially in relation to the extravagant hopes the commitment aroused. Its men made some hard summer marches in Sudan's desert and saw some action at long range but no serious combat. By June they were back in Sydney, having lost six men to disease.

Although I once hoped to visit the eastern Sudan in the course of writing a chapter for a book that was later shelved, I have not visited the country. Nor, as far as I am aware, has any other Australian military historian. Except for a flurry of books about the contingent around its centenary (the best of which is Ken Inglis's *The Rehearsal*) there is scope for a further study that takes into account the country in which the men served. There are good maps by Herb Brown in Chris Coulthard-Clark's essay, one of several in the Military Historical Society of Australia's centenary book, *But Little Glory*, which I edited.

In 2007 Australian troops returned to the west of the Sudan as peacekeepers to help to deal with the continuing tragedy that is Dafur. Like other current operations, it is no place for battlefield researchers.

South Africa

About 16,000 Australians served in the South African War, 1899–1902, popularly known as the Boer War (although the Boers weren't the only ones responsible for it). The war fell into two unequal parts. For the first six months after the Boers invaded the British colonies of Cape Colony and Natal, several sieges and set-piece battles occurred. Then the gathering might of Britain's empire brought the swift capture of the Boers' capitals. Rather than surrender, the Boers fought on for a further two years, while their families were rounded up and interned in 'concentration camps' in which many died because of starvation and disease, the result of neglect and inefficiency. Every Australian colony sent contingents of volunteers, which served as part of larger British columns, mostly fighting a dirty war against intransigent Boer guerrillas on the vast veldt of the Boer republics. Towards the end of the war, the new Australian Commonwealth sent battalions of Commonwealth Horse, but they saw little service.

The war's centenary prompted several useful products for historians, one modest, the others more extensive. Starting at the modest end of the spectrum, Peter Burness and I were commissioned to write a brief book: *Guide to the Battlefields and Memorials of the Boer War*. Peter and I had worked together on the Australian War Memorial's South African War gallery, and it was a pleasure to work with him again on this project. As with the gallery, we split the work between us: Peter did the more extensive history of the war and I compiled a brief guide to sites, cemeteries and memorials. (This was a challenge, as I only visited the South African battlefields after writing the guide.) It is a good start to a casual visit, but the serious traveller will also need to consult Craig Wilcox's *Australia's Boer War*, the major commissioned history sponsored by the Australian War Memorial to mark the centenary.

The nature of the Australian contribution makes battlefield research difficult. Australian units served as part of much larger British formations, and they mostly fought in small skirmishes, even the names of which are now virtually forgotten. The major Australian action, the ten-day siege of the Elands River camp, in August 1901, in a remote corner of the northern Transvaal, saw small numbers of men from all colonies except South Australia in an action that was briefly famous. Still, the small number of Australian volunteers means that individual stories can be followed, while the small-scale actions can sometimes be located on the ground with great precision, as David Hallett's article 'Birth of the digger?', on the Elands River siege suggests.

In 1999 I happened to travel to South Africa for one of several conferences held to mark the centenary of the South African War. I was fortunate to be able to join Craig Wilcox, who was spending two months in South Africa researching what became *Australia's Boer War*, and do a quick spot of battlefield research. I hired a car in Bloemfontein (capital of the Free State—they've dropped the 'Orange') and we headed off to find the Vlet River. I was really just a driver and observer on this trip—Craig did all the brain work. As I'd expected, he'd come equipped with contemporary maps and a good idea of what had happened in the fight at Vlet River. Essentially the Vlet was one of the lines the Boers held in trying to halt the British advance on Pretoria, fruitlessly as it turned out. Major General Edward Hutton's Mounted Infantry Brigade included contingents from every Australasian colony, as well as Canadians and British units. Early in May 1900 it was part of a column commanded by General Ian Hamilton (later of Gallipoli fame), who sent his force against the Boers defending the river line. Craig explained this as we decided where the Australian and other units had been.

What we didn't have were decent modern maps showing the detail of the terrain we were walking over. Despite this, Craig was able to trace the route taken by the New South Wales Mounted Infantry, which at the climax of the action made a wild charge down the river bed. We used the hire car like the mounted infantry we were following, driving to where we could 'dismount' and trace Hutton's troops' route on foot. In doing so, we discovered one of the great advantages of doing battlefield research in pairs—we found ourselves debating everything from the practicalities of mounted infantry tactics to the way the imperial troops might have thought about the country. The site was highly reminiscent of outback New South Wales—indeed, the pasture country around the ACT. We were able to identify the locations of the main incidents in the battle and withdrew to our car and went on to drive across the Paardeberg battlefield, though we had not light or time to do more than get a general impression of that region. Even so, the trip confirmed another benefit of field work. I had read quite a lot about Paardeberg—but I must say I had imagined it to be quite different to the scrubby country I saw that day. There is no substitute for seeing for yourself. Craig went on not just to write *Australia's Boer War*, but published an article about the battle in *Wartime* magazine based on our visit.

South Africa is a moderately difficult place in which to conduct field work. Poverty and associated crime make the visitor a potential target, and road travel is dangerous (Craig's diary alludes to the appalling accident rate on country roads that invite speeding). But language difficulties are few, even if many name changes since 1902 make for potential confusion.

North Africa

Except for the suppression of the Senussi Rebellion, in Egypt, and the Egyptian Uprising by Light Horse units in the Great War, Australia's main commitment to service in North Africa came in the Second World War. Between January 1941 and November 1942 two Australian divisions, the 6th and 9th (and the 18th Brigade of the 7th) served as part of British forces fighting the Italians and Germans in Libya and Egypt.

Australians first went into action against the Italians at Bardia, in Libya, in January 1941, the subject of Craig Stockings's forthcoming book (though he has not examined the ground: scope for a revised edition even before it appears, perhaps). The difficulties of battlefield research in the desert can be judged from John Laffin's visit to the former Italian-held desert outpost of Giarabub, which a small Australian force seized in March 1941. In 1956 Laffin described it in *Middle East Journey* as 'a lonely little village... nothing more than a cluster of small white buildings, a mosque and a central-walled fort'. The Italian defences even then had filled up by drifting sand. Laffin left, feeling depressed that 'Australians had died to capture such a forsaken outpost'. What is it like today, and might anything be learned about this early action of the Second World War from seeing it?

TOBRUK

From April to October 1941, the 9th Australian Division formed the mainstay of the garrison of the port of Tobruk, in Libya. One Australian battalion, the 2/13th, served throughout the siege, after Thomas Blamey controversially withdrew the rest of the Australian force. The siege of Tobruk became for the Second World War what Gallipoli was for the Great War, an epic of endurance. Little of any substance has appeared on Tobruk in Australia since Barton Maughan's official history in 1966.

Second World War veteran and indefatigable freelance writer John Laffin arrived in Tobruk in 1956 in a Commonwealth War Graves Commission truck carrying headstones for its war cemetery. This was a few months before the Suez crisis, and Egypt was in turmoil. Police stopped and searched Laffin's truck repeatedly. In exasperation, his War Graves Commission driver asked him to present the impressively illuminated 'Commonwealth Credentials' Menzies had given Laffin. It got them through every checkpoint to the border of Libya, then a British protectorate. Laffin searched for signs of Australian service in Tobruk, but only fifteen years after the siege he concluded they were 'hard to find'. He did locate the concrete-lined tunnels of Morshead's headquarters and some Australian graffiti, and the place in which the celebrated *Tobruk Truth* had been written and produced.

For many years the West ostracised Libya, Colonel Muammar Gaddafi's Arab People's Republic, and the Libyans returned the favour by making it almost impossible for Western tourists to visit. This changed early this century. Dr Garth Pratten, an Australian lecturing at the Royal Military Academy, Sandhurst, visited Tobruk in the course of his research for his forthcoming book *The Old Man*, on Australian battalion commanders in the Second World War. He remains one of the very few Australian military historians to have explored Tobruk and its defences. He visited the town and harbour, the perimeter and its permanent and improvised defences, which, like John Laffin 50 years before, he found to be in a remarkable state of preservation. Pratten's *Wartime* article, 'In the rats' footsteps', describes finding and exploring concrete fortified posts and even stone sangars. His observations on the location and significance of the hill Ras el Medauur bear out yet again the importance of seeing the ground before writing about the battle.

ALAMEIN

Exactly how a visit to the site of a battle can inform an historian can be seen from Mark Johnston's article, 'The Blockhouse, El Alamein', published in *Wartime*, and even more so from his vivid chapter on the defence of the Saucer in *Alamein: The Australian Story*, written by Mark and me. Informed by diligent research (drawing on Australian and German sources, both official and private), Mark described the ordeal of the battle for the Saucer lucidly. My *Wartime* article, 'Getting our knees brown', describes the field work that Mark and I did in Egypt. Our book demonstrates, we hope, the value of investigating the ground in detail before venturing to write about a battle.

Alamein has a reputation as dangerous, a reputation that's probably deserved. When in 1956 John Laffin drove south from Alamein station (in those days there was only a station—today there is an ugly township), he was taken towards a group of tanks standing unsalvaged in the desert. He drove up to them and looked about. Just as he was about to leave he heard an explosion over a nearby ridge. A Bedouin had been killed by a landmine. He suddenly realised that the tanks were untouched because they were in the middle of a minefield, and carefully retraced his wheel tracks out of the field. When Craig Tibbitts gave a talk at Tel el Eisa on a 2002 battlefield tour, hovering Egyptian police told the group to walk in wheel tracks and, in the end, stopped them from reaching the site from which Craig had planned to speak. Today,

Our first sight of the Blockhouse at Alamein (the long white building to the right of the pylon) is an excellent illustration of the way battlefields can be virtually destroyed by later development. In this case they included electricity lines, a huge quarry (note the size of the earth-movers on the right) and the multi-storey building erected in the middle of nowhere. (Mark Johnston)

Alamein is a scruffy, dirty service town on the highway and railway. But don't be put off by either the stories of mines or the look of the place. While indiscriminate urban development has blighted many sites (including Australian ones), with effort and care it is still a very rewarding battlefield to visit.

Battlefields in Asia and the Pacific

Australians first saw active service in Asia in 1900, when sailors from Victoria, New South Wales and South Australia served the empire in suppressing the Boxer Rebellion in northern China. The route that the sailors took in marching to Peking is today concealed by massive industrial and urban development, but it might be interesting to trace it.

In the Great War, Australians first saw action when the Australian Naval and Military Expeditionary Force seized Germany's Pacific colonies, notably by landing near Rabaul. No one has traced these battlefields, which are perhaps among the least changed of any in Australia's busy military history.

Since December 1941, most of Australia's military experience has been in what is today called the 'Asia–Pacific region'. This has encompassed defeat in Malaya and Singapore, major campaigns in Papua New Guinea and the islands, wars in Korea, Malaya, Indonesia and Viet Nam, and peacekeeping missions in Cambodia, Timor and Bougainville. While field work in tropical environments entails discomfort and hazards not usually encountered in temperate regions, there is great scope for battlefield research in all these places.

Malaya and Singapore

Australian airmen were in action against the invading Japanese from the first days of the Pacific War, and Australian soldiers saw a frantic and costly month of battle in southern Malaya and on Singapore island in the month leading up to the surrender of Singapore in February 1942. An early and encouraging example of the growing interest in these battles came in Peter Burness's article, 'Retracing the Malayan campaign', published in the *Journal of the Australian War Memorial* in 1985. While on their honeymoon, Peter and Elizabeth Burness traced the Australian fighting retreat from the Muar River to Johore. Peter identified the essence of battlefield research. He and Elizabeth located the scene of the terrible fight at Parit Sulong, where the retreating British Empire forces were forced to leave their wounded behind only to learn they had been massacred. Peter wrote how 'standing on the bridge at Parit Sulong, I tried to imagine the ordeal of the troops who had been trapped there'. That is the challenge that faces every battlefield researcher. Lynette Silver has risen to this challenge in *The Bridge at Parit Sulong*, her investigation into the Japanese atrocity at Parit Sulong, a book informed by detailed research on the site of the atrocity.

Yap Siang Yong's *Fortress Singapore: The Battlefield Guide* actually omits the fighting on the north-western coast of the island, where the Australian brigades met the Japanese invasion. It does contain a great deal of concise material, especially on the Singaporean experience of war, occupation and liberation, but it is not very useful to Australian researchers. Of more relevance is Brian Farrell's *The Defence and Fall of Singapore*, which is based on a thorough familiarity with the ground. While Malaysia's tropical environment and Singapore's urban development have changed many sites, enough remains of the battlefields to repay visiting them. Garth Pratten spent a week following the route of the Australian retreat through Johore and onto Singapore and found that studying the ground helped to explain many of the decisions in this lost campaign.

Papua New Guinea

Papua New Guinea is second only to the Western Front in terms of the magnitude of Australia's military experience. Several hundred thousand Australians served in what used to be called 'the islands'. The Australian battlefields there remain far less known than they should be, and only specialists have visited any except the popular tourist route to Kokoda. Travelling in Papua New Guinea demands a stamina not called upon for visits to Gallipoli or the Somme. The Lonely Planet guidebook's casual observation about the Lae war cemetery is chilling: 'there are security guards with dogs patrolling here these days, so it is quite safe to visit, even on your own'. As I have not visited Papua New Guinea I was loath to write about it in detail, but gratefully accepted Phil Bradley's kind offer to summarise his experience.

Working in Papua New Guinea imposes a particularly close relationship between researchers and the local people on whom they depend. Phil Bradley, who has trekked all over the Markham–Ramu valleys and the Wau–Salamaua regions, the latter an especially rugged area, alludes to the respect he has developed for the people he met and relied on. In *On Shaggy Ridge*, for instance, Phil thanks 'all the others of Agana Village who welcomed me onto their land'. Phil Bradley advises researchers to make the most of local knowledge. 'It is very important to find those that can help', he stresses, but warns 'often that will not be the first person who offers'.

Understanding local customs and expectations is vital. Phil advises bringing enough food for guides, and tobacco as a trading commodity, 'and you cannot help but make a good impression with a bag of rice for the local village'. As a rough guide, Phil writes, 'it should normally cost you less than a 15-minute taxi ride in Australia for a guide for a day in PNG'. Paying someone to carry your bag, he sensibly advises, 'is a good investment: the terrain and climate will knock you about; better to face that unburdened'.

Phil has had exhilarating and dramatic experiences getting around PNG. In a small boat, crossing a broad estuary he writes, when 'the mist had descended and the sea spray is coming horizontal into your face, you have to ponder your position'. Likewise, once 'while looking over the relics of Japanese aircraft at But airfield . . . a mob of hostile villagers appeared carrying bush knives, thinking we were stealing the relics'. Phil evaded conflict by 'staying calm and explaining how my father had fought there . . . I was soon their best friend'.

The problems of finding your way around rugged, jungle-clad terrain justify regarding virtually any battlefield research in Papua New Guinea as 'extreme'. Phil counsels researchers to master GPS navigation and—because satellite navigation devices do not work reliably beneath a jungle canopy—to also master map and compass navigation. Even then it is often hard to make modern and Second World War maps match. Bobdubi Ridge, for example, is bisected by two modern maps and the contour lines between 1943 and today do not coincide. Add to that the difficulty of finding routes—at Bobdubi Ridge he and his party had to hack a path up the ridge before finding the remnants of the track cut in 1943. He had to urge his helpers to cut through 3-metre-tall kunai grass, and Phil pitched in with them.

From his experience walking the battlefields of the Markham–Ramu and Wau–Salamaua campaigns, Phil advises prudence in expending energy. 'At the end of a long day's trek along Shaggy Ridge', he writes, 'I had to convince my guides as well as myself to push on further rather than take the easy option.' Phil writes that 'being able to push on and do the research when you're already knackered from just reaching the location is a key attribute of battlefield research in Papua New Guinea'.

Kokoda has become the major Australian site of memory in Papua New Guinea. In 2001 fewer than a hundred Australians made the trek from Owers' Corner to Kokoda. By the time you read this over 20,000 will have followed them over the past decade; 7000 alone in the past year, assuming frustrated traditional landowners don't close it to trekkers again.

Clive Baker's *Walking the Kokoda Trail* is nearly twenty years old, but it contains much valuable, practical advice based on many trips over the track. His book covers all practical aspects of trekking, from dress and equipment to food and medicine to track discipline, etiquette and safety. For example, Clive warns travellers from distributing sweets to children because when tooth decay

Frank Taylor, of Kokoda Treks and Tours (left), one of the most experienced Kokoda guides, with his porters on a trek over the Owen Stanleys. (Phil Bradley)

develops there are simply no dentists in the interior. It is still worth doing the track from Owers' Corner to Kokoda (or the reverse); Phil Bradley's *After the Battle* is the best recent account of how it can be done and what can be seen.

Nor is the trail limited to the young. John Newberry's article, 'Age before beauty', in *Great Walks* magazine, gives many helpful tips for over-50s contemplating the walk, both on preparing for the walk and on finishing it safely. He and his partner Robyn made the walk in ten days with Charlie Lynn's Adventure Kokoda, one of the most reputable outfits. As I write, the trail has been closed to trekkers as a by-product of the dispute over whether parts of it should be mined. Soc Kienzle (son of the legendary Bert Kienzle, who organised carrier lines in 1942), who grew up walking the track 'like my backyard', as he puts it, argues that the stretch supposedly threatened by mining was not used during the war. The argument continues: expect changes in the near future.

The main Australian historical expert on Kokoda is the historian Peter Brune, author of an epic series of books (culminating in *A Bastard of a Place*) on the Papuan campaign. Brune wrote his first books without having walked the battlefields, but for *A Bastard of a Place* he walked and flew over the Kokoda Trail. Peter visited Brigade Hill, Milne Bay, Gona and Sananada, and his later work is all the more authentic for having been there. Peter also sheds a wry insight into relations between researcher and guide in *A Bastard of a Place*. Thanking Adrian Koe of Kokoda Treks and Tours, Peter recalled an exchange with Adrian: 'Don't call me Sir, Adrian, call me Peter.' 'Yes, Sir!' Accepting that they do things in their own way is a lesson many of us need to learn on overseas trips.

Bill James's *Field Guide to the Kokoda Track* is a comprehensive combination of historical survey and practical manual, vital for the actual or the armchair traveller to the Owen Stanleys. Kokoda treks usually do not continue onto the humid coastal lowlands, to Buna, Gona and Sananada. Many people overlook the vicious 'beach-head battles' that ended the Papuan campaign early in 1943. Phil Bradley advises visiting this area with Kokoda Treks and Tours, run by Frank Taylor, one of the most experienced trekking guides in the region. Phil has walked this area alone, and tells a cautionary tale. After walking 20 kilometres to and from Siremi from Buna, he asked after a derelict Stuart tank in a nearby dump. Villagers were surprised he wanted to see the tank, but offered to take him to it. 'So off we went again,' Phil writes, 'my blistered feet screaming to stop, but I really wanted to see that tank.' Finally, they reached a patch of scrub and his guides pointed into it. 'So in I went and found...a water tank.'

Borneo

Though unfamiliar with Papua New Guinea, I am very well acquainted with Australian battlefields in Borneo, having visited virtually all of them in three visits over four years. In 1994 I was given the task of curating the Australian War Memorial's 50th anniversary exhibition, which opened a year later as *1945: War & Peace*. I was keen to take on this job, but I felt I needed to know more before I could do justice to the responsibility. While I felt that I knew the events of 1945 pretty well, I was acutely conscious that I had no first-hand knowledge of the environment in which most Australian troops fought in that year: tropical jungle.

So I planned a trip to the two main theatres in which Australians fought in 1945, Borneo and New Guinea. After some preliminary work I realised that I couldn't get from Port Moresby to Borneo (or vice versa) easily or within the time and budget available. I decided that I could visit either Borneo or Papua New Guinea but not both. I literally tossed a coin and went to Borneo. If heads had come up instead I might have written a book about the New Britain campaign—no one has yet—but instead went to Borneo and my book *Tarakan* was the result. I visited Tarakan, Balikpapan, Labuan and sites on the mainland of Borneo around Beaufort, the scenes of Australia's three amphibious landings in 1945, as well as tracing the 'death march' route from Sandakan.

On my first visit to Borneo I learned a lot about the Borneo campaign (and the ordeal of prisoners of the Japanese at Jesselton, Labuan and Sandakan), about war cemeteries—Kranji and Labuan are beautiful, sad, compelling places—and about the mechanics of researching battles on the ground. One of my first lessons came at a place that since 1945 has been known as MacArthur Road (Jalan MacArthur), on the Malaysian island of Labuan. I was able to trace a small action on the ground—a fight by a company of the 2/28th Battalion for a creek crossing—using records of the action. This proved to be a key lesson in the practicality of such research. Even though the crossing had become a busy urban road, with buildings built on positions from 1945, it was still possible to trace the event and read the ground. I applied the same technique to other sites around Borneo—and you can too.

The Australian records relating to Borneo are so comprehensive and detailed that it is possible to locate the site of virtually any incident and to work out on the ground what happened. Naturally, Borneo's prolific jungle can make this difficult (though the Malaysians are cutting down the forest with obscene fervour), but it is still possible to recapture the atmosphere and the substance of the Borneo operations on the spot.

Prisoners of war

This brings us to one of the most important aspects of the Australian interest in their military experience in Asia, the 22,000 Australians who were captured by the Japanese in 1942, a full third of whom did not return home. These men and women suffered and died in dozens of camps, ranging from remote parts of Sumatra (where the nurses were held) to the huge headquarters camp of Changi. They laboured in camps on the Burma–Thailand railway, on Singapore, and in Korea, Indo-China, Manchuria, Borneo, Hainan, Ambon, Timor and Japan itself. Some of the scenes of their ordeal are highly accessible—daily bus tours from Bangkok will give you the River Kwai Experience—while many other places have merged back into the jungle.

Some of those prisoners died working on the 'Burma' end of the Burma–Thailand railway and are buried at Thanbuyuzat, in the far south of the country. Lonely Planet's guide to Myanmar (Burma) argues that it is possible to travel to Burma without supporting businesses that will enrich the appalling SLORC military regime that continues to oppress the country. There are over 1300 Australians buried in Burma, most of whom died as prisoners of war, and another 1300 in Thailand, almost all of whom were prisoners.

In the early 1980s, the *Journal of the Australian War Memorial*, then leading the boom in academic writing about Australian military history, published an influential article by Australian National University historian Hank Nelson. Hank accompanied a party of former prisoners of war and their wives on a pilgrimage to the Thai end of the Burma–Thailand railway. He described his observations and reflections in an article, 'Travelling in memories: Australian prisoners of the Japanese, forty years after the fall of Singapore', which showed how powerful a combination of veterans and historians could be. Today, the chances of taking veterans back to the sites of their ordeal have just about disappeared, but much can still be learned by travelling to these places.

Ros Hearder, the author of an impressive forthcoming book based on interviews with former prisoners of the Japanese and their medical officers, travelled to Thailand to experience the Burma–Thailand railway first hand. Her interest was not so much in terrain as in understanding the environment in which prisoners laboured. She travelled to Kanchunaburi, three hours west of Bangkok, appropriately by rail, and then sought out sections of the wartime railway route. 'Walking along the track of the former rail line', she later wrote, 'showed the density of the topography—the impenetrable jungle foliage on both sides, and the metres of cliff rock face hand-excavated by prisoners'. Ros was moved to see poppies tied to broken spikes embedded in rock walls: these men's sacrifice has not been forgotten.

Ros found the climate 'a challenging but rewarding experience'. She was exhausted by the combination of heat and humidity and 'constantly dehydrated no matter how much water I drank'. However unpleasant, the experience paid off in historical insight. 'Imagining doing hard labour as a prisoner for months in that thick oppressive humidity and heat—all the while sick from disease, starvation and abuse from captors—beggars belief.' While conceding that the reality was 'impossible to imagine', Ros found visiting the railway invaluable—more so than Gallipoli, which she found 'increasingly touristy'.

On practicalities, Ros advises 'copious tropical-strength' insect repellent, good walking shoes (rather than the sandals you might be tempted to wear) and 'as much water as you can carry'. She also reminds us that anti-malarial medication, started before arrival, is mandatory. Ros found that the cheap and delicious food in Kanchanaburi's street stalls was safe and superior to hotel food, but cautioned visitors to drink only bottled water and to avoid iced drinks.

Korea

In 1950 Australia committed land, air and naval forces to help to defeat North Korea's invasion of South Korea, a 'hot war' that mimicked the superpower rivalries of the Cold War that dominated the 45 years following the end of the Second World War. The battlefields that lie in South Korea are rewarding to visit. South Korea has changed enormously, of course, and a developing economy has swamped parts of some battlefields.

Professor Jeff Grey, who has visited Korean battlefields in the 1980s and the early 21st century, found great changes between his visits. It makes little sense logistically, he warns, to stay in Seoul if that results in a long, slow drive to get out of and back to the capital. On shorter days this imposes a severe limitation on time, and on long hot days on energy. Some battlefields—such as Maryang San, Australia's largest fight of the war—remain completely inaccessible. Kapyong, is however, both accessible and worth a visit, not least because no one has written much about it, although it has been the subject of Robert O'Neill's official history (and O'Neill visited Korea in writing it).

My former colleagues Brad Manera and Nigel Steel have walked around Kapyong seeking to understand what went on there. Both were exceptionally well prepared. Not only had they both carried out battlefield research before, but they brought modern maps and maps from the war, had digested the war diary of the 3rd Battalion of the Royal Australian Regiment (3RAR) and had interviewed veterans and read their accounts.

In 2007 Nigel Steel took 3RAR veteran Ray Parry back to Kapyong. He was responsible for the historical content of a new diorama commissioned for the War Memorial's new Korean War gallery depicting a position defended by a handful of 3RAR men on the night of 23–24 April 1951. He had consulted the documents and interviewed veterans, but was left with a stubborn disparity between accounts of what could and could not be seen from a rifle pit on the 'island feature', the focus of the diorama. 'It was crucial to know exactly how far round the flank the pit had been', he explained, and 'there was only one thing to be done: we had to go to Kapyong to see for ourselves . . .'.

The 30 Australians captured in Korea by their North Korean and Chinese enemies endured up to three years of a brutal captivity, in which ideological terror—'brainwashing' in the jargon of the war—compounded the physical hardships they suffered. The camps in which they were held, in a North Korea still off-limits to casual visitors, are virtually lost to us. Perhaps one day an Australian researcher will be able to trace the sites of their camps.

Nigel Steel offers many practical suggestions to those travelling to Kapyong especially. First, it's now called Gapyong, and it's a couple of hours' drive out of Seoul, so you'd better hire a car and a driver. The battlefield is not, of course, in the town, but on hilltops some distance away. The Koreas remain in a state next-but-one to war, so modern maps are hard to come by. The

South Korean Army is much in evidence—tank traps line roads and hills often have prepared observation posts. It would be wise to ensure that the Australian Embassy knows who you are, where you plan to go and what you want to see. The landscape, often changed through development and reforestation, is often privately owned, and your school French won't be much help. None of this should put you off, but you'll need to plan and be a bit adventurous (in eating as much as anything). You'll also need to be fit—reaching the 'island' feature that Nigel researched for the War Memorial's diorama, he said, was as arduous as anything on Gallipoli, and it felt more remote.

Malaya and Malaysia

The long but small-scale Malayan Emergency involved British Commonwealth forces in a protracted and complex but ultimately successful war against what they called 'CTs'—'Communist Terrorists'. Fought in the mid- to late 1950s, it was a war of endless patrols and sudden ambushes by platoons and sections deep in the Malayan jungle. For that reason it is hard to find identifiable places to use as a stimulus to understanding. Visiting Malaya to see and perhaps walk in the jungle might be useful, but there is almost nothing specific to see. One of the few feasible sites is the scene of the 'Pipeline Ambush' of June 1956. Here a patrol of the 2nd Battalion of the Royal Australian Regiment was ambushed near the pipeline running from the Sungei Bemban reservoir, east of Enggor in the state of Perak. As ever, more details could be gleaned from the unit records held in the Australian War Memorial (especially AWM 9, Australian Army Commanders' Diaries). Peter Dennis's chapters in the official history that he wrote with Jeff Grey, *Emergency and Confrontation*, provide a solid starting point.

Brian Farrell's party deep in the jungle of Sarawak, wading out of a creek while following the track of a 'Claret' operation on the Malaysian side of the border. This is 'extreme battlefield research', about as far from the Claret-sipping research of the Western Front as you can get. (Brian Farrell)

Likewise, the short and sporadic 'Confrontation' between Indonesia and British Commonwealth forces, mostly in Sabah and Sarawak, in Borneo, between 1963 and 1965, has very few identifiable surviving sites. Singapore-based military historian Brian Farrell, who has trekked through the jungle of Sarawak to visit the sites of fire bases, reports that the bases disclose something of the nature of the war, though the effort may be disproportionate to the lesson. Of course, it is salutary to learn how hot and humid the jungle of Sarawak is, but at the end of the trek it may not be as rewarding as more informative battlefields in other places. While the abandoned fire-support bases of Sarawak may not be as magnetic an attraction as the trenches of France, they may be worth intensive study by specialists. Jeff Grey's chapters on Confrontation in *Emergency and Confrontation* likewise provide an entry to the sources, both archival and published. Brian Farrell warns that the locations of cross-border clashes were falsified in the Australian documents ('the only instance...I know...of Australian military records being deliberately falsified as a matter of high policy').

Viet Nam

About 50,000 Australians served in the ten-year-long war in Viet Nam (or Vietnam, as many Australians called it at the time: I've followed Gary McKay's authoritative style). Soldiers served as part of the Task Force in Phuoc Tuy and as members of the legendary Australian Army Training Team, Vietnam (AATTV). The Task Force's war can be traced in a series of both demanding patrol operations and in several major actions. With the help of the extensive official records available (under the National Archives 30-year rule they are all now open) the war is being investigated in detail. Battalion histories (some outstanding, such as Robert Hall's *Combat Battalion* and Michael O'Brien's *Conscripts and Regulars*) and studies of particular aspects, such as Greg Lockhart's *The Minefield*, his exposure of the shocking mistake of the Dat Do mine barrier, make battlefield research for Viet Nam easier than other conflicts. Many AATTV diaries and reports have now been digitised and can be found on the War Memorial's website.

Perhaps the greatest challenge for battlefield researchers is presented by the operations of the Training Team, which operated in small detachments all over the country training the Army of the Republic of Vietnam. While the South Vietnamese records are lost, the extensive reports made by AATTV men (and their American counterparts, held in the US National Archives and

Records Administration) make their war intelligible, albeit at the cost of demanding research. For Australia this task is greatly helped by the existence of Ian McNeill's history, *The Team*. It is possible that we will in future see Vietnamese-Australians travelling to Viet Nam to understand their forebears' experience of war.

Veterans have powerful reasons to return. Brian Cleaver and Peter Phillips, former members of 3RAR, tried for several years to find the graves of North Vietnamese soldiers buried in 1968 in shallow graves near a B-52 bomb crater near Fire Support Base Balmoral. Following grid references supplied by former comrades and using a GPS and compass, they eventually found and marked the graves of their former enemies.

Battlefield visiting in Viet Nam is made easier by the publication of Gary McKay's guide *Australia's Battlefields in Viet Nam*. McKay, a 4RAR platoon commander wounded in Viet Nam, has become the most prolific and authoritative Australian author writing about the war. He has written nine books on the war, beginning with his memoir *In Good Company*. His guide deals with the main areas which Australians visit (Ho Chi Minh City, Phuoc Tuy, Bien Hoa and central and northern Viet Nam), concentrating on what was Phuoc Tuy. McKay offers reliable advice on permits, security (a police escort is compulsory), tour operators, maps, and on name changes since 1975 (Phuoc Tuy, for instance, is now Ba Ria–Vung Tau Province).

McKay's guide devotes more space to the fight in the Long Tan rubber plantation than to any other action in this war. It was a messy, accidental clash, one that shouldn't have happened. It cost the lives of eighteen Australians and several hundred Vietnamese. Students and veterans of earlier wars are inclined to snort at the cost of Long Tan—single explosions on the Western Front and company-sized actions in the Second World War often cost as many men. But to give Long Tan its due, it was the single most costly action for Australia in that war. (Of course, this depends on how you look at it; veterans of the larger, longer and more costly operations around fire bases Coral and Balmoral often point out the discrepancy, but it looks as if Long Tan's drama has secured its place in popular esteem.) Long Tan needs to be considered here because the writer of the first of the Army volumes of the Viet Nam official history, Ian McNeill, himself a veteran, found that field work decisively altered the version of the battle he presented in his official history. He spent some hours sitting in the rubber plantation discussing the action with his former enemies.

So much for the theory: how does battlefield research in Viet Nam work in practice, on the ground? For Viet Nam, Gary McKay's latest book, *Going Back*, gives a graphic and often moving account of a group he accompanied in 2005. Gary's book advises the visitor (and especially returning veterans) to expect to see changes Viet Nam has undergone since 1975. The old narrow sealed road linking Ba Ria and Vung Tau 'that wound its way . . . through small villages that specialised in producing *nuoc nam* (fish sauce)' is now a four-lane highway. He warns that the Long Hai Hills are 'still a heavily mined and dangerous place', and that—ironically—D455 Provincial Mobile Force Battalion now occupies Nui Dat, precluding casual visits.

All battlefields are emotional minefields for veterans and their families, but none more so than Viet Nam. *Going Back* warns of a risk too often encountered among Viet Nam veterans. Gary talks often about veterans seeking to confront the past or lay 'ghosts' of that war to rest, so much so that the book includes a sort of Post-Traumatic Stress Disorder first-aid kit—how to recognise it and what to do about it. Gary's advice, based on several return visits, is highly practical.

How does it work in practice? For me, the answer is that sometimes it doesn't. I've gone looking for sites that I was sure existed but that I couldn't find. I've wandered about villages and trails for an hour, utterly bushed. I've quailed at reaching a place because getting there would have involved crossing a knee-deep swamp, and I've climbed to the top of a hill I knew was significant in a jungle battle, only to find that all I could see were thickets of trees and that I learned absolutely nothing despite the sweat and scratches. I've mis-located other places and have triumphantly told everyone I'd found a supposedly long-lost site, only to discover later that I had it wrong. All this could happen to you! But my colleagues and friends have also benefited immensely from taking the trouble to pull on a stout pair of boots, to see the places as well as the archival records.

PART 3

Approach march: Planning your trip

Campaigning season: When to go

At what stage should you embark on your research trip? This is perhaps a pointless question for travellers who are combining battlefield research with a holiday. Often the date is fixed; if you're a schoolteacher, for example, you have a limited time and duration, or you may have chosen to make the trip to coincide with a birthday or family occasion overseas. In that case your lack of flexibility makes preparation all the more important.

Ideally, for a substantial project such as a book, you should make at least two field trips, one near the beginning to get an idea of what you need to know, and one near the end so that you can check whether you got it right. For *Tarakan* I made two while researching (and another after the book appeared); for *Alamein* Mark Johnston and I were able to visit the battlefield once (and again immediately before publication); for *Quinn's Post* I was lucky enough to make three trips between getting the inspiration for the book and finishing the manuscript. Each trip has been invaluable in helping to get a real sense of the place, picking up clues about what it was like to live and fight there, and to check the manuscript I'd written against the ground. On Tarakan the importance of Snag's Track became immediately obvious once Sersan Sukarno, a local soldier who was helping me, and I motored along it on his scooter. At Alamein Mark Johnston and I were able to work out for ourselves why the Saucer had been such a death-trap for the defending Australians. On Gallipoli the importance—and the vulnerability—of Quinn's Post became startling once I looked down at it from Walker's Ridge. Perhaps if I'd had a Monash-like ability to interpret terrain by looking at topographical maps I might have worked this out sitting in a library. But I don't—and no one I know has either. And anyway, you can't feel the Egyptian sun on your neck or the chill of a winter's dawn on Gallipoli by poring over a map.

Your research trip should take place early enough in the life of the project to benefit from the inspiration you'll get, but late enough so that you know what questions to ask, yet not so late that your visit is superfluous, useful only as 'atmosphere', to add 'colour' or—worst of all—simply so you can say you've been. This point is a matter of calculation (particularly financial) and also of negotiation, so you can work the trip around work and family obligations. I have tended to travel to battlefields in the northern hemisphere in its early autumn, between late August and mid-October, nicely fitting in my field research between my daughters' birthdays.

The initial, obvious answer to the question 'when to go?' is 'at the same time as the battle'. For hundreds of years most battles occurred in the 'campaigning season'—basically the northern spring and summer. There were exceptions—Napoleon fought Eylau in the snow, and, of course, met defeat in the Russian winter. In the Great War there were exceptions too—the raid on Stormy Trench happened in the winter of 1916–17 and the first battle of Bullecourt was fought soon after, in the snow in April. Peter Oldham, author of a good Battleground Europe guide to the Hindenburg Line, reports that it is easier to find the remains of pillboxes and trenches in winter, when the ground is bare and the shadows are longer. There is a great deal to be said for visiting a battlefield both on a particular anniversary or at least at the same time of year as the battle took place, but you need to be sensible about this. Visiting Gallipoli in the middle of winter was among the most rewarding battlefield visits I have made, but going in summer was both more productive and enjoyable. A European winter or a tropical monsoon season can cramp your style substantially. Winter in Europe will leave you only six hours or so of daylight, and rain, mud and ice could make your limited time hazardous and uncomfortable, not to mention making sites inaccessible. There isn't much to be said for being on the spot in Papua New Guinea on an exact day if you're drenched in a tropical downpour or stranded on the wrong side of a flooded creek.

As John Laffin remarks in his thorough *Guide to Australian Battlefields of the Western Front*, 'the Diggers were not able to choose their seasons . . . and a visit to the Somme in January will give the modern visitor some idea of what the soldiers had to endure'. However, unless you have compelling reasons for travelling in the winter (or like Laffin are pretty much consumed by the need to learn about the Great War in all seasons), it is wise to travel to Europe between May and October. Other regions have different imperatives—in Asia the governing factor is often the prevailing monsoons. It's wise to check.

Money is, of course, a consideration for all but the independently wealthy, and air fares—which vary according to season—make up a good part of the overall cost. Everyone wants to travel to Europe in summer, and airline prices reflect that market force. It may be worth considering a 'shoulder' season fare, travelling in the European spring and early autumn—say April–May and September–October. August to October is regarded as the best time to visit Viet Nam. Days are long and warm enough, but demand, and therefore prices, are not so high and queues are not so long. Having said that, you can often only travel when your employer lets you go, or during school holidays, giving little room to reduce costs, so the trick is to make the best of it.

Movement orders: Planning your research trip

Travelling overseas (and most Australian battlefields are overseas) has become so much a part of our lives that many of us don't think too much about the practicalities of it. Fair enough if you're off on holiday to a Club Med resort, or if one day more or less in Provence is neither here nor there to you: you're on holiday, relax!

But the chances are that your battlefield research trip is either the only realistic chance you'll get to spend time on the site, or has to be fitted in to a family holiday, or a limited research budget. All the serious military historians I know are short of time or money, or both; they can't afford more than a few days away from jobs or family or some other pressing commitment. So let's get serious about travel. Short of buying a new car or a house, it's probably the single largest item of expenditure in your budget in any given year: let's get the best value from it.

Travel seems so easy these days because almost everyone travels and it's all taken care of, isn't it? Is it? One reason travel is such a big business is because people waste money on travelling in ways they'd never think of doing at home.

Camp followers: Battlefield research with the family

While serious battlefield research may be done alone or in the company of a co-author, we rarely travel overseas on holiday alone, so we need to consider the impact of travelling in families.

Many of Australia's historical battlefields are close to places that people will travel across the world to see. The Western Front is within an easy drive of the museums, sights and restaurants of Paris, and the heartland of Western European culture. Gallipoli is a day from Istanbul, one of the great cities of the old world, and the site of Troy is just down the road. The battlefields of Greece and Crete are close to two of the most extraordinary sites of the ancient world—Athens and Minos. Even Alamein, one of the most difficult and uncomfortable battlefields to get to and around, is close to the wonders of ancient Egypt. Visiting Australian battlefields brings you close to other, natural, wonders of the world. The battlefields of Borneo are reasonably close to the extraordinary Sepilok orang-utan sanctuary, for example, while the game reserves of the Kruger National Park are close to South Africa's battlefields.

Paying the price: Budgets

What will it cost? It depends on what you can afford, how long you'll take, the standard of luxury you expect or the amount of inconvenience and discomfort you can put up with. If you can afford to take a leisurely breakfast before summoning your driver and spending a few hours on the battlefield before retiring to a snifter on the terrace, good luck to you. I treat battlefield research as a job, starting early and finishing at dusk, squeezing the most from a trip that's always on a tight time and money budget. I have a reputation for doing field work economically, but what counts isn't what it costs, it's what you learn from it.

Even Western Europe need not be unduly expensive. For those on a budget, Martin Kerby, a Queensland schoolteacher and now PhD candidate who has spent many weeks researching Australian battlefields in Europe, advises you not to ignore the Formule 1 chain of budget hotels. Usually located off main roads, often in industrial suburbs, they offer clean and functional accommodation without the chintz, but at prices that can keep you going longer.

In my 'trip notebook' I make a meticulous record of what I bought and for how much—I'm much more organised on the road than at home. Not only does this record help me to work out what I was doing and when, it helps me to budget for future trips with increasing precision (and my trip notebooks have helped colleagues many times get a clear idea of prices).

'Pass, friend...': Visas and tickets

Most of Australia's battles have occurred in other people's countries. 'Our' war cemeteries give us no automatic right of entry, and we will often need visas, just as they often do to enter our country. Make sure that you have a current passport and the necessary visas for the trip you plan. Do you need a visa? It sounds obvious, but if you rely on an out-of-date guidebook or an authoritative-sounding but misinformed friend, you could stick yourself with an immigration problem. Check with the Department of Foreign Affairs and Trade (DFAT) website www.smartraveller.gov.au and your travel agent to ensure that you obtain the right visas in good time.

Be careful that you don't cause undue bother by applying for a visa you don't need. In most cases a tourist visa is all you'll require. Seeking a 'research' or 'business' visa can often prolong and complicate your application. Apply for special types of visa only if you are absolutely sure that you need one. For example, if you are conducting research under an academic program you may be obliged to do so by your institution. But even if you are a professional writer planning to gather material for a book, you can apply for a visa as an ordinary visitor. You obtain visas from the embassy or consulate of the countries you're planning to visit. Contact addresses can be obtained from the internet White Pages or directly from the host country's embassy website. Unless you're travelling officially, you should not ask the Australian Department of Foreign Affairs to intercede or apply for you.

Some countries have elaborate applications for visas. When I visited Borneo, for example, obtaining visas to enter Brunei Darussalam was by far the most time-consuming part of the preparation. (It was also difficult to get good modern maps of this small but secretive state.) Some countries do not require you to obtain a visa in advance of arrival, but will ask you to buy one on arrival: Turkey is one example, so you should have a handy $US20 on you when you arrive.

One of the best books of advice to the whole how-to of travelling is Edward Hasbrouck's *The Practical Nomad: How to Travel Around the World*. (The name might sound familiar. You'll have seen it on Anzac Day banners because the 1st Australian Division fought a small but very effective action in defence of Hazebrouck in Belgium in April 1918. His family originally came from there.) Hasbrouck runs a travel agency in San Francisco specialising in independent travel. His experience is vast and his advice is worth having. A fourth revised edition of *The Practical Nomad* appeared in 2007, and Hasbrouck's website (www.practicalnomad.com) is a useful source of up-to-date advice and, not least, encouragement to travel.

See a travel agent sooner rather than later, but go with a clear idea of what you want to do. Shop around; ask questions; don't be afraid to do a deal. Cultivate a relationship with one agent or one person in that branch. Over time they'll learn your preferences and needs. Don't necessarily take 'no' for an answer. Can you fly into one city and fly out of another? Of course you can. Can you break a trip or change an itinerary en route? Yes, but it will cost you: ask now to save later.

Should you use a travel agent rather than buy a ticket off the net? It depends. While the online price might sound tempting, you often have to buy there and then or lose it—specials have a short shelf life on the net. A travel agent is more flexible and the best can find you a better deal. If your travel plan is straightforward—a ticket to Paris or Istanbul—then you might as well buy online. If you have particular needs—you need to get into Borneo through Kota Kinabalu and out through Sandakan, via Singapore—then perhaps you should trust someone with that kind of experience. There are many problems with buying tickets when the only option is 'buy now' rather than 'ask some more questions'. Once you've clicked 'buy', you're committed; you have little recourse if things go wrong (or redress comes at a cost in messing about), and if you don't read the conditions you may find changes or cancellations expensive. Hasbrouck's *The Practical Nomad: Guide to the Online Travel Marketplace* tells you more than you need to know, but the headline is: 'be careful'.

Picquet lines: No-go areas?

We're familiar with the ways geo-political analysts divide the planet between the First and Third Worlds. Developed nations are regarded as 'First World'; developing nations as 'Third'—that we know from newspaper headlines. But they also talk about 'Second World'—nations formerly or still under central, usually communist regimes, and the Fourth World, the poorest, most economically under-developed and over-exploited nations, chronically afflicted with corruption, mismanagement, natural disasters or other travails. Obviously the categories are flexible and changing.

Australian battlefields and sites of military historical interest can be found in all of the world's 'Worlds'—the Western Front is First; North Korea, Libya and Viet Nam, Second; Papua New

Guinea and Malaysia and Indonesia, Third. There are Australian war graves in several of the Fourth World's poorest countries, such as Bangladesh and Burma. Travelling in these regions makes different demands on researchers. Battlefield research is possible in all places, but is clearly going to be more demanding in the poorer, more remote or less developed regions.

Some Australian battlefields are located in places hard to get to and harder to stay in. They include North Korea, Iran, Burma, Iraq and Afghanistan (for obvious reasons) and, sadly still, Bougainville. The first place to go before a travel agent is www.smartraveller.gov.au. The US Department of State (see travel.state.gov) will often explain why some regions may be risky, from an American perspective. Advisory websites will give you advice based on reports from diplomatic missions in those countries. You might still decide to go, but don't say you weren't warned.

Reports of security concerns can vary, and official warnings tend to the extremely cautious. In 2002, for example, it was absurd that Australian teachers should have been forbidden from travelling to Turkey on duty because of 'security concerns' when thousands of young backpackers and well-off over-50s went privately—and entirely uneventfully. On the other hand, take heed of the 'travel advisory' (even though 'advisory' is an adjective) for, say, Sierra Leone, Somalia, Lebanon or Georgia.

Northern Russia may be a very rewarding place to visit. Its vast fir forests may seem oppressive and monotonous, but experiencing its seemingly unchanging vastnesses would surely give a strong reminder of this neglected campaign. As I suggest earlier, finding the location of the two 'Australian' VC 'exploits' would lend purpose to visiting such a vast theatre of war. (The VCs are nominally Australian because their recipients were Australians who signed on for another go with the British regiment, the Royal Fusiliers, a battalion of which comprised mainly Australians.)

Myanmar (as the current regime calls Burma) is the site of 1300 Australian war graves, mainly around Tavoy in the remote south, but the DFAT website advises Australians to avoid Myanmar unless they have essential business. The 2008 cyclone made an impossible situation worse. North Korea is out of bounds except on bland, officially sponsored tours. This precludes a visit to Maryang San, described by Robert O'Neill in his official history as the site of 'the greatest single feat of the Australian Army during the Korean War'. Bob Breen's major study, *The Battle of Maryang San*, was accordingly based entirely on contemporary documents and veterans' memories. Perhaps one day this may change.

The Middle East continues to be risky. With the possible exception of Beersheba (the site of a 90th anniversary re-enactment in 2007) and Romani (in north-eastern Egypt, albeit off the beaten track), almost any 1916–18 battlefield in Sinai, Palestine, Israel or Jordan is either off-limits or hard to get to. If you do go, be sure to enter and leave without violating the prohibition some Islamic nations place on travellers who have visited Israel. (Entering Israel through Egypt, Jordan or Turkey seems to obviate that problem.)

But security can dictate prudence. The battlefields of the 1941 'Syrian' campaign, mostly in southern Lebanon, are located in a region that has been chronically plagued by violence over the past thirty years and has seen outright war in recent years. It is still probably not safe to visit these areas, and certainly not to be wandering the hills of Jezzine or Damour with a camera and maps. A study of the Lebanon campaign based on research on the ground seems to be a remote prospect. That battlefield researchers are both visible and suspicious-looking because of what they carry and what they do came home to Peter Pedersen at Dien Bien Phu in Viet Nam. He had to convince a local army officer and a squad of armed soldiers that he was harmless. They had seen Peter in the surrounding paddies with a camera, maps and a compass. 'It took a lot of smiling and gesticulating on my part before all was well.'

Observation post: Surveillance

Australia's battles have often occurred in countries whose governments now monitor and seek to control the ideas and attitudes of their own people—and they will probably take an interest in you too. The most extreme case is North Korea, which will not allow individual visitors to enter, and insists on guides accompanying all official groups. But other countries' military intelligence, police or security authorities will probably know who you are and, if not where you're going, at least where you've been. Visits to countries such as Myanmar, Viet Nam and even Indonesia will be the subject of discreet surveillance. In Indonesia your presence will be noted and reported by everyone from hotel staff to street vendors—all with the greatest friendliness, of course.

In Egypt, Mark Johnston and I spent many hours in polite but frustrating meetings in the office of the local deputy head of military intelligence, a Captain Mohammed. We had organised the visit through the Australian Embassy in Cairo, which had arranged for a driver to pick us up at the airport and efficiently deliver us to the train for Alexandria. It had also liaised with the Egyptian Army's Military Intelligence headquarters and—the embassy's staff believed—obtained permission for us to visit the battlefield of El Alamein. Unfortunately, in the meantime the major in charge at El Alamein had gone on leave without telling his deputy about us. The Egyptian Army does not, it seems, welcome or reward initiative, and Captain Mohammed was unwilling to let us see more than the military museum and the cemetery. His English wasn't ample (though it was a lot better than our Arabic, of course) but he knew enough to say 'no' to our requests, explanations and suggestions. Over many cups of black tea we sat and chatted—the only thing to do—with the captain answering most of our questions with a none-too-optimistic 'fifty–fifty'. All the while, we called the Australian Embassy, seeking its help. Eventually the embassy's interpreter, the wonderful Dr Mohammed, managed to broker a compromise. Officially we were not to go south of the railway line—ostensibly because of the mines—and we would have a member of the captain's unit with us.

So for the rest of our time at Alamein we had Corporal Mohammed in the back seat of our Opel. He was a genial chap, quite happy to accept our hospitality when we stopped at the fly-blown cafés at Sidi abd el Rahman and Alamein, but he spoke no English, so goodness knows what he made of our earnest conversations, pointing at maps and compass bearings at patches of desert that—to him—had little meaning. We gave Dr Mohammed, whose patience in dealing with obdurate and timid officers saved our trip, a special mention in the acknowledgements of *Alamein: The Australian Story*, and a free copy in gratitude.

Our lesson here was to be wary of getting involved with local bureaucracies, and next time we visited, with the Australian War Memorial–Imperial War Museum study tour, we simply arrived as tourists. However, even then the Egyptian Tourist Police spotted our mini-bus and stopped us. Claiming that we were in potential danger from Islamic fundamentalists, they insisted on stationing a utility full of heavily armed but bored conscripts behind us. This seemed harmless enough, but after several hours of benign indifference, our plans to hold a 'stand' on the site of Barrel Hill—a key location in the later days of the battle—entailed me stalling the captain in charge with earnest, if futile, discussion, while Chris Clark, the most experienced historian of the entire party, got on with his 'stand'. (A 'stand' is battlefield tour jargon for a talk given on a particular spot.)

Sometimes this surveillance is obvious—such as in Egypt—but it can also be simply sensed. In Brunei I followed the route of the 2/17th Battalion, which landed at Brunei Bluff on 10 June 1945 and three days later had liberated the town of Brunei from the Japanese. (The RAAF had pretty much bombed it into the jungle by then, but the Bruneians loyally did not seem to hold a grudge.) I was able to follow the battalion's route virtually from the landing beaches along what became the little state's major highways, into the capital, now renamed Bandar Sari Begawan. While I was flogging around the jungle looking for the route the troops took to move inland from the landing beaches, I realised that one of the Sultan of Brunei's many 'istana', or palaces, now stood squarely athwart the path I was on. I became aware of being watched—and decided that I need not stick around. The desire not to be caught in the wrong place equipped with camera and notebook must sometimes prevail over the desire to gather knowledge about historical sites. 'Trouble' can at best entail a protracted explanation (and remember, one of you won't have English as a first language) and at worst involve a trip to a police station or army barracks.

Head count: Who goes?

There are half a dozen kinds of battlefield visit. Each has its own advantages and opportunities and also challenges and disadvantages. You need to be certain that your visit is right for you. What are these different approaches? Let me count the ways.

Individual trips

There are many advantages to going solo. You can please yourself about where you go; you can change your plans if need be; you can focus on the task without distraction. There are disadvantages, not least being that you won't have any pictures of yourself doing what you did, unless you can find a helpful local.

Pairs

The great advantage of working in pairs is that you can apply twice the brain power to the task, while splitting the jobs between you. You can discuss what you're looking at, debating explanations and theories that individually you might gloss over or forget. At Alamein again and again Mark Johnston pointed out something that I'd forgotten, or would challenge an easy assumption I'd made, or remember a reference that helped us to solve the puzzles of the ground. Most importantly, two people can split navigating and driving. I always say that if something goes wrong, with two of you there's someone to identify the body. Nigel Steel and Peter Barton have often explored the battlefields of the Great War together. Nigel says that the most common question between them is, 'What do you think?' They have developed a rapport that multiplies the brain power they can apply to the problem of finding trenches in what are now French fields and saying something sensible about them.

Researching in pairs has worked for Craig Deayton. He traced the 47th Battalion's Belgian battlefields with a Belgian colleague. 'His English was better than mine', Craig recalled, 'and we were able to bounce ideas around, speculate, discount and propose all day to great profit.' Likewise, Peter Williams explored the Anzac area on Gallipoli for his book, *The Battle of Anzac Ridge*, with a friend, John O'Connell. (His book proposes a novel interpretation of the strength and significance of Ottoman artillery in the days following the 25 April invasion, one that makes a lot more sense than the now orthodox view that the Turks' defence was inspired by Mustafa Kemal's leadership.) In the acknowledgements in his book, Peter thanks John for having 'aided in clarifying my thoughts by disagreeing with much that follows'. That seems to express perfectly the value of having a companion with whom to bounce ideas off, even if the ball seems deflated on return.

Mark Twain, himself an inveterate traveller, wisely observed that 'there ain't no surer way to find out whether you like people or hate them than to travel with them'. Anyone who has survived a family caravanning holiday knows that travel will test the strongest relationship. This is a guide to battlefield research, not modern relationships, but be prepared for the intimacies that a shared experience of possibly arduous and certainly intense travel can bring. Apart from snoring and food preferences, pairing up on a purposeful trip can expose differences and conflict. Perhaps the best preventative is to make sure that each of you is clear about what you hope to achieve before you leave home.

Small groups

Tours of small groups—say of three to ten people—contain the ingredients of great success and of avoidable failure. Whether they succeed or not will depend upon tolerance and a willingness to compromise and accept a common view. Prima donnas and selfish people have no place in them, and you should ask 'who's going?' before committing yourself. Such groups can work. The Melbourne historian Rob Pascoe has participated in some effective small-group tours in which several friends find their way around obscure cemeteries and battlefields on the Western Front. One secret to their success is that the group comprises an existing friendship group; another is that the group members have found a working distribution of labour: one to drive, one to navigate, one to supply historical briefings from the guidebook, and a fourth to spell the others or keep them entertained. Rob's tours seem to have achieved the magical blend of personality and purpose, able to switch from banter to reflection on some of the grimmest battlefields on earth without losing balance.

Family pilgrimages

Travelling in a family group sounds dodgy from the beginning. Surely you have too many conflicting interests to contend with? Surely they're expensive? Surely most family members won't be interested to the same degree? Well, perhaps—unless you can cow your family into supporting, or at least tolerating, your obsession as a break in their holidays.

But family battlefield tours can work, as the story of the Heaths's visit to Alamein suggests. Jo Brennan and Tom Heath, children of Ted Heath of the 2/48th Battalion, had proudly shared many Anzac Days in Adelaide with their father and former members of his battalion. After he died in 2006—on the 64th anniversary of the opening of the October battle—they resolved to visit Alamein in his memory. In August 2007 they arrived in Alexandria and hired a car to travel west to Alamein, spending a day on the battlefield. They visited the Commonwealth War Graves Commission cemetery, stark in the desert sunshine, where they left tokens of remembrance to their father and to the men of the 2/48th. Then off to the German memorial at Point 26, and the Italian memorial on Trig 33. Then they looked for sites in the desert to the south. Ian, Jo's husband, used a GPS to search for the Cutting, Tel el Eisa, Trig 29 and the Blockhouse, all vital sites in the 2/48th's part in the July and October battles.

On the railway line that bisects the battlefield they found the Cutting. 'I was truly excited,' wrote Tom. 'Dad had spoken of the Cutting often and passionately.' Further on they found Tel el Eisa. 'Again, we knew that Dad had been here,' Ian wrote:

> All that was here was the railway line and then to the south desert. Tufted camel thorn dots the landscape ... the vegetation is dark green or grey and the ground and sand vary from light browns to brittle white. It is a stark place that holds little charity for defender or attacker. I wanted to just walk into the desert ...

All of them had this idea, but prudently did not act on it. They could see, though not get to, Trig 29, but they reached the Blockhouse, recognisable from old photographs. There, Tom wrote 'we contemplated the rock and sand and the men's bravery'. The group had had a long, tiring, emotional day, but were satisfied. 'We had seen the very places where Dad and his mates had fought. We had filled our pledge to him.' Tom Heath's account of their pilgrimage is a powerful expression of the importance of connecting family memory with the actual spot. On his return to Adelaide, Tom wrote a poem reflecting on their journey. It ends:

> Now rest old man, home, amongst the waving wheat.
> I've seen this place and felt the earth
> Touched the headstone and seen your grief.
> Rest well like these good men of Alamein.

Study tours

Study tours—in which groups of people travel to discuss, debate and learn about military history—are both instructive and enjoyable.

When study groups are also multinational, as was the case with several I have been involved in, the resultant discussion reminds us that history is an argument without end. Take a group of Australians, New Zealanders and Britons to Gallipoli, North Africa or the Western Front and watch as two things happen. The first is that each group tends to assert its national stance.

Canoe tutorial: Brian Farrell takes his National University of Singapore students into the jungle of Borneo while teaching a course on counter-insurgency warfare in South-East Asia. (Brian Farrell)

This leads to some robust debate. The second thing, though, is that the resultant discussion breaks down the assumptions that each group brings with it. The best study tours take on the character of a rolling seminar, with the evidence lying all around, with banter and good fellowship an emerging bonus.

School parties

Some schools take on the expensive but immensely valuable venture of allowing high-school students to travel to battlefields. One of the earliest such enterprises was organised by Mike Goodwin and Bob Shaw, who travelled with thirteen students of Mackay North State High School in Queensland to Gallipoli and Europe in 1999. They became the subject of an ABC *Australian Stories* documentary later that year. Other schools, impelled by enthusiastic history teachers, have embarked upon similar projects. Julie Reece led a 'Remembrance 2001' tour with her students from Mount Barker High School in South Australia. Her report, 'Journey of Remembrance', discusses the ingredients—notably clear direction and firm leadership—that made it such a success.

In 2002 Mike and Bob and two other teachers again took 23 Mackay North students overseas. The trip was no mere excursion. Each of the students researched individuals and arrived prepared to ask questions about the landscapes they walked over. While the students seem to have shown a worrying propensity to sentimentalise their encounters with war dead in nationalistic terms (they seem to have seen every soldier as a hero, and Australian flags were much in evidence), they nevertheless gained powerful insights into what Gallipoli and the Western Front were like.

A Scotch College student tells the group about an Australian buried on Gallipoli in Ari Burnu cemetery, with the Sphinx in the background. Such experiences, Mark Johnston writes, touch even the most blasé students. (Mark Johnston)

Mark Johnston's article on a tour he led, 'In the steps of Monash', describes how he took 28 Scotch College, Melbourne, boys to both Gallipoli and the Western Front in April 2001. Mark also used individual stories to help the students to identify and engage with the sites they visited, and as an experienced military historian was able to link cemetery and battlefield more securely than usual. It might be unreasonable to expect even motivated teenagers to appreciate the subtleties or details of tactical use of ground, but all can be moved by the personal stories so strongly apparent in cemeteries. Even so, in order to give the students more than a merely emotional experience, I would argue that leaders should try to connect cemetery and battlefield. The Scotch College party had an advantage in being led by an experienced military historian—not always on hand. But any teacher who leads such a party needs to focus on critical history as well as the natural desire to pay tribute.

Veterans' parties

Age is the great enemy of veterans' tours. Few parties of veterans will now include veterans of wars before Korea. But these visits have been and will surely continue to be among the most profound ways to understand war. I know this from leading a tour group to Borneo. It not only included men who had served in Borneo—in the artillery, the RAAF and in an Army aviation unit—but also the daughter and other relatives of Sandakan prisoners of war. This visit was no analytical study of old battlefields, though again and again the veterans pointed out things and places that even those who had studied the campaigns could not have known. The presence of the veterans and relatives formed a very powerful emotional centre to the trip, which increasingly became a pilgrimage. Perhaps the most powerful part of it was on the road between Sandakan and Ranau when we abandoned our air-conditioned bus to walk the death march route. Even a few hundred metres of walking brought home to us the suffering those men had endured.

Colleagues who have accompanied veterans' pilgrimages report similarly profound emotional responses. Michael McKernan has described some of them in his work, notably in his book about Australia in the Second World War, *The Strength of a Nation*, where he often recalls an encounter with those whom battle touched, often on a battlefield or in a cemetery. I also recall how another colleague, who had accompanied a group of 8th Division veterans (many of them survivors of captivity) on a visit to Malaya and Singapore, was powerfully affected by the veterans' dignity and stoicism, and affectionate remembrance, when they visited Muar, Parit Sulong and Singapore island. That experience—not one that our younger colleagues will ever have (just as we have never seen a Great War veteran at Villers-Bretonneux)—will stay with him for life.

I've visited battlefields in all of these ways except school visits, and all of them have advantages and pleasures. They all demand common elements—a degree of organisation and, for all but solo efforts, a need to consider the needs of fellow travellers. They are all feasible, enjoyable and productive; the choice is yours.

On your left: Guidebooks and websites

If you're finding your own way about, you'll need help, from two types of guidebooks, general travel guides to the region or country you're visiting, and guides to particular battlefields. Except for Phil Taylor and Pam Cupper's guide to Gallipoli, the two will probably not be the same book. Edward Hasbrouck recommends using guidebooks to help you visualise what your destination may be like, thereby reducing the disjunction between what you might expect and what you encounter. 'The more you can make the day-to-day reality of your destination real in your mind, before you leave', he advises in *The Practical Nomad*, 'the more prepared you will be'. This applies to seemingly familiar cultures, such as Western Europe, as much as to Borneo or Egypt.

A Lonely Planet book will probably be the most useful guide to getting into and around a foreign country, although it will not contain enough detail on any battlefield (or indeed, on many individual sites or attractions) for your purposes. Nevertheless, it will give you vast amounts of helpful information, advice and suggestions. Lonely Planet books are highly recommended, but they are certainly not the only guides—the Rough Guides series, as well as the more up-market Frommer's, can be useful, depending on the standard of luxury you expect or the size of your budget. Other series are either too much given over to glossy photographs by professional photographers or seem to be intended for wealthy travellers more intent on good food, shopping and high culture than the grubbier reaches of battlefield research.

Lonely Planet publishes guidebooks to virtually every area that Australian battlefield researchers will travel to, even though they will rarely give battlefields the same detailed coverage as they devote to cultural sites or adventure activities generally. (Lonely Planet's main readers are under-30-something backpackers, not old fart military historians, but we can certainly benefit from their authors' experience and authority.) Here we need to acknowledge the value of investing in the current Lonely Planet guide to the country or region you're visiting, advice echoed by many battlefield researchers. Lonely Planet acknowledges that the advice its guidebooks offer has a short shelf life. Its celebrated caution should make us wary of old guidebooks: 'Things change—prices go up, schedules change, good places go bad and bad places go bankrupt—nothing stays the same.' You can log on to the publisher's website (www.lonelyplanet.com) for free updates.

There are many general guides to 'popular' battlefields. The Western Front, for example, boasts guides by well-respected writers such as Michael Glover (*Battlefields of Northern France and the Low Countries*), Richard Holmes (*Army Battlefield Guide: Belgium and Northern France*), Martin and Mary Middlebrook (*The Somme Battlefields: A Comprehensive Guide from Crecy to the Two World Wars*) and Victor Neuberg (*A Guide to the Western Front: A Companion for Travellers*). All of these guides are worth reading, both in advance and on the spot.

There are also series of guides to particular battlefields, though relatively few with direct Australian relevance. The exceptions—guides to Gallipoli, the Western Front and Viet Nam—are mentioned in the relevant sections of Part 2, 'Intelligence briefing'. Series that deal with sites other than specifically Australian ones are published in the Pen & Sword Books Battleground Europe series. This series, for example, includes at least fifteen titles on the Somme, and seven on Ypres and the Hindenburg Line. Because they are specific, they are the most detailed, and make for essential reading before and during visits to those places. Ross McMullin, author of *Pompey Elliott*, recommends Peter Pedersen's *Fromelles* guide, and he has also published guides to *Hamel: Somme* and *Villers-Bretonneux*.

Nigel Steel, an historian of both the Imperial War Museum and the Australian War Memorial, has written an excellent guide in the Then and Now series, *The Battlefields of Gallipoli*. The series also includes useful guides to particular sites on the peninsula, such as Stephen Chambers's *Gully Ravine* (which I used to investigate the often overlooked service of Indian troops on Gallipoli). Each includes sections on the area today with useful 'then and now' photographs and facsimile and diagrammatic maps. 'Then and now' is a crucial idea in battlefield research. As early as 1937 a part-series of magazines entitled *Twenty Years After* appeared in Britain, advertised in Australian ex-service journals,

Then and now. The citadel at Péronne, as it was in May 1919 and as it is today, the site of the Historial de la Grande Guerre, a modern, multilingual interpretation of the causes, course and consequences of the Great War. (J.G. Roberts papers, Ms 8508, State Library of Victoria; Peter Stanley)

carefully pointing out the 'lavish' space devoted to Australian and New Zealand forces' deeds. It featured 'then and now' photographs prominently.

The British *After the Battle* series—now numbering more than 140 titles—describes battlefields, U-boat pens, V-weapon sites, prisoner-of-war and concentration camps and other war-related sites in authoritative detail. While the emphasis of the series is undeniably on European ground battles in the Second World War (exactly where Australia's troops were not), the series does include essential issues on Australian subjects. Phil Bradley's detailed *After the Battle* issue on Kokoda (no. 133) is essential reading for any historically minded walker. Other issues deal with Malta (no. 10), The Burma–Thailand railway (no. 26), Singapore (no. 31), Crete (no. 47), Tobruk (no. 51), the Sydney Harbour raid (no. 53) and the air war for Rabaul (no. 133). It's clear that many more Australian *After the Battle* titles are possible.

Phil Bradley's *On Shaggy Ridge* shows how a personal, intimate knowledge of a battlefield can infuse a historian's reading and use of the documentary sources. *On Shaggy Ridge* begins memorably: 'The feel of a battlefield is unique,' Phil writes. He describes some of the many battlefields he has explored—Austerlitz, Waterloo, the Somme, Normandy, Gallipoli and Kokoda. And he talks about how he felt when he looked over to see what Australian soldiers called the Pimple. On Shaggy Ridge, Bradley suddenly realised, that 'seeing this totally unexpected reference point that told me where I was and made me realise what the realities were of a campaign that climaxed on this very terrain'.

While these books will include many useful details on many places, you'll find that you need to compile your own dossier for the places you're interested in. In fact, such a dossier is so useful that it's worth discussing in more detail.

Key to victory: The battlefield research dossier

The battlefield research dossier is the key tool to make the most of your time in the field. It should contain everything you need to help you find your way about the area, and to understand what happened there at the time. It needs to be reasonably robust, small enough to fit into your day-pack and able to withstand much handling in climatic extremes.

Typically the dossier will contain the following:

- Your notes detailing what you want to achieve
- Maps, both historical and modern
- Copies of relevant historical documents
- Copies of the relevant pages of the official history
- Copies of relevant pages of the most useful battalion histories
- Organisation charts to summarise units and commanders
- 'Then' photographs (you'll take the 'now')
- Copies of Google maps or photographs
- Letters of introduction or explanation

All of these items will probably be annotated, to remind you to look for the location of a hill, tree or trench, and to read on the spot so you can better understand what happened there. They should be securely held within a soft plastic cover, though the individual sheets should not be sealed in plastic, because you'll often want to annotate them further.

Some items will be more useful than others. Topographical and historical maps will need to be ready to hand. The clear plastic map cases worn by walkers are very useful, especially when two-sided—modern on one side, historical on the other. Organisation charts or 'wiring diagrams' (the ones in Ross McMullin's *Pompey Elliott* are a good model) might only be used to remind you of the background, while the diary entries (keyed to location) will be essential reading when you reach the places you're looking for. Photos can be filed by place or housed in a separate section—please yourself. The important thing is that your dossier should work for you.

Craig Deayton describes the dossier that he compiled in order to walk the battlefields of the 47th Battalion on the Western Front:

> the battalion and brigade operation reports were invaluable but in addition, eyewitness accounts—private soldiers' diaries, letters or memoirs—are important, especially for Dernancourt, where the official records are directly contradictory. At Dernancourt also, the prisoner of war accounts were of the greatest assistance in throwing light on events where the official record was silent.

What do you do with the information in your dossier? Again, Craig Deayton's description of his method shows how to use this repertoire of sources:

> I found sketching the ground from key points important and, on returning to the hotel to process the material overnight, re-reading the official history and operations reports before returning to the battlefield for a second, third or even fourth day.

Craig was honest enough to acknowledge something that all serious battlefield visitors will encounter: 'even after several close re-readings of the primary and secondary sources, it was still sometimes very difficult to hold together a coherent mental picture'. Inconsistencies and disagreements often create a complex picture but, Craig wrote, 'the sight of the battlefield often brought a sudden, sharp and unambiguous clarity'. It is these moments of clarity (what Jeff Grey calls 'ah ha!' moments) that the battlefield researcher seeks above all.

Based on experience, I strongly advise that you do not seal your maps in plastic. While plastic makes them impervious to moisture, it also makes them hard to handle—I struggled with a documents case twice before giving it away as a bad job—and makes them impossible to annotate. Still, in the tropics especially, maps (and just about everything else on paper) will become moist and tatty and in extreme cases will fall apart by the end of the trip. While they may no longer look pristine, these fragments will serve both as a reminder of the trip and a source of wonder that any of the records made in Borneo, Papua New Guinea or Viet Nam survived at all.

Under no circumstances should you carry original documents with you on a trip. The idea of bringing Great Uncle Joe's diary back to the place where he wrote it might seem romantic and fitting, but if you damage or lose it, or if it's stolen, you know you'll regret it forever. Photocopies are perfectly adequate.

The bearer: Letters of introduction or explanation

Sometimes you'll need to approach an embassy, to obtain a visa, or in the hope of some advice. Some embassies are helpful, even enthusiastic (I found Czech, Greek and Turkish diplomats in Canberra exceptionally helpful). But take care. The battlefields you are looking for are very important to you—they may be the resting place of a relative or the scene of dramatic and heroic events of importance to Australia—but from the point of view of the diplomatic mission the events of 1916, 1941 or 1945 or 1963 may be an irrelevance; at worst they may be an event they want to forget. A developing country's representatives will invariably be polite, but they may well be more interested in trade or development than helping a tourist. So think about whether you need to seek diplomatic help and be careful how you go about asking for it. Many people think that they can obtain information from embassies that in fact is not available. However pleasant and co-operative embassies might want to be—they usually wish to present a positive face—bear in mind that they aren't information or reference services. A lot of advice that you want can be found from libraries, books generally, and especially the internet.

If you're going anywhere out of the way, or to a country where English is not likely to be widely spoken, you might think of obtaining a letter of introduction from an appropriate authority in Australia. This does not necessarily mean you should ordinarily bother the Greek or Turkish embassies or consulates for letters, but it could help. You might ask a local Honorary Consul, but you could also get a local cultural group to help you with an appropriate letter. The only essential requirements are that the letter says who you are and what you're doing, and that it should be written in the host country's language. An impressive letterhead is handy but not essential, but the letter ought to be typed. Here's a sample:

> To whom it may concern
>
> The bearer of this letter, Mr John Smith, of Werribee, Victoria, Australia, is travelling to Crete in order to visit the places that his great uncle, Joe Jones, served as an Australian soldier in Crete in 1941. Mr Smith's Great Uncle Joe was captured by the Germans and spent three years as a prisoner of war.
>
> Mr Smith would like to see the country where his great uncle fought. He will be bringing maps of Crete in 1941 and today, and will be taking photographs to show his family the places where his great uncle served.
>
> I would ask you to extend to Mr Smith the courtesy all Cretans give to all who visit our country in friendship.
>
> Signed
> President,
> Melbourne Cretan Association

Notice how the letter is written for its recipients. It doesn't tell you that Great Uncle Joe was a member of the 2/7th Battalion—that is meaningless to all but specialists, even in Australia—or that you're interested in finding the farmer who hid him until the Germans captured him. It states what you're about in straightforward language.

To be sure, you'd better take a copy, and a translation, just in case.

When should you use this sort of letter? I think you should have it handy whenever you're wandering about on someone else's land, which means more or less all the time in the field. At the very least, if you meet a shepherd or a farmer on a remote hillside, he's going to wonder what you're doing on his land, and he probably won't speak English. He'll probably be friendly on principle, but if he is suspicious (or, and it's unlikely, hostile), what do you do? The answer is that you whip out your letter of introduction. He's reassured that you're not looking for oil, you're relieved, and he points you towards a roadside shrine remembering victims of the occupation that you would have missed. Everybody's happy and you have a more interesting story to tell at home.

Be prepared to get more out of an encounter from such a letter than you may have bargained for. If you flash it about to all and sundry, you'll probably make a lot of new friends. This can have unexpected and productive consequences. In Crete the 2002 Australian War Memorial–Imperial War Museum study tour set up in an olive grove on Forty-second Street. The noise of me singing *Forty-second Street* in Forty-second Street—the song was, after all, the origin of the name—attracted the owner of the olive grove, Michalis. He emerged, learned of our purpose and invited us in—all twenty of us—to the impromptu hospitality of cake and raki. We learned that his family had owned part of the battlefield in 1941, and we saw (rather than merely heard of) the fierce local patriotism of the people of Crete.

A friendly encounter with local people: Michalis describes to interpreter Sevastianna (centre) his family's memories of the fighting on Crete in May 1941. Members of a battlefield tour group, including Brian Manns of the Army History Unit (left), listen. (Peter Stanley)

'Kit inspection': A pre-departure checklist

Call me an old fogey, but I don't think that packing the night before departure is conducive to successful travel. While I no longer pack three weeks in advance (as I did for my first visit to the barracks and battlefields of the raj, which lasted exactly the same duration as the packing), I still use a checklist, now refined after a dozen or more battlefield research trips. Here's my packing checklist:

- Passport (including necessary visas)
- Tickets
- Insurance documents
- Secure wallet with money (whether traveller's cheques, cash card or cash, or a combination)
- Domestic and international driver's licence (if necessary)

- Documents relating to bookings and reservations
- Photocopies of essential documents (e.g. passport, visas, prescriptions)
- Spare passport-sized photos

- Notebook
- Camera and lanyard
- Batteries (and, Aaron Pegram adds, 'spare, spare batteries')
- Research dossier
- Letter of introduction (if required)

- Walking stick (if necessary)
- Water bottle
- Mobile phone and charger
- Adapters/chargers
- Spare glasses; repair kit (if necessary)
- Sunglasses

- Clothing (according to climate)
- Trousers, dresses, shorts, belts
- Socks/stockings
- Hat (rain or sun, or both?)
- Shirts, blouses, T-shirts
- Underwear, sleepwear
- Walking and evening shoes
- Sweaters
- Raingear (coat, Drizabone, poncho or umbrella to taste: but remember weight and bulk)

- Toiletries (in travel-sized containers)
- Medicines and first-aid kit
- Knife (NB do not include in cabin baggage)
- Alarm clock, watch, torch
- Laundry bag
- Insect repellent, sunblock

Peter Pedersen (right), persuading a tour member away from a Great War excavation that has opened in a field by the Australian cemetery at Noreuil in France. Note the angler's jacket Peter favours, allowing him to stow compass, binoculars, water and so on. (Diane Melloy-Follet)

It's important to anticipate when you'll be likely to be able to wash clothing. If you're going to be in one spot for several days (assuming that a visit could last between three and five days), you'll need to take enough changes of clothing to last. And you should anticipate that you may need more than one change of clothing in a day. In hot conditions, such as in deserts, you'll return to your base sweaty and dusty. In tropical areas you'll get sweaty within minutes of breakfast and stay that way all day. Even in Europe, a day's tramping overland (especially if it rains) will encourage you to change for dinner. (That's why those English gentlemen dressed for dinner in the jungle: sweaty cotton drill is not conducive to an enjoyable meal, especially a shared one.) Either way a laundry bag to separate dirty and clean clothing is essential, as are bags to quarantine muddy or dirty boots. And do take light, comfortable shoes to change into and to travel in.

Some cultures deprecate clothing that is too brief. Shorts, for instance, might be acceptable in Australia in summer, but in Egypt long trousers might be more sensible, even for men. (In Egypt, Mark Johnston sensibly dressed in cricket gear; I favoured White Hunter attire.) Women are often subject to cultural rules, which need to be taken into account. There's not a lot of point arguing the toss on this one: stay safe and sensible is the only rule.

A word on boots. Your footwear needs to be sturdy enough to stand country walking, but in reality, the boots shouldn't be too 'stout'. I've made right and wrong purchases over many trips, including buying boots so sturdy that I could barely move in them. I wore out the best boots I ever bought between Borneo in 1994 and Gallipoli in 2004 and have now settled on good walking shoes: heavy enough to stand country walking but light enough to not use up too much of the baggage allowance on their own. Everyone's needs and preferences differ. The best advice is to choose and break in your footwear well in advance of departure. Blisters and battlefield research aren't a good combination.

Toiletries and medicines

You may need to bring tissues, toilet paper or sanitary items (remember in some cases local supplies may not be available or adequate). You should bring enough proprietary medicines (e.g. painkillers, heartburn tablets, hay fever spray) to last you, as local products may not match your own. You will often need to bring prescription medicines, including prescriptions and repeats if necessary, and not just for medical reasons. In some countries (including those you may only pass through) you may need prescriptions to justify carrying particular drugs: be warned and be wary. Take Imodium so tummy upsets don't knock you out of action for a few days—you can't afford to be sick on a tight schedule.

Insurance and inoculations

Always get travel insurance, and make sure it covers you for what you're going to be doing, where you'll be and what your state of health is. You should consult your doctor in advance of any trip that is any more adventurous than a European holiday. If you'll be travelling to malarial areas, make sure you have *and take* the necessary prophylactics. There's not a lot of point objecting to this: a bout of malaria is the worst sort of writer's block you can get.

Long-haul health: Travelling healthily

Airline travel is as safe as it's ever been, and it's much safer than land transport, especially buses and cars in developing countries. British figures suggest that flying is 176 times safer than walking and 300 times safer than riding a motorbike. These figures are less reassuring when adjusted for the number of hours spent in these forms, but passengers (or, as they are now charmlessly described, 'customers') on major airlines can fly with complete confidence. Airlines in less developed areas can be less secure, as can passengers in smaller aircraft regardless of the region, but getting there and back isn't your biggest worry. You can dismiss the threat of terrorism as a real danger—the security theatre at the airport is more of an irritant than a reassurance.

Long-haul trips are simply a part of Australian military historians' expectations. When the world history congress was held in Australia a few years ago, the hosts—us—were often surprised to learn that many delegates, especially from Europe, had found the journey a once-in-a-lifetime ordeal. Indeed, some colleagues had simply not come because the journey was 'too long'. Australian historians, like their sporting teams, understand that if they are to do their job properly, they must travel long distances.

Your comfort in the air will depend to an extent on the airline you choose. Often this won't be a real choice, because of routes, schedules or prices. Still, you can tell your travel agent your preferences, and which airlines to avoid. Even if you have no choice over whether to take a particular carrier, the 'Skytrax' website (www.airlinequality.com) will at least tell you what to expect in terms of the size and pitch of seats (a crucial factor in comfort) or what services you can expect to enjoy. It's based on reviews by people who've actually flown with the airlines you may be considering.

Still, you need to be aware of the health risks of long-haul flights. Now that airlines have banned smoking on planes, respiratory complaints are no longer a hazard for battlefield researchers, though hypochondriacs complain that airliners are breeding grounds for coughs and sneezes. But hazards remain, and it's possible to minimise or reduce their impact.

Low air pressure and humidity

One of the less obvious or talked about hazards of long-haul flights are the effects of the low air pressure and humidity maintained in aeroplane cabins. To reduce stress on their planes' fuselages, most airlines maintain the pressure of passenger jets not at sea level but at about 2500 metres above sea level (that's about 270 metres higher than Mount Kosciuszko). This can lead to respiratory complaints and a form of mild altitude sickness.

Cabin air is also very dry—drier than the driest desert, drier than you would normally ever experience on the ground. (More humid air could cause condensation and therefore electrical faults.) The dangers of dehydration can be combated simply by drinking more water, before, during and after the flight. The best airlines understand this and offer liquids to passengers throughout the flight (Japan Airlines is especially good at this practice); it's much better for you than free grog and ice creams. Much of the feeling that people ascribe to jet lag is actually a consequence of the low humidity of the cabin air.

DVT

Medical science has known about Deep Venous (or Vein) Thrombosis for about 30 years. Hardly anyone gets DVT, but if they do it's serious. Essentially it involves clots forming in the veins deep within the calf, which can travel to the lungs and kill you. The ancillary effects, such as ulceration, could really muck up your trip. Many factors can contribute to the condition, but they include sitting immobile in restrictive seats for long periods, hence its colloquial misnomer, 'economy class syndrome'. Activists claim that out of a typical Jumbo-load of about 400 passengers perhaps three or four might develop symptoms, but an Australian study by the Chief Medical Officer found that for a middle-aged traveller DVT would occur once in 40,000 flights. Airlines take the prospect of DVT claims seriously and many offer advice about it and encourage you to exercise moderately in flight. Clinical trials suggest that wearing knee-length compression socks has a measurable effect in reducing DVT. I choose aisle seats, which make it easier to get up and move about. Action that might counter DVT also helps to combat more common effects, such as jet lag, dehydration and low air pressure.

Jet lag

Jet lag is, of course, the result of shifting across time zones, upsetting the body's rhythms. Biologically, everyone will suffer from jet lag to an extent, but it's not as serious as it's made out, and you can minimise its effects. Some people profess to be badly affected by it, but it can be ameliorated by approaching the journey sensibly.

Beating jet lag is as much a matter of attitude as medication. Sleep as much as you can on the plane; avoid alcohol but drink lots of fluid. Typically you'll adjust by one hour per day for every hour of difference between your home and destination, so by the end of your first week you should be adjusted, more or less. But the most important element in this adjustment depends on your activity. Hitting the ground running—waking early (you will anyway) and getting underway actively is the best way to adjust. By the day's end you'll be ready for bed, though you may hit a slump around late afternoon and need a nap or (and I swear by this remedy) several hits of hot chocolate. You can make your adjustment more difficult by sleeping out of kilter with your new time zone, whinging that you're tired or by constantly reminding yourself that it's 3 a.m. at home. So what! Let them sleep—you've got work to do!

There are dozens of preventatives, palliatives and curatives for jet lag—take your pick. Remedies range from Charles Krebs's self-administered acupressure system ('if the Chinese had airplanes 5000 years ago, they would have used acupressure to eliminate jet lag!') to adopting a nocturnal life for a fortnight before departure. There is a plausible theory that the noise of aircraft engines aggravates jet lag. Wearing earplugs will help you rest better. You can reduce noise-induced fatigue further by wearing noise-reducing headphones—available for between $150 and $300. Whatever you do, be wary of listening to music through earbuds or headphones all the way. You may be tempted to turn up the volume to beat the engine noise, but in doing so you might damage your hearing—be careful.

Physical fitness

On the positive side, battlefield research is likely to help you stay healthy. Overseas travel, especially if it will entail tramping over battlefields—and that's exactly what this book encourages you to do—will be one of the most invigorating experiences you can have, especially if, like me, you're a not especially fit 50-something. It makes sense to make sure that you're in reasonable shape before you leave. This isn't much of an ask. The sorts of trips this book discusses usually aren't mounted at the spur of the moment. You'll have months to prepare your documents and maps; it makes sense to also take the time to prepare your body by taking more moderate exercise to get in shape for the demands travel will make.

Travelling library: Books on the battlefield

One of the great pleasures of battlefield research is the experience of sitting in a place where an event happened and reading about it. I have had extraordinary times reading about battles in the places in which they happened. I've done this in the United States and India, and on a dozen 'Australian' battlefields. In Borneo I read accounts of the fighting at 'Freda' on Tarakan, 'Parramatta Ridge' at Balikpapan and 'The Pocket' on Labuan. It is remarkable what a difference being on the spot makes. You can look up from the page and follow the route a unit or group took, and see where an incident occurred. It makes sense to take with you copies of war diaries or other documents, memoirs or secondary sources, and the essential maps needed to understand them.

However, weight is always a consideration. While you may want to take several reference books with you, do resist the temptation. You won't read all of them, and you'll just become exasperated with a travelling library, particularly as you accumulate stuff along the way. It's best to copy the chunks of books you'll most need (the official history, unit histories, secondary works you may want to rely on or check). You can always annotate them as you go, or even ditch the pages you no longer need along the way.

So you're now equipped for your battlefield field work. What happens on the ground?

PART 4

Crossing the start-line: On the battlefield

Jumping-off trench: Making a plan

Your bags are packed, and you're sitting on the plane taxiing down the runway to start your trip: what happens next?

Exactly what you'll do and the way you'll do it in depend very much upon your purpose. A two-member party getting a grasp of complex operations over several months will obviously differ from an individual investigating the experience of a small group of soldiers on one small part of a battlefield—I know because I've done both. But there will be common elements, and one thing is certain: you'll have to have a plan. You don't want to slap your forehead as you reach for the peanuts on the flight home, saying, 'Damn! I forgot to...' I know, because I've done that too.

Soon you'll be landing, taking a day or so to sort yourself out, perhaps, and will then be collecting your hire car or (depending on the country) meeting your driver, and you'll be off! But still: what are you going to do?

The answer is that well before you even get on the plane you'll have devised a list of what you want or need to do. You'll have been studying the relevant maps for weeks, of course, mulling over combinations and possibilities of time and distance. Should you look for Scott's Post first, because that's a key position, or for map reference B5.3.5, because that was the starting point and that'll provide a fixed point to work from? You know that you're looking for 'the Butte', but exactly where is that, here or here? If it's here, then the company probably went up that spur, but if it's here, then it could have... And then there are places named in men's diaries but not marked on maps in the brigade or battalion war diaries. Preparation is largely a matter of imagination.

It's important to point out—to anyone who'll listen—that field work like this isn't simply a matter of stepping out of an air-conditioned car, strolling over to a viewing platform, taking a few snaps, and retiring to a hotel terrace for a few cold ones. Most of the time you'll have to search for what you're looking for—whether it be a long-lost trench or a jungle-clad hill or a sandy hillock looking a lot like all the other sandy hillocks in the vicinity.

But when you've weighed all of the relevant questions, you can in the end draw up a list that will give you something to work with. This shouldn't be too rigid, but amid all the excitement of the trip and the novelty of arriving in an exotic destination, not to mention the jet lag, you need to have a plan to work from. I'm particularly convinced of the need for a provisional priority list because in 2002, on my first visit to Gallipoli, I arrived without one. I had planned to write a book about the hundred-odd Australians who had been awarded the Distinguished Conduct Medal for deeds on Gallipoli. I thought that a study of a manageable group of relatively well-documented men would reveal something more about the volunteers of 1914. I'd done a heap of research on their deeds but when I reached the peninsula I found that I had no list of what to do first. As a result, I explain in the introduction to *Quinn's Post, Anzac, Gallipoli*, when I got to Anzac

Cove on the scooter I'd hired, I simply walked up Shrapnel and Monash Gullies (partly to prove wrong a patronising person who told me it couldn't be done) but without a real plan. That chance decision took me to Quinn's Post. On the spot, struck by a certainty that it was Quinn's I wanted to write about, I immediately abandoned plans to write about DCM winners. Had I been better organised I might have produced a very different book; perhaps the lesson is to be flexible and organised, but not too organised.

What you do when you reach the battlefield depends on the sort of study you're undertaking and the stage you're at. If the focus is a grave in a cemetery, it's hard to resist the temptation to go straight to it. And why not? It represents the motivation that has led you to commit so much time and money to the venture.

If your study focuses on a place rather than one person (such as my books on Quinn's Post and Mont St Quentin), you'll be inclined to go straight to them. And again, why not? You'll come back to them several times in the course of a typical research trip, and each time will bring new questions and insights. Peter Pedersen has a method that's worked for him. He works from prominent terrain features he can see from anywhere on the field. 'They are an essential aid because the orientation process is continuous.' Then he relates the map to the ground in detail—friendly and enemy locations, start-lines, forming-up positions, axes, limits of exploitation, fields of fire (as a former army officer Peter has a command of the technicalities). Then he'll investigate aspects in detail, for example, 'walking to retrace an attack, getting a feel for the steepness of a route'. He frequently checks what he can see from the enemy perspective. I learned too late that several key witnesses saw Mont St Quentin from a nearby ridge, one that I'd flashed past in my hire car on the way to the Mont. Fortunately I returned soon after—though at my own expense.

One technique recommended by some veterans of field work is to approach the site of your investigation from the direction (if not perhaps in the form of transport) your subjects used. Assuming that your main focus is on Australian troops, that means approaching Pozières from Albert (rather than Bapaume), Alamein from Alexandria and Balikpapan from the sea. It's a method that doesn't always work, however. Others will emphasise the need to see the battle from both sides. At some point in your visit to Pozières, for instance, you should go to the German side of the line and try to see what they saw. At Alamein, Mark Johnston and I made a point of trying to work out what the German view was from Sidi abd el Rahman. We lacked powerful Zeiss binoculars (and we weren't game to try to get inside the mosque, as had *Deutsche-Italienische Panzerarmee* artillery observers), but we still marvelled at the difficulties of identifying places, let alone targets, in the desert.

Stand here long enough and...: Starting points

The novelist Ralph Mottram, author of the *Spanish Farm Trilogy*, three of the great novels of the Great War, returned to the Western Front in 1936. He found himself in a landscape at once familiar and absolutely foreign. In place of trenches and shattered villages he found green fields and new buildings. He was momentarily disconcerted, but realised that he had found 'enough that is unmistakeable to guide me'. The battlefield researcher is in a similar situation—with the additional problem that in all likelihood he or she will not have visited these places before. But the task, to find 'enough that is unmistakeable' to form the basis of a physical investigation of the ground and its meaning, remains the essence of the problem the battlefield researcher faces. Sometimes that starting point is a memorial—at Alamein the big German and Italian memorials at either end of the Point 26–Trig 33 ridge provide reference points visible from almost everywhere in the Australian area of the battlefield. Sometimes it is a distinctive feature (a hill or gully) or a road, bridge or crossroads that you can be certain has remained unchanged in location from the time you're studying.

One of the most absorbing and rewarding parts of battlefield research comes when you are able to stand on the exact spot where something happened. This doesn't come by chance: it's the result of careful preparation and usually a lot of legwork—literally. Sometimes these sites are important and well documented—the site of the Windmill at Pozières, for example. Other places are obscure, known only to you, or hugely important, but only to particular people: 'This is where Great Uncle Joe was wounded—and over there is where he died.' It was very important to Mark Johnston and I to trace several actual spots. We walked along the railway line at Alamein to the Blockhouse, and the surrounding area, known to the Australians as the Saucer. We walked to the Cutting, which the 2/23rd had captured on 16 July. Mark and I drove back and forth along the coast road, progressively locating Ring Contour 25, known to the men of the 2/24th Battalion as Baillieu's Bluff. That place was most important to Mark—he would write the chapters about the fighting there in our book *Alamein: The Australian Story*.

The place that gave me the most satisfaction to find was a low, scrub-covered hill by the roadside, the location of the 9th Australian Division's Tactical Headquarters on the eve of the opening of the first great attack at El Alamein on 23 October 1942. Earlier in 1997 Mark and I had consulted Alec Hill, who in 1942 had been a captain on the staff of Morshead's division. He had told us how at dusk on the evening the battle began, with all the plans made and orders written, he had sat on the sand on this hill and watched silence settle over the desert, a brief lull before the storm of the British bombardment, which opened at exactly 9.40 p.m. Using our maps and taking bearings by compass, we found the otherwise unmarked knoll. It was intensely satisfying for me to find that place, and to imagine the scene almost exactly 55 years before. Sadly, Alec died in 2008.

A key word here is 'imagine'. Visiting battlefields is all about imagination. In his diary of one of his visits to South Africa's battlefields, Craig Wilcox described tracing the route of the 1900 campaign. Conscious of both the physical landscape and the historical reality, he commented: 'Driving across a huge plain of yellow grass under a china blue sky and hot midday sun—surely, I think to myself, it would take a day to cross this on horseback, and the whole time you'd be visible to the enemy.' Applying the historical imagination like this is essential. Because no battlefield is the same as it was in history, travelling to them in the hope that all will be revealed is in most cases naïve. Only in a few places—parts of Alamein, and perhaps jungle battlefields where little seems to have changed—can we see more-or-less what the subjects of our research saw. But for some fortunate and insightful researchers, being receptive to what the landscape can tell them brings moments of revelation. Craig Deayton, travelling by train through the Somme, described the moment when his train rounded a curve before crossing the Dernancourt battlefield of 1918. 'I will never forget rounding a sweeping bend... as the battlefield came into view with all the features I'd tried so hard to picture from maps and records—the cemetery, the quarry, the sunken road, the broad exposed hillside. It was breathtaking.' Every battlefield researcher hopes for such moments of clarity, and many are fortunate to look back upon them.

For some researchers, encountering the actual spot can bring a jolt. Andrew Faulkner visited Pozières as part of the research for his recent biography of Arthur Blackburn, VC. At Pozières ('a village built on a graveyard') he took a while to get his bearings in 'a place I'd imagined and studied from books and letters for countless hours'. At first the topography threw him: 'All the accounts talk of Pozières being on a ridge, but it was more of a slight rise than a ridge in the Australian sense of the word.' Walking the fields where OG1—the German line—had been 90 years before, Andrew found the spot where Blackburn had performed the 'deed' that gained him a VC. 'This is Blackburn's battlefield,' he wrote:

> Stand here long enough and you get a feel for the geography. The ground does fall away subtly, but steadily, to the south, down towards where Black Watch Alley wound its way through the slosh. The German machine gunners were behind us, near the Bapaume road, looking down on the attacking Australians. The height advantage is even more apparent from the sunken road some 300m to the south. The 3rd Brigade's first waves jumped off from here...

Andrew could imagine on the spot what he had read and written about. Imagination is necessary on the green fields of the Somme, and on many other battlefields. Think of the Nek, perhaps the most famous Australian battlefield on Gallipoli. The Nek (presumably named by a soldier remembering the narrow saddles of South Africa) was a patch of scrub at the north end of Walker's Ridge. The Australians held one end, the Turks the other. In 1915 the Nek was seamed by barbed wire and trenches—Australian and Ottoman—separated by a narrow no-man's-land less than 30 metres wide. Artillery shells had blasted away much of the scrub.

As everyone knows who has seen that extraordinary film *Gallipoli*, Australian light horsemen went over the top against Turkish machine-guns. The Nek battlefield today is almost completely covered by the Commonwealth War Graves Commission cemetery in which the remains of many of the attackers lie. Though there are headstones marking the graves of only ten soldiers, 216 bodies lie under the neat turf. The Nek cemetery is the embodiment of the beautiful and moving cemeteries the Commission has created from Reykjavik to Rabaul. But it doesn't seem to tell you much as a military historian, except that perceptive visitors—Bill Gammage and Mark Johnston among them—made a point of asking what could be seen *from* the Nek, not just *of* the Nek.

Finding exact spots will often depend upon you bringing 'then' photographs, which can guide your search on the ground. The places you are visiting have often changed a great deal. If you go to, say, Ieper hoping to simply see the landscape of Ypres in 1917, you will surely be disappointed. Where are the trenches? Where is the mud? You'll see trees bordering broad sealed roads, neat houses and carefully tended cemeteries. If it rains (and it probably will), you'll be able to reach even Passchendaele from the Menin Gate in about twenty minutes, even if the traffic lights are against you. So you'll have to use your imagination.

Interrogation: Looking and asking questions

So you have your list of what to do, where and in what order. But what do you actually do? What you do is what any historian does when he or she sits down to read a document: you ask questions.

Here's one of the basic differences between the guided tour of the battlefield that a tourist can expect to pay for and the field work that a battlefield researcher will undertake. One has questions answered before they have to ask them—they are fed a prepared, often pre-digested story—look here, look there, listen to me, I have the answers. The other—the battlefield researcher—starts with some knowledge, of course—often a very detailed knowledge—but their basic approach is to treat the ground as a gigantic primary source. They'll ask questions all the time, often implicit ones, sometimes obvious ones, but always trying not to make up their minds before the ground (read in combination with the maps, documents and photographs they've brought with them) provides tentative answers.

Your research dossier will be your guide here. Over the weeks (or months or even years) that you've been compiling it, you will have recorded, explicitly or not, dozens of questions. Now is the time to begin to unpack the dossier and to use it to start to find answers to the questions you've posed while looking at the documents and writing drafts at home.

What you need to ask depends on the battle you're researching. But there are several common elements:

- Where were the combatants at the beginning of the battle; and where did they go during the action?
- What was the weather like?
- What time of year was it; when was sunrise and sunset?
- Where were the units you're mostly interested in?
- Where were their flanking units?
- What route were casualties evacuated along?
- Where were the medical units placed?
- Where were the guns (that is, artillery positions) and their observers?
- What could they see?
- What was the effective range of infantry weapons and artillery?
- Where were the headquarters that controlled them—battalion, brigade, division, etc.?
- What could 'your' unit see?
- From where could it have been seen?
- How long would it have taken to get from A to B, and in what conditions?

- Where were the enemy: what could they see?
- What's missing: what was present then that isn't now?
- What's here now that wasn't then?

All these questions will suggest conclusions but more likely other questions. The questions you'll pose will depend upon the type of project you're conducting, and that depends in turn upon what sort of historian you are. Some operationally inclined historians will ask about command and control arrangements, dispositions and decisions, and only later will take an interest in cemeteries and memorials. Culturally inclined historians may begin with the cemeteries and memorials that dot many battlefields, and use them as the fulcrum of their enquiry. To these historians the positions of units at various times, and commanders' decisions and dispositions are less relevant. Military social historians—and that's what I call myself—might be more interested both in what happened at the time, and in the changes that have occurred since.

Let's look at three representatives of these types of historian, and see what they do on the battlefield.

Jeff Grey of the Australian Defence Force Academy is a military historian in the classic mould. He does not try to do a Bean and take his readers into the front line, but analyses the currents of command and their impact on operations. He is also a leading Australian exponent of the 'staff ride', having taken groups of US Marine Corps officers on study tours to battlefields in Turkey and South Korea.

In taking student officers to Gallipoli, Jeff has noticed how they react and what they do. Of course they respond to the drama of the campaign as Jeff outlines it, and the pathos of the cemeteries. But they also use their training to put themselves in the place of their counterparts in 1915. He encourages them to ask 'what happened here, and why?', and to think what they would have done in their place. While not shrugging off their training—amphibious warfare officers make some interesting observations on the sense of landing at Cape Helles—Jeff tries to get them to think like company commanders. Jeff takes them to places likely to stimulate 'ah ha!' moments. He took one group on a trek around newly ploughed fields in the highlands overlooking Suvla Bay. From a now obscure spot—not the site of a cemetery or a memorial, deep within Turkish lines—Jeff asked them to look out towards the coast. 'Ah ha!' they said. They could see what Turkish artillery observers saw in August 1915—the whole Suvla position, open to observation, and therefore to artillery fire. That explains the failure to advance at Suvla as much as any dissection of General Stopford's character or visits to Green or Chocolate Hills, easier to reach from the sealed coast road.

Research for Craig Deayton's history of the 47th Battalion has drawn on family papers from all over Tasmania and Queensland, official records, and the 47th's battlefields. In the course of his research, Craig has learned not just about the history of the 47th (a run-of-the-mill battalion, but unique in its way, like all of them); he has reached profound conclusions about the value and methods of battlefield research.

Craig remembered reading (in John Keegan's *The Face of Battle*, a seminal, inspirational book for so many military historians) how a simple walk around a battlefield could prove a participant's account of a battle to be nonsense. (This might seem to be heretical to those brought up to revere either eyewitness evidence or soldiers, but be patient.) Craig himself doubted this 'very much'. Then he tramped the Somme, Ypres and Dernancourt in search of what had happened to the 47th. To his surprise, he found Keegan's observation to be absolutely valid. 'On more than one occasion', he writes, 'after having inhabited the battlefield vicariously through maps, personal accounts and official records, the experience of walking over the ground brought almost instant answers to some previously intractable problems'. As a battalion historian, Craig found a manageable scale of inquiry. At Passchendaele, for instance, the battalion's frontage was 250 yards (230 metres), and the depth of its attack 500 yards (460 metres). He found at Messines that he could cover, in a 15–20-minute 'easy stroll', the distance that the battalion had advanced in eight to ten hours.

Ross McMullin is a versatile freelance historian who has produced several noteworthy books (including a study of the cartoonist and war artist Will Dyson) and has lived off his keyboard. His *Pompey Elliott* is a detailed and authoritative study of one of the most inspiring commanders Australia has produced. Ross visited the Villers-Bretonneux battlefield and, as well as reflecting at the memorial there, he looked about and understood the battle that Pompey helped to win better than he could have in a library.

It is fitting that the Australian national memorial to the missing in France should be located at Villers-Bretonneux. Some 15,000 Australians became casualties in the battles to halt the German advance. Visiting the memorial and its adjoining cemetery (which actually contains more British than Australian graves) is a sobering experience. But what does a battlefield researcher see on the ground? Ross explained that 'if you position yourself near the Australian memorial, you can see the sloping ground Pompey's brigade covered in its famous counter-attack'. There, he says:

> You can appreciate the complexity of the task, with multiple changes of direction in the dark (with no artillery support). On a clear day you can see Amiens in the distance, a view that brings into sharp focus the significance of Villers-Bretonneux as the key to Amiens. Anyone positioned where you are could direct artillery fire onto the city and its vital railway junction. It explains why there was such relief among senior officers when the counter-attack proved successful.

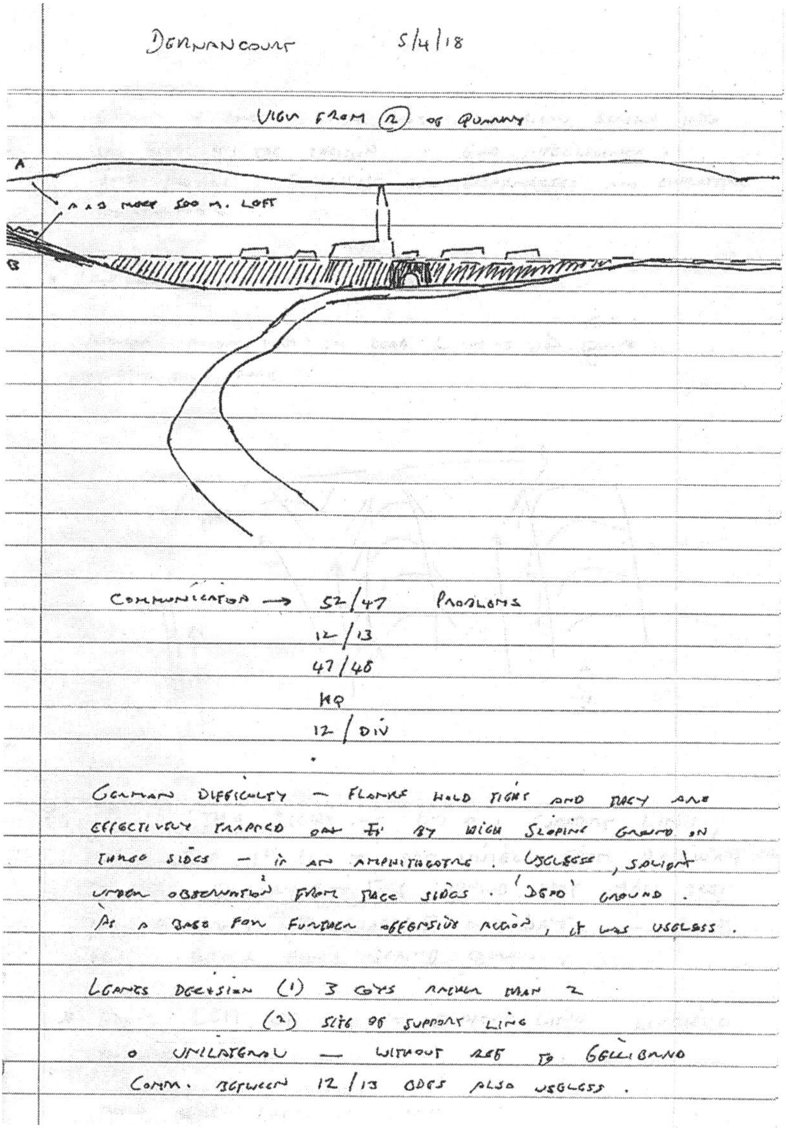

One of Craig Deayton's on-the-spot sketches of the Dernancourt battlefield is in the same tradition as the drawings in Charles Bean's notebooks. (Craig Deayton)

You can see why experienced battlefield researchers urge novices to keep looking up and around. It's far too easy (especially on battlefields like Gallipoli, where we always hope to find a 'relic') to look at the ground rather than the horizon. Ross's use of the physical setting of Villers-Bretonneux explains why you need to enlarge your focus and not just look at headstones, however moving they may be.

One key idea that you can use while thinking about the battle when walking the ground is Lieutenant Colonel Alfred Burne's concept of 'Inherent Military Probability'. This might best be defined as 'what a trained and competent officer would most likely have done in the circumstances'. It can help to answer questions that the documents can't. It doesn't always work: at both the Nek and at Fromelles trained officers devised and persisted in foolish attacks, while in Malaya and on Singapore officers withdrew when the textbooks would have urged them to hold. But applying the idea of IMP on the battlefield can help to make sense of oddities and anomalies that persist even when you are reading the actual orders or reports in a library at home. And if your battlefield companion reaches a different conclusion, so much the better!

This method presumes that battlefield research is an active process of asking questions and seeking and pondering answers, effectively using much the same approach as any other sort of research.

There are other models, though they are not recommended. What might be called the Les Carlyon school of battlefield research entails visiting battlefields to soak up the atmosphere. Page after page of Carlyon's *Gallipoli* passes with lyrical descriptions of the landscape and Carlyon's observations of the country and its inhabitants: 'The tomatoes are going in on the red-brown dirt of the Suvla plain. Everyone is out in the fields, as if to celebrate the land coming alive again...' Carlyon uses the landscape as a palette to add colour to his writing, but he doesn't ask questions of it. Human character—mostly flawed—is the engine room of his narrative. In his *The Great War* he does refer to travelling to the battlefields of the Western Front. 'It is better to see the ground', he acknowledges, but concludes 'it doesn't necessarily lead you to the truth'. I take the opposite view.

Random shots: Photographs

As this book shows, photographs are an invaluable tool in comparing what exists today with what was there then. Because military historical field work is so bound up with the ideas of 'the ground', it is vital to record as much as possible on the spot. The photographs merely document the insights you gain from seeing the ground. On my first visit to Mont St Quentin I hadn't identified the sites from which Charles Bean observed the fight or from which Arthur Streeton painted the Mont. Some work with map, compass and camera on a subsequent trip enabled me to do so, and to photograph what they had seen.

Naturally, weather, technical malfunctions and accidents such as dropping your camera in a water-logged ditch can get in the way of perfect photography. (Aaron Pegram, a former colleague at the National Museum, has explored the battlefields of the Western Front, and suggests keeping 'all your paraphernalia stored in zip-locked bags for when you fall into that drainage ditch in Polygon Wood'.) However, we are better able now to get decent shots of what we seek than ever before. The challenge now is getting the best shots and making them as useable as possible. The advent of digital photography had made it seemingly ridiculously easy to photograph sites and sights. However, the old problem of 'great subject, lousy shot' remains. We can still commit all the old sins of shooting into the sun, leaving the subject in shadow, or composing and framing the shot badly;

Nigel Steel photographs the battlefield of Kapyong, South Korea, from a rock on the 'island feature'. (Nigel Steel)

digital photography has not solved these problems. There are any number of guides to taking photographs, both in popular and specialist magazines to books.

Phil Bradley reports that he has used a digital camera that attaches a ten-second audio grab to an image. He uses this to identify the patch of jungle at which he is pointing the camera. You can also attach GPS devices to cameras that then record the exact position of an image in the camera's meta-data. Having experimented with this type of camera in France, I decided that it was an unnecessary refinement in a well-mapped landscape, but it may be vital in desert or jungle terrain.

Digital cameras have intensified the problem of identifying and sorting the images. Craig Deayton solved this problem by reviewing and selectively deleting the images he had taken each evening of the trip. This is onerous but sensible, and asking 'what will this shot add to my knowledge?', 'what does this add to my interpretation?' (or indeed, 'why did I take that?') will make the selection smaller but stronger. Even more onerous, but even more sensible, is to list and comment on the images remaining after your cull.

Ideally the researcher should return with lists of photographs identified by location, subject and (crucially) the direction in which the photograph was taken. At the time the reasons for a photograph and the subject of it seem so obvious that listing seems tedious or superfluous. But what was obvious on the spot may be obscure weeks or months later.

Some researchers—Mark Johnston and Peter Pedersen included—take video footage of battlefields. This makes sense if you need a broader focus than the viewfinder of a still camera. I recall Mark taking long sweeping shots of the southern horizon at Alamein—the area we were forbidden from reaching—and Peter Pedersen remarks that he refers to his footage often in writing his books and guides to battlefields.

Ratting: Picking up souvenirs

Almost all battlefield visitors hope to return with souvenirs as well as memories and photographs. All of us will hope to find what Charles Bean called 'relics'—the tangible (and takeable) stuff left lying about for decades after battle.

The most visited battlefields are, of course, empty of the detritus of war. The ridge road on Gallipoli has been picked over by generations of trippers, Turkish and otherwise. The finds you'll make will depend on what has been flushed out by each winter's rains—visiting in the early spring of 2008, Peter Dowling found bones on the road verge. Elsewhere, and especially on less visited battlefields, you may come across bullets, shrapnel fragments, bits of bully beef tins—the leftovers of combat that we now treasure as ways of connecting with what happened on the spot. You will feel a compulsion to pick them up and carry them away. Be wary. The first thing to make sure is that you're not handling something dangerous—see 'Achtung! Safety on the battlefield', page 190. While on the RMC staff tramp along the Black Cat Trail in Papua New Guinea in 1977, Peter Pedersen came across a weapon pit on the edge of a clearing. It was 'still in reasonable nick with a dozen or more Australian grenades, which looked ready to throw, arranged in rows at the business end'. He sensibly left them alone and moved on.

It's often very likely that what you pick up has no necessary connection with Australians; just because you find it on the Somme or at Polygon Wood or on Gallipoli doesn't make it an 'Anzac' relic. If the battlefield was the scene of only a brief and clearly identified action, and if you can be sure of where it was and where you are, then you may have something worth cherishing. For example, on the Alamein battlefield we visited localities that were the scene of fighting for just a few hours. In that case the items we found were probably directly related to those events. But a .303 bullet on the Chunuk Bair range on Gallipoli is far more likely to have been fired by a rifle aimed by a British soldier than an Anzac one.

This pile of Great War ordnance in the yard at Mouquet Farm, awaiting collection by French army bomb disposal teams, is a striking reminder of the potential danger facing visitors to even an apparently 'tame' battlefield like the Somme. (Aaron Pegram)

That's assuming you'll find anything. After any war, large-scale official salvage and small-scale local scavengers would have cleaned up anything big or valuable. In tropical and temperate regions most metals and all organic material (such as webbing, leather or rifle stocks) will have corroded or rotted away years ago—remember, we're only thinking of stuff that you can see; we're not digging anything up. Areas like the Somme have been reoccupied and put under cultivation for getting on for 90 years. Gallipoli has been well and truly picked over in the last twenty-odd years, though rusty stuff can still be seen in the more remote parts. (Much of the rusty stuff seems to be in the little museum at the crossroads at Alçitepe, most of it utter tat.) Battlefields in dry desert climates such as Alamein and Tobruk will offer the best opportunities, but only in relatively out-of-the-way localities, and you'd have to be sharp-eyed even there.

But if you do make a find, should you put it in your rucksack and bring it home? The argument that we should leave the battlefields as they are has long ago been lost. We've been changing battlefields since the moment the last shot was fired, and we still are. If you don't take it, you can be sure that someone else will, and with the greatest charity towards the theory of material heritage, it's not now going to make much difference. If you find a bullet in the scrub behind Lone Pine, I think you're morally entitled to pocket it. All the formal museums of the Great War have as much rusty kit as they need to interpret that conflict, so you're not even imperilling the world's material heritage (as you would by, say, buying a piece of ancient Egyptian pottery).

But be careful. Under a strict interpretation of the relevant Turkish law you're not supposed to take anything away, and foreigners have been arrested and held for picking stuff up. The best advice is to be selective. Don't rat the whole area, collecting as many bullets and rusty tin cans as you can find; choose one item of particular significance from an area of meaning to you. My favourite battlefield relic is a rusty tin lid that I found on Point 24 at Alamein. Someone—probably an Australian infantryman—punctured it to create a crude grater to make porridge out of his biscuits. Less is more when it comes to meaningful relics.

If you do decide to take your find home, make sure you put it in your checked luggage so it will come home to rest on your mantelpiece or bookshelf as a memento of your trip. Carrying it in your pocket through an airport metal detector is foolish. Yes, it's a 90-year-old bullet, but it's still going to cause you problems, especially these days. You don't want to be put in a position where you have to explain why you've come to have it on you.

Battlefield burial: Bones

The most common things you'll find on some battlefields are bones. Battlefields are full of bones. The numbers are staggering. There are 200-odd bones in the human body. Even before we speculate on bones shattered by shrapnel and grenades, the numbers of dead mean that at Anzac there could be a couple of million bones in an area a bit bigger than Fountain Gate Shopping Centre. On Gallipoli there are still drifts of bones—mostly Turkish—in the gullies and washaways inland from Anzac Cove. By the same reckoning, at Pozières there could be a million fragments in an area the size of your average Australian suburb, though the wetter conditions there mean that they're less likely to be preserved.

What do you do if you find bones on a battlefield? It's often a shock: you are looking at the piece of a man (probably) who (again, probably) died in the events you've come to try to understand. The first thing to do is to stop, look and think. This is ultimately what it's about; it's a sobering moment. It's possible to speculate on the events that might have brought the bones to this spot. Whole bodies—identifiable ones—are still being found by chance, to be interred respectfully in Commonwealth War Graves Commission cemeteries.

But what should you do? There are different schools of thought. Some say you should do nothing; leave the bones in place. They'll be washed further down the hill and eventually will merge with the earth, just as all the other bones have. Others argue that these bones deserve respect, like those that were recovered and interred in a war cemetery. In this case you might want to carry the bones to the nearest Commonwealth War Graves Commission cemetery and leave them by the Cross of Sacrifice. This is a good place to think about remembering.

Reverse arms: Remembering on the battlefield

Everyone who visits a battlefield cemetery should be thinking of the relationship between you, now, and them, then. The most obvious difference between the two is that you're alive and they're not. And because of the reading you've done, you know—sometimes in more detail than you'd like—why they are not.

However focused you may be on tactics, positions or manoeuvres, I suggest that at some point in your visit you should call in on a cemetery. Phil Bradley writes touchingly about visiting the graves of the men about whom he has written in *On Shaggy Ridge* and *The Battle for Wau*. 'For me it is like meeting long-lost friends,' he says, a feeling I and others have echoed.

You may think of this as paying your respects to those who did not live to enjoy the benefits of the free, safe, prosperous and

Cemeteries are an essential part of visiting battlefields: Australian historian, soldier and now lecturer in War Studies at Sandhurst, Garth Pratten, in the solemn Commonwealth War Graves Commission cemetery at Suda Bay, Crete. (Peter Stanley)

democratic country we're lucky enough to inhabit. You might think of it as a gesture of acknowledgement to victims of war. I don't think why we remember matters. Not everyone who has died in Australia's wars gave their life for this ideal—some deaths were futile—but there is every reason to simply pay respects to those who died in the events which we study. This desire has a disadvantage historically, in that excessive veneration or unthinking remembrance can blunt an historian's most important tool, their critical faculty. But a regard for those who died can also immeasurably empower a military historian's insight.

In 1993 the Australian War Memorial popularised the slogan 'Lay a Single Poppy' to accompany the interment of the Unknown Australian Soldier. (Very sensibly, the Memorial didn't want the tomb to become overwhelmed with floral tributes—it could have looked like Lenin's Tomb within hours.) I've taken that as a motto in visiting battlefields. As well as laying single poppies in cemeteries and on memorials, I now place them at sites that have an especially powerful meaning. In 1997 Mark Johnston and I identified the Cutting, a place where the 26th Brigade's units fought hard actions in July 1942. Going there helped Mark to write two chapters of our book, *Alamein*—'A Hot Spot' and 'Vigorous Local Actions'—and it was important to both of us to lay a poppy.

Before you leave home, buy enough poppies to cover your needs. You can buy plastic poppies around Remembrance Day in most places, but if your local florist or the local RSL can't help, the shop at the Australian War Memorial, the Shrine of Remembrance in Melbourne or similar location in other cities will be happy to sell you some for a modest price. Some people take the little wooden crosses that organisations such as the War Widows' Guild place in their 'Fields of Remembrance' around Anzac Day. The great advantage of them is that you can write on the cross, explaining what or who it is that you're both researching and commemorating.

This desire to connect research and commemoration is of course not an exclusively Australian impulse, but it is one that many Australians share. That it is not universal is suggested by a letter I received from Milson Milkias, the English teacher who helped me so much when I visited Tarakan on my second research trip in 1997. Having accompanied me to battle sites around the island (several of which I would not have found alone), Milson wrote that he had 'learned something special when I saw you in Tarakan... watching you honouring the war dead with the red flowers from your hand-bag. I wondered if all historians were just like you.' You too will have special places where you'd want to lay a poppy in memory of those you've researched and travelled many thousands of kilometres to visit.

Achtung! Safety on the battlefield

By definition, battlefields are dangerous places, now as well as then. Wanting to stay safe is not just a reaction from a paid-up member of the Nanny State—everyone wants you to come home safely. You'll face many possible hazards, natural and human, some more important than others, some more lethal than you'd like. The trick is to anticipate and prevent as well as deal with them.

You may fear terrorism or air accidents. Statistically, though, these are negligible risks. International air travel is safer than it has ever been. So safe travel isn't about avoiding getting on the six o'clock news for the wrong reasons. Safe travel is not really about the spectacular; it's about avoiding the filler paragraphs on the margins of the morning paper, the ones that tell you that 'Two Australians were among the dead when a mini-bus plunged off a mountain road in ...'. It's really about what could go wrong, not what probably will. It's also about having the right attitude towards what may go wrong. The first hazard you face is an undue or unjustified fear of what could go wrong, but probably won't, provided you're careful. Let's run through the major hazards.

Weather

By definition, you'll be tramping about in the open air, and paying the price for it. Australian battles have been fought in climatic extremes. While 25 April 1915 was a beautiful spring day, the first battle of Bullecourt opened in a snow storm, and summer temperatures at Tobruk were hotter than most Australians experience routinely. Serving in the tropics, anywhere from Darwin to Phuoc Tuy, involved the heat and humidity of a South-East Asian climate.

All of these climatic extremes present hazards. On the Western Front and Gallipoli in winter you must dress for the climate. That involves thermal underwear, layers of warm clothing and especially warm headgear (heat loss is greatest through the head) and decent footwear. Most Australians don't live where it is cold and wet. Despite the tedious chiacking about their city's cold weather that Canberrans like me put up with, I have never experienced such bone-chilling cold as I did in two weeks on Gallipoli in December, and wish I had invested in thermal underwear. Plan and prepare.

Australians are more used to high temperatures but, like the Americans in Viet Nam who knew more about ambushes because they were ambushed more often, we tend to take the sun for granted. As we are reminded every summer, wear a hat (one with good neck protection), take and use sunscreen, wear long sleeves and drink lots of water. Remember, you're likely to be in the open for ten or twelve hours a day; dress and act accordingly.

Much the same advice applies to the humid tropics, especially about drinking enough water. In the tropics you are likely to encounter heavy rain, sometimes all through the year, sometimes only in the monsoon. Take rain gear by all means, if only to keep your kit and documents dry, but if you are rained on in the tropics nothing you can do will keep you dry, so accept that you'll get wet and plan accordingly.

The extremes of both heat and cold are your greatest threats. If you do feel the symptoms of heatstroke, get out of the sun, drink water and if the symptoms persist, seek medical aid. Hypothermia occurs when the body's temperature falls below 35 degrees. It is dangerous, especially because one of the symptoms is often a misleading sense of well-being. If one of your party suffers hypothermia, get them into shelter, wrap them in a thermal 'space blanket', and call for medical aid. The latest edition of Peter McKie's *Active First Aid* gives further details, as do all good first-aid manuals. You probably won't take a manual with you, but you should be conversant with the main points of first aid, preferably having completed a course, such as those run by St John Ambulance.

Natural hazards include dangers from animals. The most notorious are the ferocious dogs that roam Gallipoli (they seem to be free-range guard dogs; I just out-distanced some on my dinky scooter in 2002), but there are also snakes, on Gallipoli and elsewhere. In 2004 I narrowly missed what looked like a brown snake in the Quinn's Post cemetery. Like Australia, Papua New Guinea has some of the most dangerous snakes going, and fewer facilities to treat you if bitten. Mosquitoes are an obvious hazard in tropical areas, as are spiders. Peter Pedersen recalled spiders 'that could easily cover your face' on the Black Cat Trail, and on the same trip he had to be pulled out of a rushing torrent by a human chain of his fellow RMC cadets. Near Messines, in Belgium, Craig Deayton was zapped by an electric fence while photographing bison: about as improbable an Australian battlefield injury as you could imagine.

Human hazards

Tourists in the cities battlefield researchers use as bases, such as Cairo, Istanbul, Ho Chi Minh City and Paris, are often the target of 'crimes of distraction'—pickpockets or conmen, often operating near tourist attractions. For example, near the Musée de l'Armée in Paris in 2007 Michael McKernan and I separately encountered conmen playing the 'wedding ring' trick. They 'find' a ring on the ground and while inviting you to wonder how it came to be there, an accomplice tries to pick your pocket. Neither of us fell for this blandishment, and the conman hastily retreated when I took his photograph when he tried the same trick later the same day. In the field you are refreshingly free from these annoyances. Battlefield research usually occurs in rural areas remote from the hazards of tourist traps. Even so, however immersed you become in your field work, you should observe ordinary prudence. Take all the usual precautions, such as not leaving cars unlocked, not leaving valuables visible, keeping an eye on your camera and your bag, and so on.

Up to twenty Australians are murdered each year overseas. Expert commentary observes, somewhat obviously, that many of these people paid insufficient attention to 'personal security'; that is, they placed themselves at some risk by where they went and what they did. Be careful; no book is worth dying for before it's written.

Car accidents

About 40 Australians die in road accidents overseas each year, and you're more likely to be killed driving to the airport than in the air, especially in countries, like Egypt and Turkey, with a more casual attitude to road safety. As I finished this book, a Melbourne coroner investigated the deaths of six Victorians killed on the desert highway near Cairo after visiting El Alamein in 2006. Developing countries have accident rates up to twenty times those of the developed world. This is due to poorer roads and lighting, poorly maintained cars and aggressive car cultures. Various measures can be used to compare the hazards of driving in the First and Third worlds, and the less developed world comes off worse by all of them. Measuring deaths per 100 million kilometres driven, Egypt rates at 43.2 and Turkey 22, compared with the United States at 1.1. On the measure of road accidents per 100,000 of population, Australia comes out at 9.3, Greece 22, South Africa 26.5, South Korea 30.4 and Malaysia at 31.

Explosives

Assume that any grenade, shell, bomb, bullet or mine is dangerous no matter how corroded it may be. Don't pick them up to find out; leave them be. The temptation is obvious: something rusty

The shell game at Alamein. This Egyptian labourer is about to belt these shells together; we didn't stick around. (Mark Johnston)

makes a wonderful souvenir, and even experienced battlefield visitors can make stupid choices when faced with old ordnance. A colleague brought home a Mills bomb from France and was killed tinkering with it. In Egypt Mark Johnson and I encountered a labourer chipping rust off old shells. We didn't get a good look at him, but made a hasty retreat. Peter Pedersen had a much closer call deep in the jungles of Saipan, the island American forces took in 1944 at such great cost. He almost walked into a Japanese grenade placed at head-height in a tree as a booby trap.

Guns

When visiting the battlefield of Fromelles in the northern autumn, Ross McMullin, biographer of both Pompey Elliott and Will Dyson, tells the story of how he found himself caught up in a hunt. He saw a line of green-clad men carrying guns approaching him across the ploughed fields. Was this a time-travelling platoon from 1916? No, it was a party of French farmers out for a day's shooting. They greeted him gruffly—they were after quail, not Australian historians—and he made a prudent retreat out of the line of fire. Other battlefield researchers' encounters with guns have been more direct. When visiting the site of Stalag Luft III at Sagan, Poland, Nigel Steel wandered beyond a fence in a wood. Before he knew it, he was surrounded by Polish troops wearing 'Noddy suits' (equipped for nuclear, biological or chemical warfare), with coloured smoke thunderflashes going off.

Even more chilling is the story Garth Pratten tells of when he and Brian Farrell explored the Johore Strait in a 'tinny'. A Singapore Defence Force Apache attack helicopter saw and shadowed them. Both of our heroes had enough military experience to realise that the Apache's observer was probably ranging his rockets on them, in case they were Jemaah Islamiyah arms smugglers or terrorists.

Garth and Brian decided that they had seen enough mangrove swamps for the day and retreated to the Malaysian shore.

Mines

In North Africa in general and around Alamein in particular there are thought to be a couple of million landmines left over from 1942. John Laffin certainly encountered live minefields in Libya and Egypt in the mid-1950s. Mark Johnston and I were warned of this by several people, here and in Egypt, and we solemnly believed them. I'm not so sure any more, though Mark reminded me of the military compound we saw at Alamein containing mine-clearing equipment. The most prudent advice seems to be to act as if the place is still mined. The same caution applies in Viet Nam, Cambodia and Laos. Greg Lockhart, Viet Nam veteran and author of *The Minefield*, has drawn attention to the problem mines still pose in Ba Ria–Vung Tau Province. Old minefields are a problem elsewhere in Viet Nam—'The locals know they're there but you probably won't,' Peter Pedersen warns. At Dien Bien Phu he learned later that he had unknowingly walked through a field in which a French visitor had lost his leg a year or so before. Peter is an ex-regular officer and an experienced battlefield researcher, but he commented, it 'shook me up a bit, I can tell you'. Be careful.

And while you're about it, don't think about taking a metal detector with you. A metal detector will—surprise, surprise—detect metal. And what do you do when it does? Well, you'll be tempted to dig it up. That could result in two undesirable outcomes. One, you get monstered by the local police for digging stuff up, and you waste a lot of time in explaining or, worse, cooling your heels in the local chokey. Or, two—you've located a Mills grenade in a rusty case and ... don't try it.

Tunnels and caves

You can find tunnels and caves on many Australian battlefields—on Gallipoli and on the Western Front, and in Papua New Guinea at Salamaua, on Bougainville and New Britain, and at Balikpapan in Borneo. Peter Pedersen warns from experience, 'Be wary about

Battlefield researchers are often faced with opportunities to enter tunnels, excavations, dug-outs or other dangerous places. Aaron Pegram, mindful of his promising career as a military historian, wisely chose not to enter this pillbox at Hill 60, Belgium. (Aaron Pegram)

tunnels . . . Not only can they be unsafe but getting lost is a real risk in the more labyrinthine ones.' He went with a guide into the Malinta tunnel complex on Corregidor, in the Philippines, but when he thought that the guide seemed unsure said 'enough's enough', and headed out. (This is another good example of where the visitor rightly retains control of the visit they are probably paying for.) The temptation to get into pillboxes and tunnels on the Western Front should also be avoided.

Food poisoning

If you're lucky, you'll be researching a battlefield in a region of Europe famed for its cuisine, or a city in Asia noted for its cosmopolitan restaurants. If you're unlucky, you'll catch a dose of upset tummy. This is often described as being down to a change in the water, and indeed, water does contain bacteria, harmful and otherwise. In some places upset tummy is to be expected. At Alamein I ate everything (partly, I'm now prepared to admit, because my companion was very fussy). I had the trots every night, worst of all after the camel-meat kebabs, and we stayed in a large hotel that catered for Western visitors—though clearly not well enough. Mark survived for a week on bread, potato chips and soft drink. Ordinary prudence should suffice.

Accidents

It's odds-on that something will happen to you that you'd wish hadn't. I've been lucky so far—touch wood. On Gallipoli I lost my glasses, flicked off by a branch halfway up the slopes below Quinn's Post. On Gokçeada, Turkey, I climbed through a barbed-wire fence and heard that familiar ripping sound. On the Lucknow battlefield in India an insect flew into my eye and simultaneously I cut my thumb (ironically while peeling fruit to make it safe to eat). I'd rather not remember the effect of the camel-meat kebabs at Alamein, and there was that snake at Quinn's Post—the manuscript was more-or-less finished and I suppose someone would have brought it out posthumously... But perhaps I've also been better prepared by experience.

Finding your way: Maps

Just as commanders can't fight battles without maps, you just can't do military history without them. Nigel Steel describes the natural condition of the experienced battlefield researcher as 'map obsessed'. They are the essential foundation of field work. With maps, you are merely confused; without them, you will definitely become lost, both 'now' and 'then'.

You'll need several different kinds of maps, before, during and after your trip, so before haring off to order a copy of ten situation maps from the Australian Corps war diary or satellite images from Google Earth, let's run through what maps you might need.

Assuming you'll need to drive to your destination, your first need will be for road atlases. Even in countries where it's customary to be driven (India, Indonesia, even in my recent experience, Turkey and the Czech Republic) I like to know where I am even if I'm not behind the wheel. This desire to navigate silently gave the irrits to my companions on a film project in Turkey. Since the driver knew where he was going and you won't presume to know better, they reasoned, why not just sit back and relax? It does seem a bit up-tight, I admit, but keeping your finger on the map and noting where and how the country changes adds to the geographical knowledge that a military historian ought to have. In the Czech Republic I realised—just too late—that we'd driven across the site of one of Frederick the Great's battles; the road passed between the Austrian and French lines. Even on a group tour it makes sense to keep your eye on the compass and your finger on the map: you never know what you'll pass by.

European countries are wonderfully well served by detailed, reliable road atlases. For France the Institut Géographique National *Atlas Routier* is ideal for getting from Paris, the Channel coast or airports to the battlefields. Other European countries are covered in a companion atlas. Many countries are covered by maps produced by Freytag & Berndt, Periplus, Berndtson & Berndtson, Collins or Michelin. All these, and more, in various scales, are available from your local map shop. There are specialist Mapworld shops in several capital cities, and it has a good website (www.mapworld.com.au). A competitor, Mapland, operates in Melbourne. These shops and their local counterparts will hold or be able to order most maps (and guidebooks) you are likely to need. Countries with a more restrictive attitude towards geographical information, such as Indonesia, Viet Nam and South Korea, will need special attention, but maps can often be found through the map librarians in the various state libraries, or the excellent National Library of Australia map library.

Once on the battlefield your cartographic needs will depend on your project and your level of interest. Again, you'll need modern and historical maps, and will continually switch between the two in navigating around the present in search of the past. At the very least you'll need a modern road map to get you there and the maps used by units at the time, so you can understand what the war diaries record. A fundamental rule is to try to use the maps the subjects of your research used, or at least maps of the same scale.

Jeff Grey offers a useful hint for finding your way around battlefields that are dotted with cemeteries, such as the Ypres Salient and the Somme. Having done it, he advises that 'it is often most useful to triangulate off the cemeteries, since their position is marked on virtually any map you'll use'. He warns

Mark Johnston comparing compass and GPS over a map at Alamein, looking south from Ring Contour 25, on the anniversary of the battle, 1997. (Peter Stanley)

with the voice of experience that 'road signs are often inadequate, non-existent or only face one way—usually the other way'.

In trying to understand what happened at Quinn's Post I needed everything from the most general topographic maps of Gallipoli and especially the Anzac area to the most detailed plans possible of Quinn's Post's trenches and tunnels, an area of only a couple of hundred metres long by 50 metres wide. Ultimately I needed the detailed trench plans (showing underground saps and surface trenches) made by an Australian sapper later in 1915. For *Alamein: The Australian Story*, which took in the 9th Division's part in the setting of the entire Alamein battlefield (an area about 20 by 30 kilometres), Mark Johnston and I mostly worked off 1/40,000 scale maps found in unit and formation war diaries and copied from the Australian War Memorial's collection. Obtaining maps from the War Memorial used to be expensive but necessary, though the Research Centre's curators sweetened the price with

Then and now: Mont St Quentin photographed by Hubert Wilkins as men of the 6th Brigade 'hopped the bags' at 1.30 p.m. on 1 September 1918, and by the author exactly 89 years later (J.G. Roberts papers, Ms 8508, State Library of Victoria; Peter Stanley)

efficient and knowledgeable service. Craig Tibbitts points out that the maps in war diaries can be downloaded gratis. They can be printed commercially if you need a paper copy.

For Mont St Quentin I used the modern 1:25,000 Institut Géographique National topographical maps, sheet 62C of the British 1:20,000 maps showing trenches as they were in the summer of 1918 (including versions from the 21st Battalion war diary showing the positions of companies and platoons at key times), a very large scale map of the battle published in the *History of the Fourth Army* (written by its Chief of Staff), and, at the other extreme, a scrappy sketch made by a platoon sergeant. All of them enabled me to get to and around the battlefield, but I still had to ask many questions and to make many deductions moving between different maps and sources as I walked around the battlefield, now greatly changed in many ways.

Digital research: Google Maps

We're used to googling just about anything these days, sometimes using up-to-date sources unimaginable a decade ago, but often lazily, to save ourselves the trouble of doing some real research. But your Google home page now includes a feature that can be of vital assistance, in battlefield research: Google Maps. This feature enables you to call up maps of many parts of the world which can be viewed as maps, as satellite images or as a combination of both. They can be viewed at various levels of detail, viewed on screen or printed out and taken with you.

The value of Google Maps is incalculable. At the very least it can give you colour images of actual terrain and its visible features. Aaron Pegram has found traces of trenches still visible in the chalky pastureland of the Somme, but even where such detail is not visible, you can gain a picture of the ground you are going to walk over. I laboriously located 'Brewery Farm', in Querrieu, where Charles Bean lived with the 21st Battalion in 1918, by walking around the village with a 1918 photograph.

Afterwards, I consulted Google Maps to find that it allows you to zoom in on the individual buildings that survive at the farm. The value of this tool can only increase as it becomes more sophisticated and we learn how to get the best out of it.

Google Maps is of course only the beginning of the popular application of digital satellite imagery. Soon we will be able to locate places through what is known as 'geotagging', something that will probably be familiar to some readers of this book by the time it is published. It involves linking images to GPS coordinates. In time, as the database of images with embedded geographical coordinates grows, we will be able to plan routes and view sites not just in the vague locality, but in the actual spot, correct to within a few metres.

Report location: Place names

Be aware that often place names will differ from what you might expect. This may be due to political changes and linguistic politics, but also to decisions made by military forces and historians decades ago that are no longer relevant; sometimes names were never known by or relevant to local people. Either way you need to know what to look for.

Sometimes the names familiar to us (derived usually from the official history) are anglicised versions of names that staff officers or official historians decided were unpronounceable. For example, on Crete the Australian official history talks about 'Retimo' and the German sources 'Rethymnon', while the locals live in 'Rethymno'. Likewise there's confusion between 'Chanea' and 'Hania' and Heraklion and Iraklion. The problem is compounded by the use of Greek script, of course. While you'll want to use the 1941 names in describing operations, you'll need to know and use the modern Greek names if you're asking your way or finding a bus. Fortunately Cretans are overwhelmingly welcoming to those interested in their history and you should have no hesitation in seeking help.

Sometimes linguistic politics plays hell with military historical topography. In Belgium, for example, the perpetual conflict between Flemish and Walloon means that the names 'Ypres', 'Warneton' and 'Lille' are now 'Ieper', 'Waasten' and 'Rijsel'. Again, use 'Ypres' in writing about 1917 but under no circumstances ask for directions to 'Ypres' today.

After the Great War, Turkey expelled the substantial Greek population of the Gallipoli peninsula, so the Greek places named on 1915 military maps as 'Krithia' and 'Helles' are today 'Alçi Tepe' and 'Ilyasbaba Burnu'. Turks are reluctant to discuss the messy ethnic cleansing that accompanied the establishment of the modern Turkish republic, so you won't get anywhere mentioning this linguistic oddity.

A more subtle problem occurs on Asian battlefields. Often localities either had no name (or no name that was known to colonial mapmakers, especially in wartime) so military staffs simply renamed features with code names that would be most useful to both combatant troops or naval gunnery observers. So around Balikpapan almost every hill was christened with names according to rough alphabetical groups—Muffle, Marshall, Mackay, Joint, Junior, Judge—and so on. On Tarakan many a feature was given a girl's name: Agnes, Freda, Helen, Susie, and so on. Only Gunung Api—'Fire Mountain' was left unchanged—and contrary to what you might think it's merely a low sandy hillock. None of these code names appears on Indonesian maps. There's no point asking locals today for directions to Agnes or Freda (in any case most will be immigrants from islands to the west)—they have no idea of Tarakan in 1945. The same problem is apparent in Korea, though less so in Viet Nam.

Axes of advance: Compass and GPS

A compass will be your best friend on the battlefield (and also when finding your way around the subways of a strange city). It will enable you to quickly orient yourself according to your maps. A compass is relatively easy to manipulate, especially for an old Scout or Guide. Those needing a refresher on taking bearings and using one in navigating should read Peter Simmonds's chapter on navigation in the authoritative and recommended *Royal Geographical Society Expedition Handbook*, in which he gives an essential primer on using this vital tool. Across the world magnetic variation, well... varies, and it is important to use a compass that has a 'global' needle.

Don't get snowed: you won't need a GPS to know where you are on most battlefields. No one is going to get lost at Pozières or Retimo. Simmonds, Navigational Instructor at Britain's Royal School of Military Survey, left GPS to last in his survey, and not just because satellite navigation is several hundred years younger than using a magnetised needle. 'GPS is a very good aid to navigation, but that is all,' he warns. Batteries can run out, the receiver could be damaged and in some terrains you may not be able to track the satellites GPS depends on. 'Becoming over-reliant on GPS is bad practice,' he says, advising travellers not to forget basic navigational methods. For further tuition on navigational theory, Pete Hawkins's *Map and Compass: The Art of Navigation* will give you as much as you'll need.

For the historian there are actually advantages in using maps and compasses. Remember, for most of Australia's military history that's how commanders found their way about; I have just such a military compass, used by an Australian officer in 1941, on my shelf. In Egypt Mark Johnston and I marvelled at how easy it would have been to become disoriented or lost in the desert using the same maps and tools as the men of the Eighth Army and

Panzerarmée Afrika. As well as understanding better how mistakes happened, we also appreciated the skill of officers who found their way in seemingly featureless desert. In many cases a compass and a decent topographical map will be all you'll need. For some Asian battlefields even a decent road map will let you find your way around, say, Labuan or Singapore.

But a GPS—especially now they are both simpler and cheaper—can be anything between very handy and a lifesaver in many places. Even on Gallipoli, with its well-marked cemeteries, the country can become a wild and even a dangerous place off the beaten track. In 2005 Christina Spittell and Peter Londey walked along Monash Valley, becoming disoriented in thick, thorny scrub before they pushed up the north-western face of the valley and emerged on Walker's Ridge. This happened a few hundred metres from Anzac Cove, in a landscape overrun by thousands of visitors every year. About twenty years ago Sydney tug-boat skipper Joe Crumlin followed the track of Monash's 4th Brigade in the August offensive. Like Monash, Joe walked into the scrub north of Anzac Cove aiming to come out on the Chunuk Bair ridge. Unlike Monash, Joe kept his bearings, despite the twisting, bush-choked gullies, heat and maps that made no sense. (Of course, unlike Monash, Joe didn't have to contend with hostile Turks.)

Had Joe used a GPS—this was before they were available—he would have been sure of his position at all times: assuming that his position could be plotted on a modern map. But that wasn't available either—this was when the Turks were frightened that the Greeks were going to invade. So the combination of modern navigational technology and a 1915 map may not help you as much as you'd think.

Still, using the best features of both and some initiative can get you to where you need to be. When the Heath children visited Alamein in 2007 they took the trouble to get GPS coordinates for all of the locations where their father had served with the

2/48th Battalion. They had no coordinates for the Blockhouse, the scene of some of the most desperate fighting later in the battle. Tom Heath transposed a large coloured map from Barton Maughan's official history over the computer screen while running Google Earth and identified key points close by. On the ground they were able to find the feature relatively easily. And when driving in a strange city an English-speaking GPS unit can be a lifesaver, though a recent experience in Rouen, where my GPS simply got streets wrong, provides a caution against assuming that technology will answer all our problems.

At sparrow fart: Making the most of your time

Making the most of your days on the battlefield can involve keeping the same sorts of hours as the subjects of your research. Experiencing a battlefield at dawn can be one of the most illuminating and—dare I say it—magical experiences. In December 2004 I was fortunate to go to Gallipoli in the middle of winter. Being on Gallipoli at a time that no ordinary visitor in their right mind would think of arriving was truly wonderful. First, we were able to experience Gallipoli as the Anzacs did—in winter. We had the dubious comfort of the Kum 'motel', but then the Anzacs had only dug-outs and trenches. We were able to get a very clear idea of what a winter at Anzac had been like. But it wasn't only cold and windy. It was also still and clear at dawn, and standing on Baby 700 as the sun rose over where the Turks would have been in 1915 was one of the most transcendent moments of my encounters with battlefields.

Peter Pedersen has sound advice based on solid experience. He starts early and continues until dusk and after, 'based on my dictum that I can't come back tomorrow'. He observes that British historians, within easy reach of the Western Front, say, often take a more relaxed approach. I'm with Peter on this. 'Wherever possible', he writes, 'I like to get onto the battlefield at night too'. So much military history occurs in the dark that he sensibly wants to see what can be learned in the same conditions. But more than that, he writes, 'I find that the solitude gives me a terrific empathy with what went on.' Ross McMullin makes a similar point in a passage quoted by Phil Taylor and Pam Cupper in their Gallipoli guide.

Making the most of your trip can entail going beyond the familiar routes and places. Try to think of things other people haven't done. When I visited Gallipoli in 2002 I made sure that I took my scooter on the ferry from Kaba Tepe *feribot* terminal to Gokçeada. Where's that, digger? It's the island the Anzacs called Imbros—the smudge on the western horizon on everybody's Gallipoli photographs but which hardly anyone visits. It was also the place where Charles Bean rented a little stone cottage in the autumn of 1915. He probably edited *The Anzac Book* there. It stood in 2002. I hope it still does. Likewise, when Peter Londey and Christina Spittell visited Gallipoli in 2005, besides doing the essential rounds of Anzac, Helles and Suvla, they also made for the narrow isthmus of Bulair, where you can still trace the Lines of Bulair, left over from exactly 60 years before 1915, when Gallipoli was a British staging area for the Crimean War (when Britain fought Russia alongside its ally, Ottoman Turkey).

Not everyone is as driven, though. Often battlefield research will be part of a trip that's broadly rather than narrowly educational—go to Troy, Petra or Reims while you're in the neighbourhood—so don't make a fetish of doing it cheaply or running yourself ragged by imposing unrealistic limits. Often you'll think of places to see or check, or find connections between what you've seen, but it will be too late to do anything about it, so program in a break before finishing your field work. This will allow your mind to frame the questions and make the connections and give you time to revisit and look again. I now try to program this sort of break into my research. In doing the first field trip to Mont St Quentin, for example, my break was a driving tour of the 1918 battlefields from Villers-Bretonneux to Montbrehain, and on the way some ideas bubbled to the surface that I was able to check on the Mont on my last two days. If you think of a battlefield as a source, you can return to it with fresh questions over again.

Movement orders: Getting around

There are two main ways to get around: self-drive and its variants and being carried by taxi, bus or other public transport. We'll deal with each under the headings 'driving' and 'driven'.

If you use a taxi, make sure you understand the local customs. Do you pay in advance, by the meter or at the end of the day? Do you negotiate or accept or decline? If you do use a taxi, remember that you're paying for this gig, so you're in charge. Be clear where you want to go, and for how long, and be prepared to bargain if the asking price seems high compared with what a guidebook, hotel or a previous visitor recommends. Western visitors do often seem to have 'EXPLOIT ME' tattooed on their forehead in ink only taxi drivers can read.

But you're the paying passenger, so make sure that you get out of the trip what you want. Be wary of accepting excuses about why you can't go a particular way. This can be the most stressful part of a trip. The sensation of rocketing along at a speed greater than the legal and the safe limit, without a seat belt, unsure where the taxi is or is going, for how long and at what price, is not a good feeling. But be careful of getting involved in a stoush. Having an argument with the taxi driver is not conducive to the frame of mind necessary for battlefield visiting. On my first trip to Delhi, in search of the sites connected with the siege of 1857, I had a raging row with a rickshaw driver. I refused to pay what I thought was an outrageous price because I was sure he'd gone the long way round to the Kashmir Gate. I gave him what I thought the trip was worth and stormed off. I saved about ten rupees—about a dollar—but at the cost of not actually taking in where I was or what I should have been looking for. I had wanted to work out where the moat had been that British and Indian sappers had crossed to blow a hole in the gate and allow the storming parties through. While I walked off with a photograph that proved I'd been there, I was so angry that I didn't actually do the looking and thinking I'd come for. What I saved cost me heaps in failing to make the most of my opportunity. Not until eighteen years later did I again visit the Kashmir Gate to do what I should have done the first time.

Don't assume that you'll have to use taxis (invariably the most expensive form of transport). Public transport is often quite acceptable. You can visit many battle sites in Crete, for example, by using buses (and being prepared to hoof it). In Indonesia I found share taxis were perfectly useful for getting around Tarakan and Balikpapan, and they allowed me to practise my rudimentary Bahasa, to the amusement of all. But often a taxi (or a hire car and a driver) makes sense. A local driver will know the car and the road rules, and can often act as interpreter and guide. As a navigator they can be irreplaceable, even if there are no or poor maps, they can ask directions more easily. And if a car breaks down they are often able to fix it.

Don't be afraid to ask. Edward Hasbrouck, who has spent many years pondering how First World travellers behave overseas, observes that 'Self sufficient First Worlders think it a sign of incompetence to ask directions from people along the way'. They often prefer to follow maps that might be inaccurate, incomplete or out of date, when 'there are plenty of local people around who actually know exactly where local places are and would be happy to tell them if asked'.

Drive on, corporal: Self-drive car hire

Battlefields are often relatively remote and public transport won't take you to where you need to go. If you're driving yourself you'll need to learn the basics of both the road rules and the road signs in your host country. Be prepared to come to grips with a driving style that may differ markedly from the one you're used to. If you hire a car in Istanbul to drive to Gallipoli you'll find that Turkish drivers go faster, take greater risks and indicate less than we do; some describe them as driving like maniacs. In some countries drivers use their horns when passing; in others they only turn their lights on when they see an on-coming vehicle.

Self-drive touring gives you flexibility and freedom, and many other incidental benefits. In Malaysian Sabah, for example, I had my first sight of the magnificent bulk of Mount Kinabalu through the windscreen of a big Toyota. I was driving up the highway from Sabah's capital, Kota Kinabalu, over the flank of the mountain and on to Ranau, the terminus of the Sandakan death march. I was able to explore the area (and stop at the extraordinary Kundasang war memorial, set on a hill overlooking a vast alpine valley in Kinabalu's shadow) and find several sites connected with the tragic events of 1945. Stopping and thinking in the jungle east of Ranau, listening to it and feeling the heat and humidity, gave me a powerful insight into the ordeal of the death march.

If you do hire a car, don't just hop in and drive away. Take your time to learn where the controls are and what they do. Find the controls for the fuel cap, and establish what sort of fuel it uses—and what that type is called in the language understood by local bowser boys. And don't just work out how to drive the car forwards. At the Alamein Military Museum, Mark and I scratched our heads trying to work out how to put our Audi into reverse. Eventually we hailed a passing group of Egyptian soldiers, who cheerfully pushed us backwards out of a carport. Then we went into the museum and found that we'd had a hand from the colonel in charge.

There's an element of danger in driving overseas. I was almost wiped out by a Belgian driver on the battlefield of Waterloo because I didn't look to the left, or so a white-faced Claire told me—I never saw him. And I almost died on the Civil War battlefield of Fredericksburg in Virginia, because I unthinkingly turned right onto the left-hand lane of a bridge. I'll never forget the face of the man who saw me driving towards him. But it is possible to drive in an unfamiliar system. Once you feel you have the hang of driving on the 'wrong' side of the road—well, that's the time to be really scared.

In some countries it just isn't wise to drive yourself, especially if you're on your own. In India, for example, you'd be well advised to hire a car and a driver rather than just a car, and finding your way around Indonesia can be just as hard. Road signs are rare (and anyway often in an unfamiliar script) and navigation is a challenge to say the least. If you have a driver you can devote your time to keeping track of where you are and what you're looking at. At Balikpapan, Indonesia, for example, you orient yourself around the battlefield by identifying the hills on which the battle was fought. You can't drive around a busy Indonesian city—or any city—and do that at the same time.

The combination of jet lag, left-hand drive, unfamiliar road rules and paying more attention to the landscape than the road can be fatal. It would be interesting—and a real caution—to know how many Australians have died or been injured while trying to find trenches or hills in foreign fields. In the sadly neglected 'English' cemetery in Canakkale there are the graves of at least two visitors who died in car accidents while visiting Gallipoli. How many others have died but been returned home? Craig Wilcox's diary of one of his tours of South African battlefields includes a sobering passage: 'Steve's a little shaken this morning, having seen a pedestrian run over on his way to where we're staying. In a few days we've passed two serious motor accidents and heard radio reports of two more "horror smashes"'. Nearly a thousand people die every year in accidents involving mini-buses in South Africa. And they don't just hit other mini-buses, so watch out.

But one of the most satisfying memories of a battlefield trip is finding your own way around a strange place. On the way back into Alexandria in 1997 I drove the car in which Mark Johnston and I had travelled about the Alamein battlefield and navigated, somewhat apprehensively, back into Alexandria. The roads were busy, and all the road signs were in Arabic. I turned left at a point that I thought might work and—to Mark's lasting astonishment—brought us straight to the door of the celebrated Hotel Cecil. I take a certain pride in this. Being driven by a talkative guide may be handy and convenient, but it doesn't beat the feeling that you've taken on the traffic of Paris and won. (Incidentally, I was horrified to learn—after I'd successfully negotiated Paris's ring road, the Boulevard Périphérique, with my fifteen-year-old daughter as navigator—that it is among the half-dozen most dangerous roads in the world.)

You can be lucky. But if you can't count on being lucky—and you can't—you need to prepare carefully, or work out what you'll need. Even in the age of GPS you'll often be looking for places not altogether findable on the sat-nav.

Navigating around a strange city is probably the most terrifying experience. Some hints. First, do your homework: study the maps, note or mark the best routes to get you to your destination, memorising landmarks on the way. Study the maps and note the names of major roads and landmarks *not* on your route, because if you come to them you'll at least know you're off-course. Be prepared to stop and ask locals. Allow plenty of time. Drive more slowly than you would at home. It will give you more time to decide on upcoming ramps or turns. If you possibly can, try not to drive into cities at rush hour, into the sun or at night. But don't get spooked. You may be honked or abused, but you won't get rammed, even in aggressive car cultures.

Often hotels or other businesses will helpfully supply directions, on paper or on a website. These are a mixed blessing. The problem with putting your faith in written directions is that if you happen to depart from them, they give no idea of how to get back on track. A map is much better. Some would argue that a GPS navigational system is best of all, and so it might be. You could buy a hand-held GPS device for a few hundred dollars, and it will at least be useful in getting around Western Europe, if not countries further afield. At best it will help you get through Brussels at rush hour and find a hotel in the dark. It is less fun than a map, though...

The best way to navigate is with a... well, a navigator. If there are two of you, one needs to take on this job. This can become a stressful test of your partnership. You are trying to find your way around a place neither of you has ever seen before, probably driving a strange car on the wrong side of the road, and possibly in heavy traffic, in the dark or (you hope not 'and') in the rain.

Some rules. First, if you're the driver: trust your navigator. You may think you remember that the road curves to the right and you take the second turn on the left, but your navigator will have the map on their lap. If they tell you that the turn is further on, trust them. If they're wrong, they'll be big enough to admit it. Bring a torch so you can read the map without having to put on the interior light, and if possible a mobile phone so you can telephone the hotel or whatever—hopefully not the police to report an accident.

Honda rash: Scooters and mopeds

Scooters or mopeds could be good means of transport on battlefields in Europe, Gallipoli, Indonesia and Malaysia. Be wary about the obvious business of which side of the road to drive on. Most of the world drives on the right rather than the left, and most Australian battlefields are located in right-hand-drive countries, except Papua New Guinea, Indonesia, Malaysia, Brunei, Singapore and Thailand. Whether left- or right-hand-drive, scooters give way to just about everything except push bikes.

Some battlefield areas are particularly suited to getting about on scooters. You can go places on a scooter you might not with a car, and will certainly see things you won't see from a car. They're smaller, cheaper to hire and run and easier to get on ferries, and they free you from many of the problems of car parking. Sure, you're more open to the weather, but you can often travel when it's more likely to be dry (or, as my old geography teacher used to stress, 'drier'). While ideal for individuals travelling alone, you can also easily travel in twos or threes, which could be a lot of fun.

They are also extremely dangerous; even in Australia motorbike accidents kill disproportionately. About ten Australians die each year in motorcycle accidents overseas. I would urge you not to hire powerful motorbikes. You don't need a 500cc bike to find your way on rough country roads. Safety is paramount. It's tempting to scooter without a helmet—it's often either not mandatory or not enforced. Riding a 'fun' machine you might feel like a wimp wearing one—but do ask for a helmet and wear it. Not only is the risk obvious, but not wearing one might well nullify your travel insurance.

Mopeds or scooters are extremely vulnerable. What might be a minor (if irritating) bingle to a car could leave a motorbike rider immobilised if not dead. Broken bones, gashes and burns (if you fall under a hot exhaust—'Honda rash', as it's known) will be serious matters if you're far from medical treatment. And you probably will be: Australian battlefields are often (though not always) in the country. This means that traffic on battlefield roads will probably be lighter than elsewhere. But you'll often stay in a town or city and 'commute' to the area you're interested in—most of the sites around Ypres, for example lie on quite busy roads.

Having made those necessary cautions, I'd encourage you to try a scooter, in France or Belgium, and especially on Crete, where the roads are full of tourists on scooters—but be careful. Gallipoli by scooter is exhilarating—I became so enthused by visiting battlefields by scooter I wrote an article for *Two Wheels* magazine. A practical hint: natty scooters can be hired from the reliable Varol Bisiklet in Canakkale (Kemalpasa Malt. Tekke Sk.No. 37/1—it's a narrowish lane on the southern side of the main street, a couple of streets from the clock square). You can contact the helpful Varol at varol@rentabike@hotmail.com.

Vivid green vegetation: Battlefield research and the environment

The battlefield traveller gets close to the environment; sometimes, when you're batting away flies on Gallipoli or mosquitos in Borneo, too close. But the physicality of the battlefield is one of the most important justifications for making the effort. Feeling the enervating humidity of Thailand—and wondering how on earth half-starved prisoners could labour on that bloody railway—is exactly why you should go to Hellfire Pass.

Research is partly about noticing the environment of the battlefield. The landscape you walk over will probably be different to the way it looked in wartime. For example, Pozières today is utterly different to Pozières in 1916. Tropical and desert battlefields might look superficially similar, but in fact there, too, huge changes could have occurred. Desert winds shift vast amounts of sand—at Alamein Mark Johnston and I found weapon-pits barely discernible beneath drifting sand. Rapid economic development can alter the landscape surprisingly thoroughly. On Tarakan I walked the length of a road for about 5 kilometres and told the world that I'd walked down Snag's Track—until I went back and found the real Snag's Track. The one I'd mistaken for the real thing had been made after 1945.

The important things are to look and think, and ask questions. In tropical environments, especially, battlefield researchers need to be aware of how rapidly and dramatically vegetation and land use can change. Visiting the area of the ambush at Gemencheh, near Gemas, Malaysia, in 1982, Peter Burness looked for its site. He found that the bridge across the river had been replaced a couple of times since the original wooden structure had been blown up in 1942. The roadway, too, had been moved and widened. However, Peter found that 'a short way off the new road, almost hidden under the heavy vivid green vegetation, is the bitumen strip marking the original roadway. Alongside it rises the bank from which the Australians poured down their fire'. Peter took the trouble to poke around and, in many places, to ask. It is vital not to expect that what existed in 1942 (or whenever) will still be in existence. The remnants fuel the imagination. Peter reflected that 'It was hard to imagine that in this still, lush spot the silence had once been shattered by gunfire, explosions and screams.' Brian Farrell, the foremost expert on the Malayan campaign, has visited this spot at least eight times ('and learnt and felt more every time'). Brian investigated the action from both Japanese and Australian perspectives to understand why it was such an effective ambush position.

Environmental matters are also relevant to battlefield research in another sense. Everybody's concerned about the environment

Dan Crosswell photographed by Brian Farrell from the top of the cutting at Gemencheh near Gemas, Malaysia, showing the view that the Australian ambushers had of the Japanese trapped below. This view makes plain the tactical advantage the 2/30th Battalion enjoyed. (Brian Farrell)

A Japanese-eye-view of the 2/30th's ambush site at Gemencheh near Gemas, Malaysia. (Brian Farrell)

today, or ought to be. Environmental considerations might seem to be remote from battlefield visits, but they're not.

Before you even book your ticket or step onto the air bridge you'll need to consider (as the old wartime slogan put it) 'is your journey really necessary?' I'd argue it is. You're travelling with more than pleasure in view. You're gathering evidence or deepening understanding, perhaps writing a book or an article, almost certainly visiting the graves of those killed in battles long ago. As a purposeful traveller you can feel superior to the tourists who are simply going to lounge on a beach at Pattaya or enjoy the attractions at Euro Disney. Your journey will enrich you in ways you can't even anticipate.

However justifiable your trip may be, your plane will still spew clouds of gas into the atmosphere. If you are to travel and add to greenhouse gases, you can help to redress the damage by subscribing to a 'green' scheme, such as www.greenfleet.com.au. These schemes basically seek to 'offset' the damage we do in travelling by planting oxygen-making trees. I was horrified to learn that my research trips in one year produced several tonnes of gas, requiring an offset of up to twenty trees. It may not be a perfect solution, but it's a gesture.

While overseas you may feel overwhelmed by the environmental problems of the Third World. Cairo's traffic on a bad day—well, any day—may leave you despairing about the prospects for meeting the challenges of global warming. But so many Australian battlefields are, if not pristine, at least in country that is impressive, and even beautiful, and you will feel a hope that they remain that way. Even when the country you're in is very obviously not 'unspoilt'—such as in Egypt or parts of Indonesia—you'll want to not follow the local custom and just chuck your rubbish away. If there's nowhere else to dispose of it, you should put rubbish in a bag and take it back to your hotel.

Can I help you? Local assistance

A battlefield belongs to someone else. Even if you feel that you have a 'moral' claim to be there, remember the reality. Peter Oldham, author of *The Hindenburg Line*, offers useful advice to travellers searching for the remains of the Hindenburg Line, that the land we call a battlefield is today owned by somebody. 'Whereas access is unlikely to be denied, normal courtesy, in the form of not leaving litter and closing gates, should be shown.' While you may encounter suspicion, hostility or (more often) incomprehension, the great majority of battlefield visitors meet nothing but a warm welcome and find invaluable help.

Indeed, you'll often encounter striking kindness. On Tarakan a sergeant in the local Commandar Militar, Sersen Sukarno, took pity on me and helped me find my way around the island. I travelled the length of Snag's Track—the real one, not the one I had thought I was on—on the back of his scooter. Then he arranged for a friend to give me a lift to the northernmost tip of the island, travelling in the most beat-up vehicle I have ever travelled in, on the worst road I have ever experienced. The local school principal and especially his English teacher, Milson Milkias, also took time to drive me to places on Tarakan that I would never have found, or seen as easily, on my own. Many other battlefield visitors have struck similar goodwill on the part of local people who have no personal interest in the obscure events that preoccupy us.

Peter Pedersen describes a typical encounter, on the Magersfontein battlefield in South Africa, in 2000. Late one afternoon he stopped by the road near Graspan, by some hills the Boers had held, now on fenced-off farmland. Peter was tempted to hop the fence (a frequent opportunity on the battlefield) but in the end just took some photographs from the fence line. Suddenly 'a giant Boer' appeared and asked Peter what he was doing. Peter (relieved at not having hopped the fence) explained. The farmer, whose land it was, took Peter home for a cuppa and next day showed him sites Peter would never have known of. Peter looked back, reflecting, 'Had I jumped the fence he probably would have killed me!' It just shows how serendipity is always present.

Encounters such as these are humbling, and you'll often want to express your appreciation accordingly. You may need to take some small gifts to give to particularly helpful local people. You might get away with some kangaroo stick pins or 'Australia' badges, especially for children. In Papua New Guinea or Egypt it may be a couple of packets of cigarettes—forget the health aspect: it's the done thing. In other countries you could follow the example of Ewan McGregor and Charley Boorman (who famously rode their motorbikes the *Long Way Round* from London to New York), who offered miniature bottles of whisky to the many Mongolians and Siberians who helped them out of jams. (This won't work in Indonesia or Egypt, of course.)

When you strike difficulties, especially with officials in the Second or Third World, think carefully before resorting to bribery. It may seem worthwhile—a friend of mine was able to offer 100 dollars US to a Vietnamese official to gain entry to an area supposedly off-limits. In Indonesia I found myself paying a derisory sum—which we all agreed was an 'administrative fee'—to eliminate supposed problems in loading my tour group's luggage. Perhaps Mark and I were just too obtuse to understand that our odds at El Alamein would have become better than 'fifty–fifty' if only we had converted the odds into dollars. The problem is knowing the rules: who to approach, what to offer, how to offer it. It isn't as simple as waving a 50-dollar note. Putting aside the questionable morality (because it may just be the *only* way you're going to get on the once-a-week plane off the island), the most practicable advice is to not offer an inducement unless you get a clear signal from a local that one is needed.

Making the most of local help depends crucially upon language, rather than money. Much can be communicated in mime (though I'm glad that *Australia's Funniest Home Videos* was not around to expose some of my efforts at miming 'Excuse me, is there a Japanese bunker at the bottom of your garden?'), but we also need to understand and be understood in words.

Or words to that effect: Communicating

Australians have largely succeeded in fighting their many wars in someone else's country. Even Australia's first war, against the Aboriginal occupiers of the continent, happened at first in a country that—by definition—belonged to other people. Since then, as we've seen, not only have Australians always fought nations whose people spoke a different language—Turkish, German, Italian, Japanese—but they've always fought in countries whose inhabitants spoke a different language again—French, Arabic or Hebrew, Malay or Pidgin. Having something of the language of your hosts can be to your advantage. It can be daunting and discouraging when it doesn't work (Mark Twain quipped that in Paris people simply stared at him when he spoke French—'I never did succeed in making those idiots understand their language'). When it does work you may find or be shown something that no visitor has seen before.

Even in countries that might seem to be English-speaking, the actual enemy spoke a foreign tongue, and still does. In South Africa in 1999 Craig Wilcox and I drove through the Free State in search of the battlefields of the Boer War. We reached a pretty little town near Bloemfontein and I approached an older man—a European—for directions. He looked at me quizzically and shrugged—and then replied in Afrikaans. Neither of us could understand the other, and that was in a country that counted English among its official languages.

Language is crucial to the battlefield visitor. You might think that your maps and dossiers will insulate you from contact with locals, but you will need to communicate. At the most basic level you'll need the Big Five of international phrases:

- Hello
- Thank you
- How much?
- Please, where is the toilet?
- Goodbye

Acquiring these phrases is both a basic courtesy and a prudent necessity. In most countries local people will appreciate you going to the trouble to learn these words and phrases, even if you must then point, gesticulate or mime (and never raise your voice) to make yourself understood. Having a go at 'bonjour' or 's'lamat datang!' in France and Borneo respectively can help to grease the wheels of international diplomacy in a way that no amount of finger-clicking and waving of US dollar bills can achieve.

Don't fall for the easy reassurance that 'most people speak English these days'. Battles almost always happen in the most inconvenient places (traditionally, according to soldiers, 'at the join of three maps, in the dark and in the rain') and usually in rural regions, often quite remote ones. While hotel clerks and often taxi drivers will have modest (or at times embarrassingly good) English, they often won't be on the spot when you need the advanced language skills required for:

- Where is the cemetery? (often, 'the English cemetery')
- Can you tell me where is the...?
- Do I go north or south?
- Where can I get petrol?
- Please, I need a toilet, now!

It's important to understand the psychology of these exchanges. You can't rely on a yes or a no in reply to a question seeking directions. It isn't only 'foreigners' who will send you anywhere rather than admit they don't know—a recent survey disclosed that a good fifth of Britons will misdirect enquirers, out of an unwillingness to admit ignorance, or sheer perversity. So asking, 'Is the temple this way?' may elicit a 'Yes' rather than a 'Don't know'. Instead, ask, 'Which way is the temple, please?' Then ask several other people and make your judgement accordingly.

Don't necessarily expect people of other countries to be as familiar with maps as you are. Military historical researchers are particularly adept at using maps, but Australians generally, members of an open, highly literate society, are more familiar with maps than most. In many countries where Australians have fought (such as Turkey, Egypt or Indonesia) governments have actually kept maps out of the hands of their people, and the average passer-by might be even more confused if you helpfully offer them a map. In India, where I've traced remnants of the raj and the 1857 mutiny war, requests for way-finding advice can turn into kerb-side seminars, in which bystanders offer voluble and vehement opinions. This is entertaining, but not always helpful. A useful hint is to become familiar with common words for likely features (such as church, temple, wood, etc.), which can help you follow directions, if not the detail of the ensuing argument.

You may need to give taxi drivers directions. You can make do with sign language and basic English, but you'll probably need:

- How much?
- Turn right
- Turn left
- Straight on
- Go back

- Wait here
- Please
- Thank you

The features you'll be looking for are often so minor as to be unmarked on either topographic maps or on modern digital aids (another reason to use old rather than new technology). But often they are familiar to the local people, who would be helpful if only they knew your needs, though the features may have names unknown to outsiders. In France I was looking for a long brick wall that I now know had marked the southern edge of the village of Mont St Quentin and has now been knocked down. In the first days of my field research there, I was looking for this wall (about half a kilometre in the wrong direction, because I had not brought a key source). So I was wandering about the village of Halle and the banks of the Canal du Nord trying to ask people if they had seen a brick wall . . . but not actually knowing the French word for 'brick wall'. After 'Pardon, monsieur . . .' I was reduced to drawing a picture of a brick wall and—because I was half a kilometre out—getting 'Ah non . . .' and a shrug. All this might have been avoided if I had bothered to learn the right expression (or, indeed, to have remembered that source).

For my second trip to Borneo. I had taken night classes in Bahasa Indonesia in preparation for research in a very remote area where I could not count on anyone speaking English. Once there, I was quite well equipped to ask questions and understand the answers. Of course the short-term effects wore off and now I can only gabble random words in Bahasa, but for that trip I was able to guide my drivers and understand local people's replies to my awkward questions, and—perhaps most importantly—to preface each exchange with the courtesies of that graceful language. Often, though, words from a long-ago war pop up in conversation. Seize on them. On Tarakan I somehow heard the words 'Markoni' and

'Kampong Enam'—the names of two districts of the straggling town of Lingkas. 'Markoni' was where the old Dutch Marconi radio station had been (and where Australian Catholic soldiers had rebuilt a local church), while Kampong Enam was the Indonesian name of what the Dutch had romantically called 'District VI'—'enam' being Bahasa for 'six'. I was able to visit the church—a powerful physical connection with men I knew who had worked on the job. Kampong Enam had been the location of a nationalist protest abetted by Australian communists, one of whom I was also later to meet, and I was able to visit the remains of the 'Native Theatre' where the protest occurred.

Of course, it's also true that a lot of the features you're seeing either no longer exist—such as trenches, light railways, command posts and dumps—or they do exist but have no association with what you're looking for in the minds of local people. For example, in Crete, Forty-second Street has probably existed as a country lane since Minoan times—it's worn quite a deep groove in the land running from near what is now the Suda Bay war cemetery towards the Malaxa Escarpment. In May 1941 it became the scene of a dramatic bayonet charge by Maoris of the 28th New Zealand Battalion and Australians of the 2/7th Battalion, AIF. But to Cretans that event is one tiny moment in a 3000-year history. They are very happy to celebrate the event once they know about it—the owner of the olive grove in which it happened welcomed twenty or so British and Australian strangers into his home because they represented the forces that had tried to defend it from the Germans—but they don't call that road Forty-second Street. So asking a taxi driver in downtown Hania to take you to 'Forty-second Street' won't get you anywhere. I hoofed it with a map and compass and sure enough found it. In this you're on your own, and a mixture of good map reading, good communication and luck will get you there.

Look to your right: Guides and guided tours

It may be wise to engage a local guide; I've done so in Borneo. There are several considerations to think of. First, do you think you'll really need one? One of the main reasons you're considering walking Australia's battlefields is that you want to find out what happened for yourself. Part of that self-reliance is eroded if you are then steered around by someone else.

There are many companies that take you about the Western Front and the Mediterranean especially. The biggest and longest-established of the tour companies is Major & Mrs Holt's Tours (now called Holts History and Battlefield Tours) of London. In their book *Dark Tourism*, John Lennon and Malcolm Foley described a Holts tour to the Western Front departing from Victoria Station in London as 'a well-organized affair, encompassing almost military discipline upon customers to ensure efficient and effective embarkation'. This is certainly true. I took a Holts tour to Ypres, some years ago, and while it got me to places I couldn't have reached in the same time, I found their method uncongenial. (But not everyone does—Holts handed out medals and bars to those who came on five, ten and more tours. Some people obviously loved it.) I prefer to make my own way to battlefields, to find my own way about them, and to form my own conclusions from looking at the ground in the light of the documents and other sources. If you're reading this book you may be inclined that way too.

In some places a local guide is sensible and necessary. In both Indonesia and Malaysia I have engaged a local travel company to act as a guide (each time when travelling with a group). The local guide found transport and liaised with hotels, though in neither case did they help to get us to historical sites, which I knew better from my research and recce trips. I would counsel against guides unless you either doubt your own ability to navigate around a strange place (on the 'wrong' side of the road) or if you are short of time. But hiring a guide may still be mandatory in Libya (for visits to Tobruk) and is highly advisable in Viet Nam.

However, if you do engage a guide, make clear your needs. Tell them what you want to do. You may be more interested in the history of the thing. Or you may be more interested in commemoration, in finding cemeteries and memorials.

A bad guide will give you the bog-standard spiel they give everyone. A good guide will establish what you are interested in and what you most want to see. Most importantly, they will give you space and privacy. Be wary of a guide who seems to insist on you taking a particular route to suit their own needs, or one who sticks to a familiar screed, or who spends too long telling you too much. It's hard to know before you agree to take on a guide, and hard to re-negotiate afterwards, but it's up to you to make clear to a guide what you want, just as you would with a provider of any services. If you think they are talking too long or telling you too much, say so—'I would like to spend only fifteen minutes here' or 'I'm not very interested in the Minoan period—I want to know about Crete in 1941'.

In your old kit-bag: Luggage

The question of what you should carry your gear in is as important as what you should pack. Don't skimp: bear in mind that you'll have to manhandle your luggage in and out of taxi boots and trains, on and off airport luggage belts, up and down stairs. Bear in mind:

- its empty weight
- what you'll acquire on the way

- what sort of travel you'll be doing
- the environment you'll be travelling in
- your own physical state and capabilities.

The kind of journey you're planning is the single most important factor. If you're planning to walk any distance make sure the case can be wheeled or carried on your back. If you're a youngish person and are expecting to climb stairs in backpacker hostels or Greek pensions then a case with back straps might be better. If you're older, expecting to stay in hotels with lifts, then a straightforward trolley suitcase might be ideal. Don't over-pack—you'll come to curse your folly. If you do have too much, you can always either post unwanted stuff home or even simply discard some. Learn from experience. My weakness is books. I often take more than I need, and buy more along the way; or I used to.

The golden rule in packing is 'if in doubt, leave it out'. Remember that as fuel costs rise airlines will increasingly enforce their weight limits for luggage. That varies, but it's commonly 20 kilograms per person, and they can enforce the limits on cabin baggage that they often ignore. It's best to check, by phoning or consulting their websites, well in advance. Always be prepared to check your luggage, except for the essentials you will carry on in a hand bag.

A Christmas tree: Kit

In *Goodbye to All That*, his classic memoir of the Western Front, Robert Graves describes reporting to his new battalion in 1915 carrying 'the usual furnishings'—revolver, field glasses, compass, whisky flask, wire-cutters, periscope, and a lot more. 'A Christmas tree that was called,' wrote Graves. I've had cause to recall Graves's passage when taking with me more gear than I needed.

You can carry too much gear; be sure you'll need it. The type of research you're planning should be your guide. Whatever you do, be sure not to go mad in travel shops with a credit card. You'll be tempted to buy all sorts of gizmos and gadgets—head torches, inflatable neck cushions, eye shades, travel-weight clothes lines, and so on. Think carefully before shelling out for this sort of gear—it will cost you money, space and weight. However exciting it seems (buying this stuff is almost as good as going), a lot of it is useless, but you know what's best for you. Some travel accessories are vital, such as adapters to enable you to use electrical appliances and charge phones or whatever.

One item that I've changed my mind about is a mobile phone. At first I was deterred by the bother of unfathomable rates and whether a phone had 'global roaming' or not, and had been inclined to be scornful. Now I'm a convert, especially if your trip involves more than one person. Avoiding the aggravation of losing each other (especially in strange cities) alone makes the mobile phone a vital accessory, not to mention its value for keeping in touch and in case of emergency.

The essential items (besides your dossier) are:

- reliable non-ticking travelling alarm clock (possibly with a torch)
- compass
- camera
- notebook
- small torch
- neck cushion (to help you sleep easily on the plane or train)
- mobile phone.

Some people swear by walking sticks. I don't understand the physics of them, and don't see how they help, though I have used one on Gallipoli. A map tube is certainly a needless encumbrance—better is a clear plastic envelope able to be slung around the neck when on the spot and folded into the day-pack when travelling.

Whether you carry a whisky flask, wire-cutters and revolver is up to you…

PART 5

Stand down: Home again

Bread and butter letters: Essential paperwork

On your return—as soon as you can—write and post thank-you letters to all those you met who helped to make the trip easier or possible. This is a courtesy I've regretted not meeting, and there's usually no excuse besides laziness, at least in my case. A quick 'thank you' to a helpful guide or a local museum official, or a farmer who saved you a 3-kilometre tramp is a basic courtesy. It also helps to smooth the path of those who may follow you. You'll become the resident expert on 'your' battlefield, and others will seek your advice. Having written bread-and-butter letters you'll be confident in recommending others to follow your path.

If you've been funded by any other body besides your credit card—your university, a philanthropic institution or—best of all—the Army History Unit—you should always send it a report immediately you return. This is not only courteous but prudent (and probably an obligation). Those who don't meet the conditions of research grants can't expect to get others, and getting a reputation for not delivering would be fatal.

Patrol reports: Keeping your own records

Even if you aren't inclined to introspection or record-keeping, do try to keep a trip diary. Each night, write a record of what you've done and what you saw and even felt. This will become of particular value after you return. You may feel that that first view of the Nek was an unforgettable experience while it's happening. But if you return to the same spot several times, your knowledge might become deeper but your recollection of your initial impressions might become murkier.

Whatever you do, write or otherwise record your impressions of your visit and share them with others. You needn't write a book—though you might be surprised by the effect a battlefield can have—but you may enjoy writing an article for a popular or scholarly journal.

But you should write *something* about what you've seen, and discovered and realised. My mum, an inveterate camper-van traveller into her 80s—usually keeps a diary of her trips around the country with her bloke, Willy. She records where they went and what they did—a handy reference in months or years to come—and notes points of interest, encounters with people along the way and the sorts of details that blur over time. Even if your record is in the form of a serial e-mail to the family, postcards to workmates or a notebook of jottings, it will have enduring (and, indeed, increasing) value as the years pass. If your battlefield visit matures into a serious interest, you will find your notes become the basis of paragraphs, sections and even chapters in whatever you write.

While the heyday of the 'slide night' is (mercifully) over, you should think about taking the chance to talk about your trip in public. One of the battlefield tourists that Craig Wilcox guided around South Africa mentioned that he would speak at a service or social club about what he'd seen. 'It helps you put into place what you've seen,' he said. Craig agreed with his companion that 'no matter how often you read about it, however many photos you pore over, there's nothing like being there'.

This is one reason why it's worthwhile keeping a diary of your trip; to fix the sequence of events of what you looked at and what you noticed or concluded, or what further questions the day's explorations prompted. I don't keep a diary ordinarily, but I have at stressful times, and the discipline of recording thoughts and impressions seems to help impose order on the assimilation of new details and knowledge.

At the very least, I keep a 'trip notebook', in which I record all expenses and many other details, including information I collected en route, inscriptions on graves, names and addresses of those who've helped and (before photography went digital) details of the photographs I took, in order. My family regard the trip notebooks as a bit of a joke, evidence of incipient obsessive-compulsive disorder, but they mean that over the years I have created structured records of many trips. Your trip may well be the visit of a lifetime, but your memory of the details will erode as time goes by. You may never want to know what you had for dinner on 15 July 2004 (I can tell you what I had—an over-priced omelette and cheesecake, 17 million lira in Istanbul), but one day you'll want to remember whether you saw Pozières before Bullecourt or whatever. A trip notebook will help you remember. Needless to say, mine are just that, notebooks, small enough to slip into a shirt pocket, but you may use your Palm organiser. I don't care what you do as long as it works for you. Again, you may think that my family are on the right track in thinking me somewhat over-organised, but we're not talking about a Club Med holiday. If you're a purposeful traveller and battlefield research is your purpose, even just for the duration of this trip, you will probably need to be somewhat more methodical than you usually are.

If you haven't indexed or listed your photographs while you were away, it is time to do so as soon as you return.

Chapter 1: Writing about battles

You come home inspired. If you hadn't been planning to write something about the history you've walked before you left, you certainly want to now. How do you go about making something of your visit, turning what you've seen and found and realised and learned into the basis of a piece of historical writing?

It's not easy, not the first time anyway, and even after your tenth or twentieth book or article there are pitfalls and obstacles. But you can write an article, or a book, making your battlefield research the foundation of something others will want to read and will value.

Good history starts with a question; the word itself comes from the Greek word, 'to ask'. You start with a question and by thinking about the evidence you come to an interpretation. That 'come to' is important. You don't start with an interpretation and spend your time collecting evidence to substantiate it; that's why history isn't really like the court of law it's often superficially compared to.

You need to be realistic about what you will be able to produce. Start off at the modest end of the spectrum and you won't disappoint or embarrass yourself. Tell people that you're doing some research; until you have a good chunk of first draft down, don't tell people that you're 'gunner' do a book: there are too many gunners about. Write the draft and then tell the world you've finished.

But start small. Craig Tibbitts is a good model. He has just been awarded a grant from the Army History Unit to do the field work in France for the history of the 56th Battalion that he and

Nick Fletcher will write. Craig is a part-time historian, researching and writing history in his own time. He wrote a long article about Tel el Eisa (which he was able to check by visiting Alamein with the Australian War Memorial–Imperial War Museum Joint Study Tour in 2002). He read his way into the Great War and began to become interested in the 56th Battalion, writing several short articles and blogs about Australian actions in 1917 for a War Memorial exhibition project. Now he's ready to move on to a full-length book. His co-author, Nick, has followed a similar trajectory. They are both now ready to produce a 60,000- to 80,000-word battalion history, but the process of gaining the requisite skills has taken them about five years of dedicated preparation.

You might start small. The sheer quantity of sources available for even a small action or a unit history can be daunting, especially given Australia's superb system of archival preservation. You can almost have too much of a good thing. For example, if you plan a battalion history of a unit that served from, say, early 1916 to mid-1919 (like many Australian infantry battalions), you will be well advised to consult about 40 months of unit war diaries, as well as search for private sources in several archives and libraries (at the very least, the War Memorial, the relevant state library and probably a local library or two), as well as newspaper sources and … You can see the problem. If you choose a division-sized operation to examine, you may have perhaps twenty war diaries to consult, though for a shorter period, and many more official and private records to find. (The bibliography for my *Tarakan*, for example, a four-month-long, brigade group operation, lists over 200 official records files.) This is a lot of reading and noting, especially if you're working on weekends and evenings. You'll need motivation to start and stamina to finish.

But you can finish. It takes a degree of organisation and discipline. There isn't a cast-iron set of rules for starting and finishing articles or books based on your battlefield research, but there are some principles of advice that have worked for me.

Get it written! Some principles for research and writing

Research is about making meaning in your head. It precedes writing, but is intimately linked to it by the process of asking questions, looking for answers and thinking about the evidence and what it reveals and suggests about the historical experience you're investigating. Some principles:

- Research should be directed towards a product; never just 'do research'
- It's about judgement: what to consult; what to note; knowing why you're noting
- Devise a research plan and schedule, but revise both as you go
- Plan ahead, adapt to blockages and take advantage of serendipity
- The internet is a source of sources not a source of knowledge
- 'Evidence' is not 'information'
- Take notes in relation to your questions, but remember—enough is enough
- Note where you got it: exactly, even if you don't use footnotes
- Beware of the tyranny of the file card: don't just use it because you've got it
- Control the material: don't let it control you

Writing is about transmitting meaning to someone else. It is a skill we can all practise and master, and the more we do the better we get. Some principles:

- Write early; write often; keep writing; don't wait for inspiration

- Hank Nelson says: 'A page a day is a book a year'
- Remember your readers; but you'll want to write more than they want to read
- Anything can be said in any amount of words; don't write more than they need
- Don't use lengthy quotes: they're lazy; find your own voice
- Get it down and revise brutally
- Don't let the chimera of absolute accuracy paralyse you: don't get it right, get it written!

An example: Terry King

What's the point of the investment in time and money that battlefield research demands? It may be a private amusement, but almost everybody wants to write something. Terry King of Bundamba, Queensland, offers an inspiring example of what one dedicated individual can achieve. Terry's grandfather, Lieutenant Charles William King, had served with the 3rd Field Company on Gallipoli and on the Western Front. And Terry had the detailed diary that Lieutenant King had written throughout his service. Terry has made three trips to trace his service. He has travelled to Egypt, Gallipoli (twice) and France. This was no mere pilgrimage, though Terry writes of the pride he felt when reading his grandfather's words on Gallipoli (and indeed, reading them out on a broadcast made in the hours before dawn).

Because his grandfather's diary was often cryptic (lacking place names, for example), Terry had to find records that complemented the diary, such as unit war diaries and other men's diaries. Terry and his wife Marianne visited Gallipoli with a tour group but split off to trace Lieutenant King's sites, using Phil Taylor and Pam Cupper's *Gallipoli: A Battlefield Guide*, and he admits to being 'quite task oriented' in field work. In Egypt he had many places to visit, but having had experience of Egyptian roads and drivers, he hired a car and driver. Terry and Marianne visited Tel el Kebir, Ismailia and other sites along the Suez Canal. At Kantara they were stopped by Egyptian soldiers, who confiscated their passports and after a two-hour wait escorted them to the Kantara war cemetery. They were allowed to take photographs of the war cemetery but not of the sensitive Canal Zone. They were forbidden from getting to Serapeum, east of the canal.

Battlefield research is often an intensely emotional experience. Terry King at the grave of a member of his grandfather's field company, in the cemetery at Flers, France. Terry has travelled three times to the battlefields of the Great War in the footsteps of his grandfather, Lieutenant Charles William King. (Terry King)

In France, now experienced battlefield travellers, Terry and Marianne decided to travel independently, seeking out the places described in his grandfather's diary. In France he relied on Mat McLachlan's *Walking with the Anzacs* and the relevant Michelin maps. In a four-day, self-drive tour they found most sites, though their visit to Ieper coincided with (and was disrupted by) a car rally, inevitably.

Back in Australia, they visited King George Sound, in Western Australia, where the first convoy assembled in 1914, an odyssey in itself for a Queensland-based researcher. Terry is now assembling and integrating his grandfather's diary and the many other sources and sites he and Marianne have found and visited. 'My footsteps have barely made an impression and there remains a yearning to return to complete at least a few further pieces in the puzzle. Once you start on a journey like this,' Terry writes, 'it is amazing where it takes you both physically and metaphysically. It takes a hold of you and keeps drawing you back.'

Terry's writing is still in progress, but he already has a manuscript of 80,000 words written, and is gradually revising and refining the product of the research and travel he has invested in. We wish him well.

Many other, more modest products show what is possible. 'Why has it taken 90 years for our family to visit this land so far away?' Robin and Del Hart asked in their 44-page booklet *Visit to the Battlefields*. Robin and Del followed in the footsteps of Robin's uncle Morris, who was killed at Ypres on 3 October 1917. They were pilgrims, tourists and researchers. At Ieper they followed the route Morris's battalion, the 42nd, took from its bivouac west of Ypres towards the Menin Road. Morris was killed in the battle of Broodseinde, but his body was never recovered. Robin and Del remembered him at the Menin Gate Memorial, Ieper, the site of the moving nightly ceremony of remembrance. Their booklet provides a permanent record for their family, and others, in memory of one casualty of the Great War. They did it, and so can you.

Combat stress: The emotional reaction

Returning from a European research trip can only make you more sophisticated and worldly wise, you might think. Returning home after spending time in a Third or Fourth World country, especially for a prolonged period, can result in a degree of culture shock.

Visiting historical battlefields can be a stressful experience. Every battle brings loss, of course, and wounds, mental and physical, for many survivors. If you visit these sites in company with someone who knew or was close to a casualty, the experience can be moving in the extreme. In 1997 I travelled around Borneo, visiting battlefields and the route of the Sandakan death march in company with both veterans and—most memorably—the daughter of a prisoner of war who never knew her father. That was a most upsetting but also memorable and worthwhile reminder that war involves real people, and that its effects last for decades.

Don't think that because your interest is in the detail of, say 'the changing tactics of the Australian infantry platoon 1916–18', you'll be immune from the emotional consequences of visiting a war cemetery or of standing on a spot where death occurred. It may hit you suddenly or hit you in the places you expect, but it may well disorient or even disable you; be prepared for unforeseen consequences.

These consequences may not always be unpleasant. Margaret Hadfield, an artist from Queanbeyan, New South Wales, first visited Gallipoli in 2004 with a group of friends. Uninterested in Gallipoli before she arrived, the place soon captivated her. She has since painted many aspects of Gallipoli, and won the inaugural Gallipoli Art Prize in 2006. Margaret intertwines images of the landscape

Margaret Hadfield with her painting *Rhododendron Ridge*, one of her *Gallipoli Series* paintings. A visit to Gallipoli in 2004 transformed Margaret's artistic life. (Peter Stanley)

with mythic elements to explore how the Gallipoli of 1915 is present when we visit today. A visit to Gallipoli has utterly changed the direction and nature of her art. The same thing could happen to you by visiting any powerful site of memory: be warned.

The magnitude of the emotional reaction to a battlefield can be seen even among hard-headed military historians. On his last evening at Anzac in 1981, Peter Pedersen had the place pretty much to himself. After a hard day walking in the footsteps of Monash, he sat on the grass near North Beach in the quiet dusk. Then he felt it 'shattered by the shouts of men climbing Ari Burnu, the rattle of machine-guns and rifles on Baby 700, the incessant explosion of bombs at Quinn's'. Peter has returned again and again to the battlefields of the world, often Australian ones. He has devoted a second career, as a writer of military history, to understanding and explaining what happened on the battlefield.

Adequately equipped—intellectually, physically and emotionally—you could too.

Glossary

Military history is full of jargon; some necessary and useful, some not. This list helps to explain abbreviations and terms often found in contemporary documents and in memoirs. Words marked with an asterisk are themselves defined elsewhere in the Glossary. Military history often demands the use of terms precisely. For example, tyros often confuse 'strategy' and 'tactics', or use 'attack', 'assault' and 'offensive' as if they are interchangeable. They may also mistakenly assume that military history demands copious use of jargon and abbreviations. Often the best military history is that which avoids the use of jargon altogether. Writing good military history depends upon reading good military history.

Anzac 'Australian and New Zealand Army Corps'; applied only as an acronym to military formations in 1915, 1916–17 and 1941; otherwise 'Anzac' as a word

Approach march the movement of troops to the positions from which they attacked

Armoured denoting a unit* equipped with tanks

Army a grouping of two or more corps*

Artillery the arm of the Army equipped with field or anti-tank guns, firing at targets at a distance

Assault an intense attack against a specific objective

Attack a tactical operation intended to gain a goal or advantage in the face of the enemy

Barrage closely controlled and targeted artillery fire ('a wall of shell-fire', Bean writes), directed at specific places and times. Later in the Great War the 'creeping barrage' was devised, protecting attacking infantry as they advanced. Machine-guns fired barrages as well

Battalion the standard organisation of infantry; nominally about 750 strong but often weaker due to casualties*

Battery a sub-unit* of field, anti-tank or other guns, usually numbering four to six

Bay a portion of a trench between traverses*

Bombardment not really a technical term—more a description of prolonged or intense shelling

Bombstop a barrier, usually of sandbags, blocking a trench

Brigade before 1918 a formation* comprising four battalions*; after 1918 three, when the idea of the 'brigade group' (a brigade plus its various supporting units) became current. In the Great War a 'field artillery brigade', comprising three batteries, was the standard artillery unit

Casualties any losses due to deaths, wounds*, illness or capture; not just dead

Company the largest sub-unit of an infantry battalion*, nominally 100–200 strong; also engineer and other semi-autonomous units* (e.g. engineers were organised in 'field companies')

Corps a formation comprising two or more divisions; in 1918 the Australian Corps was unusual in comprising the five Australian infantry divisions

Dead ground ground that, although within range, cannot be seen or fired at directly

Division a formation in the British/Australian armies comprising three brigades*

Enfilade firing along a defended line; also 'flanking fire'

FDL Forward Defended Localities, a Second World War term

Fire Base also 'Fire Support Base'; a Viet Nam era term meaning a fortified post equipped with artillery* able to fire in support of infantry operating in the neighbourhood

Flanks the sides of a position, a unit*, an advance, etc. 'Flanking fire' comes from the flank; a flank 'in the air' is one unprotected by friendly troops

FOO Forward Observation Officers, 'spotting' targets for batteries; generically 'artillery observers'

Formation the conventional term for a grouping of units—brigade, division, corps, etc.

Foxhole the American counterpart of a rifle pit*

Jumping-off trench a Great War term for the foremost trench from which attacks were launched

Light Horse the Australian term for mounted infantry units which moved mounted but usually fought on foot

Machine-guns rapid-fire guns operated by infantry. They came in several varieties: in the Great War Lewis (light) and Vickers (heavy); in Second World War Bren (light) and Vickers (heavy)

Motorised in Second World War applied to infantry units or formations equipped with their own mechanical transport

Offensive a series of major attacks across a front, intended to gain a strategic advantage

Order of battle a list of units arranged by their place in the organisation of a force (e.g. division-by-division, in order of battalions)

Pillbox a concrete fighting post, ranging in size from small ones holding a handful of men to large posts holding several platoons

Platoon a sub-unit of about 30 infantrymen, comprising several sections*

Redoubt a defensive entrenchment able to be defended all-round; also a 'strongpoint'

Re-entrant a concave line; the reverse of 'salient'; also a valley (a term in vogue in the Great War)

Regiment the standard Light Horse* or armoured* unit; the mounted counterpart of the battalion*. In the Second World War a field regiment comprised the standard artillery unit. In German, French and American usage, the equivalent of a brigade

Retreat a movement to the rear under enemy pressure

Rifle pit a small hole dug and protected by two or three men

Salient a projection in a trench line

Sangar a small fortified post built of loose stones

Sap a trench dug outwards from a fire-trench (*see* 'trench')

Section the smallest infantry sub-unit, usually led by a corporal; nominally ten strong

Squadron in the Light Horse, the component sub-unit of a mounted regiment* (e.g. 'C' Squadron, 7th Light Horse); in the air force, the standard operational unit (e.g. 452 Squadron, RAAF)

Strategy the conduct of military operations to gain broad goals. National or inter-allied strategy is often called 'grand strategy'

Sub-unit a company*, platoon*, squadron* or battery* forming part of a unit

Tactics the conduct of military operations in the face of the enemy, on the battlefield; at the lowest level, 'minor tactics'.

Traverse a 'zig-zag' in a trench, protecting the occupants of bays* from fire or blast

Trench a linear excavation; may be a fire or a communication trench; the former with fire-steps to enable troops to defend it; the latter wider to allow movement. Both may have traverses* to protect men against fire or shelling

Unit a military organisation of battalion or regimental size. Several such units combine to make the formation of a brigade*, or in later usage, a task force

Withdrawal a movement to the rear made on a commander's own initiative

Wounded non-fatal casualties intentionally inflicted by an enemy: injuries are incurred accidentally—the modern media seems oblivious to the distinction

Zero-hour the time at which an attack opened; time before Zero-hour is called 'minus' and time after 'plus'; later 'D-Day' used the same principle

Bibliography

Roger Absolom, '"Another crack at Jerry"? Australian prisoners of war in Italy 1941–45', *Journal of the Australian War Memorial*, No. 14, 1989

Patsy Adam Smith, *The Anzacs*, Melbourne, 1978

Eric Andrews and B.G. Jordan, 'Second Bullecourt revisited: The Australians in France, 3 May 1917', *Journal of the Australian War Memorial*, no. 15, October 1989

Clive Baker, *Walking the Kokoda Trail: Do-it-Yourself Trekking Guide*, Sydney, 1994

Charles Bean, *The Official History of Australia in the War of 1914–18*, Vols I–VI, 1921–42

——*Gallipoli Mission*, Sydney, [1948] 1988

Joan Beaumont, *Gull Force: Survival and Leadership in Captivity 1941–1945*, Sydney, 1988

Geoff Blackburn, *Conquest and Settlement: The 21st Regiment of Foot (Royal North British Fusiliers) in Western Australia 1833–40,* Carlisle, 1999

Allan Box, *Footsteps of the Diggers: A Travel Guide to the Australian Battlefields of the Somme*, Leongatha, Vic., 1996

Phil Bradley, *On Shaggy Ridge*, Melbourne, 2006

——'The Kokoda Trail', *After the Battle*, no. 137, 2007

——*The Battle for Wau*, Melbourne, 2008

Bob Breen, *The Battle of Maryang San*, Sydney, 1994

Richard Brown, 'Defenders of Newcastle: The tank traps of Belmont', *Wartime*, no. 5, 1999

Peter Brune, *A Bastard of a Place: The Australians in Papua*, Sydney, 2003

Peter Burness, 'Retracing the Malayan campaign', *Journal of the Australian War Memorial*, no. 7, October 1985

——*The Nek: The Tragic Charge of the Light Horse at Gallipoli*, Sydney, 1996

——'The last shots: The capture of Montbrehain, 1918', *Wartime*, no. 4, 1998

——'Then and now: A camera on the Western Front', *Wartime*, no. 8, 1999

——'A chateau in France', *Wartime*, no. 27, 2004

——*Fromelles and the Somme 1916*, Canberra, 2006
——'Australia's worst experience in war', *Wartime*, no. 39, 2007
——and Peter Stanley, *A Guide to the Battlefields and Memorials of the Boer War*, Canberra, 1999
Les Carlyon, *Gallipoli*, Melbourne, 2001
——*The Great War*, Sydney, 2006
Stephen Chambers, *Gully Ravine*, Barnsley, Yorkshire, 2003
Bill Chapman and Richard Taylor, *The Pocket Medical Travel Guide*, Perth, 1995
Peter Charlton, *Pozières 1916: Australians on the Somme*, Sydney, 1986
Chris Clark *see* Chris Coulthard-Clark
Manning Clark, *A Historian's Apprenticeship*, Melbourne, 1992
Brian Cleaver and Peter Phillips, 'Reconciliation at last', *Wartime*, no. 28, 2004
John Coates, *An Atlas of Australia's Wars*, Melbourne, 2006
Anne-Marie Condé, 'In search of the Cowra breakout', *Wartime*, no. 27, 2004
John Connor, *The Australian Frontier Wars, 1788–1838*, Sydney, 2002
Rose Coombs, *Before Endeavours Fade: A Guide to the Battlefields of the First World War*, London, 1976
Robin Corfield, *Don't Forget Me, Cobber: The Battle of Fromelles 19/20 July 1916: An enquiry*, Melbourne, 2000
Chris Coulthard-Clark, *The Encyclopaedia of Australia's Battles*, Sydney, 2001
Joe Crumlin, 'In the steps of the 4th Brigade', *Journal of the Australian War Memorial*, no. 16, April 1990
Charles Darby, *Pacific Aircraft Wrecks and Where to Find Them*, Melbourne, 1979
Peter Dennis and Jeffrey Grey, *Emergency and Confrontation: Australian Military Operations in Malaya and Borneo 1950–1966*, Canberra, 1996
David Dexter, *The New Guinea Offensives*, Canberra, 1961
Val Dickinson, 'The old battlefields—now', *Listening Post*, vol. 31, no. 8, December 1952
——'Battlefields of France, today', *Reveille*, vol. 26, no. 6, 1 February 1953
——'Battlefields of France, today', *Reveille*, vol. 26, no. 7, 1 March 1953
A.H. Edmonds, 'The Coral Sea battlefields', *Reveille*, vol. 31, no. 8, March 1958
Brian Farrell, *The Defence and Fall of Singapore 1940–1942*, Stroud, 2005
Andrew Faulkner, *Arthur Blackburn, VC: An Australian Hero, His Men, and Their Two World Wars*, Adelaide, 2008
Sebastian Faulks, *Birdsong*, London, 1993
Peter Firkins, *The Australians in Nine Wars: Waikato to Long Tan*, Sydney, 1982
Roger Freeman, *Bases of Bomber Command: Then and Now*, London, 2001
Bill Gammage, *The Broken Years: Australian Soldiers in the Great War*, Canberra, 1974
Michael Glover, *Battlefields of Northern France and the Low Countries*, London, 1987
Mike Goodwin, *Lesson of a Lifetime: An Anzac Day Pilgrimage: Mackay North State High School Anzac 2002 Commemorative Tour*, Mackay, Qld, 2002
Al Grassby and Marji Hill, *Six Australian Battlefields*, Sydney, 1988
Robert Graves, *Goodbye to All That*, London, 1929
J. Glenn Gray, *The Warriors: Reflections on Men in Battle*, New York, 1970
Neville Green, *Broken Spears: Aborigines and Europeans in the Southwest of Australia*, Perth, 1984
Jeff Grey, *A Military History of Australia*, Melbourne, 2008

Robert Hall, *Combat Battalion: The Eighth Battalion in Vietnam*, Sydney, 2000
David Hallett, 'Birth of the digger?', *Wartime*, no. 15, 2001
Bob Halstead and Tim Rock, *Diving and Snorkelling Papua New Guinea*, Melbourne, 1999
Peter Harries, 'Frontier and Section: An Analysis of... the so-called battle of Pinjarra', BA (Hons) thesis, Curtin University of Technology, ACT, 1998
Robin and Del Hart, *Visit to the Battlefields 6th–9th May 2007*, privately published, 2007
Edward Hasbrouck, *The Practical Nomad: How to Travel Around the World*, Emeryville, CA, 2000
——*The Practical Nomad: Guide to the Online Travel Marketplace*, Emeryville, CA, 2001
Pete Hawkins, *Map and Compass: The Art of Navigation*, Milnthorpe, Cumbria, 2003
Les Hetherington, 'The Kangaroos March: Wagga Wagga to Sydney, December 1915–January 1916', *Journal of the Australian War Memorial*, no. 26, April 1995
Alec Hill, *Chauvel of the Light Horse*, Melbourne, 1978
David Holdsworth, *Papua New Guinea Battlefields*, Adelaide, 1974
Richard Holmes, *Army Battlefield Guide: Belgium and Northern France*, London, 1995
——*Riding the Retreat: Mons to the Marne 1914 Revisited*, London, 1996
——*Complete War Walks from Hastings to Normandy*, London, 2003
David Horner, *General Vasey's War*, Melbourne, 1992
James Hurst, 'Raid on Gaba Tepe', *Wartime*, no. 16, 2001
——*Game to the Last: The 11th Australian Infantry Battalion at Gallipoli*, Melbourne, 2005
Garrie Hutchinson, *Pilgrimage: A Traveller's Guide to Australia's Battlefields*, Melbourne, 2006
——*Gallipoli: The Pilgrimage Guide*, Melbourne, 2007
K.S. Inglis, *The Rehearsal: Australians at War in the Sudan, 1885*, Adelaide, 1985
Bill James, *Field Guide to the Kokoda Track: An Historical Guide to the Lost Battlefields*, Sydney, 2006
Mark Johnston, 'The Blockhouse, El Alamein', *Wartime*, no. 8, 1999
——'In the steps of Monash', *Wartime*, no. 18, 2002
——*That Magnificent 9th: An Illustrated History of the 9th Australian Division 1940–46*, Sydney, 2002
——*The Silent 7th: An Illustrated History of the 7th Australian Division 1940–46*, Sydney, 2005
——and Carlos Chagos, *The Australian Army in World War II*, Oxford, 2007
——and Peter Stanley, *Alamein: The Australian Story*, Melbourne, 2002
Ian Jones, *The Australian Light Horse*, Sydney, 1987
Nigel Jones, *The War Walk: A Journey Along the Western Front*, London, 1983
John Keegan, *The Face of Battle*, London, 1976
Jeff Kildea, 'Easter Rising', *Wartime*, no. 36, 2006
John Laffin, *Return to Glory*, Sydney, 1956
——*Middle East Journey*, Sydney, 1958
——*Guide to Australian Battlefields of the Western Front 1916–1918*, Sydney, 1992

——*Digging Up the Diggers' War: Australian Battlefield Archaeology*, Sydney, 1993
——*A Kind of Immortality: An Autobiography*, Sydney, 2000
Peter Leggat and John Goldsmid, *Primer of Travel Medicine*, Townsville, Qld, 2002
John Lennon and Malcolm Foley, *Dark Tourism: The Attraction of Death and Disaster*, London, 2000
David Lloyd, *Battlefield Tourism: Pilgrimage and the Commemoration of the Great War in Britain, Australia and Canada, 1919–1939*, Oxford, 1998
Cecil Lock, *The Fighting 10th*, Adelaide, 1936
Greg Lockhart, *The Minefield: An Australian Tragedy in Vietnam*, Sydney, 2007
Peter Londey, 'Observing in South Lebanon', *Wartime*, no. 3, 1998
——*Other People's Wars: A History of Australian Peacekeeping*, Sydney, 2004
——'Bulair: The attack that didn't happen', *Wartime*, no. 34, 2006
——'Fifty years watch', *Wartime*, no. 35, 2006
Gavin Long, *Greece, Crete and Syria*, Canberra, 1953
James McAllester and Syd Tregellis-Smith, *Largely a Gamble: Australians in Syria June–July 1941*, Sydney, 1995
Ian McGibbon, *Gallipoli: A Guide to New Zealand Battlefields and Memorials*, Auckland, 2004
Gary McKay, *In Good Company: One Man's War in Viet Nam*, Sydney, 1987
——*Australia's Battlefields in Viet Nam: A Traveller's Guide*, Sydney, 2003
——*Going Back: Australian Veterans Return to Viet Nam*, Sydney, 2008
Michael McKernan, *The Australian People and the Great War*, Sydney, 1984
——*The Strength of a Nation: Six Years of Australians Fighting for the Nation and Defending the Homefront in WWII*, Sydney, 2006
Peter McKie, *Active First Aid*, Canberra, 2005
Mat McLachlan, *Walking with the Anzacs: A Guide to Australian Battlefields on the Western Front*, Sydney, 2007
Ross McMullin, *Pompey Elliott*, Melbourne, 2002
Ian McNeill, *The Team: Australian Army Advisers in Vietnam, 1962–1972*, Canberra, 1984
Martin and Mary Middlebrook, *The Somme Battlefields: A Comprehensive Guide from Crecy to the Two World Wars*, London, 1991
Roger Milliss, *Waterloo Creek: The Australia Day Massacre of 1838, George Gipps and the British Conquest of New South Wales*, Sydney, 1994
Michael Molkentin, 'The Westhoek five', *Wartime*, no. 40, 2007
Hank Nelson, 'Travelling in memories: Australian prisoners of the Japanese, forty years after the fall of Singapore', *Journal of the Australian War Memorial*, no. 3, October 1983
Victor Neuberg, *A Guide to the Western Front: A Companion for Travellers*, London, 1988
John Newberry, 'Age before beauty', *Great Walks*, December–January 2008
Michael O'Brien, *Conscripts and Regulars with the Seventh Battalion in Vietnam*, Sydney 1995
Office of Australian War Graves, *Annual Reports*, Canberra, 1982–95
Peter Oldham, *The Hindenburg Line*, London, 1997
Robert O'Neill, *Australia in the Korean War 1950–53*, Vol. 2: *Combat Operations*, Canberra, 1985
J.A.B. Palmer, *The Mutiny Outbreak at Meerut in 1857*, Cambridge, 1966

James Payne, 'A Digger returns to Egypt and Palestine', *Mufti*, 1 October 1938
Howard Pearce and Bob Alford, *A Wartime Journey: Stuart Highway Heritage Guide*, Darwin, 2006
Peter Pedersen, 'The ghosts of Anzac', *Journal of the Australian War Memorial*, no. 2, April 1983
——*Monash as Military Commander*, Melbourne, 1985
——*Hamel*, Barnsley, Yorkshire, 2003
——*Villers-Bretonneux*, Barnsley, Yorkshire, 2004
——*The Anzacs: Gallipoli to the Western Front*, Melbourne, 2007
Yvon Pérusse, *Bushwalking in Papua New Guinea*, Melbourne, 1993
Garth Pratten, 'In the rats' footsteps', *Wartime*, no. 15, 2001
Nigel Prickett, *Landscapes of Conflict: A Field Guide to the New Zealand Wars*, Auckland, 2002
Julia Reece, 'Journey of Remembrance: An account of Mount Barker High School's Remembrance 2001 Project', Adelaide, 2002
Richard Reid, 'Up north: The Australia Remembers veterans' pilgrimage to Papua New Guinea, 29 June to 13 July 1995', *Journal of the Australian War Memorial*, no. 27, October 1995
——'The virtual Anzac walk', *Wartime*, no. 30, 2005
John Richardson, *A History of Australian Travel and Tourism*, Melbourne, 1999
Peter S. Sadler, *The Paladin: A Life of Major General Sir John Gellibrand*, Melbourne, 2000
Bruce Scates, *Return to Gallipoli: Walking the Battlefields of the Great War*, Melbourne, 2005
——'Soldiers' journeys: Returning to the battlefields of the Great War', *Journal of the Australian War Memorial*, no. 40, February 2007, www.awm.gov.au/journal/j40
Dirk Schroeder, *Staying Healthy in Asia, Africa and Latin America*, 5th edn, Emeryville, CA, 2000
Lynette Silver, *The Bridge at Parit Sulong: An Investigation of Mass Murder*, Sydney, 2004
John Siseman and John Brownlie, *Bushwalking and Touring in the Bogong High Plains Alpine National Park*, Sydney, 1994
Tony Spagnoli and Ted Smith, *Celtic Wood: The Anatomy of a Raid*, Barnsley, Yorkshire, 1998
Charles Spencer, *Blenheim: Battle for Europe*, London, 2004
Peter Stanley (ed.), *But Little Glory: The New South Wales Contingent to the Sudan, 1885*, Canberra, 1985
——*The Remote Garrison: The British Army in Australia 1788–1870*, Sydney, 1986
——'Sniffing the ground: Australians and Borneo—1945, 1994', *Journal of the Australian War Memorial*, no. 25, October 1994
——*Tarakan: An Australian Tragedy*, Sydney, 1997
——*White Mutiny: British Military Culture in India 1825–75*, London, 1998
——'Being dead, yet speaketh: Berhampore, a Bengal cantonment', *Soldiers of the Queen*, Spring 1999
——'Getting our knees brown: exploring the El Alamein battlefield', *Wartime*, no. 8, 1999
——'A good dishing on 42nd Street', *Wartime*, no. 15, 2001

——'Our little Imbros cottage', *Wartime*, no. 21, 2003
——'Battlefield archaeology: Illustration and interpretation from the Australian experience', National Army Museum 'Battlefield Archaeology' conference, 24 July 2004
——'Turkish delight: Gallipoli by scooter', *Two Wheels Scooter Magazine*, 2005
——*Quinn's Post, Anzac, Gallipoli*, Sydney, 2005
——'Death on the last day', *Wartime*, no. 35, 2006
——*Invading Australia: Japan and the Battle for Australia, 1942*, Melbourne, 2008
Nigel Steel, *The Battlefields of Gallipoli: Then and Now*, London, 1990
——'Getting the measure of Kapyong', *Wartime*, no. 39, 2007
Alan Stewart, *Persian Expedition: The Australians in Dunsterforce, 1918*, Sydney, 2006
Andrew Stone, *A Walk in their Footsteps: A Kokoda Trail Experience*, Sydney, 1997
Phil Taylor and Pam Cupper, *Gallipoli: A Battlefield Guide*, Sydney, 1989
Glenn Wahlert, *Exploring Gallipoli: An Australian Army Battlefield Guide*, Canberra, 2008
Jonathan Walker, *The Blood Tub: General Gough and the Battle of Bullecourt 1917*, Staplehurst, Kent, 2000
Mark Whitmore, 'A Waikato tour: Australia and the New Zealand wars, 1863–64', *Wartime*, no. 7, 1999
Craig Wilcox, 'The "prettiest" bit of fighting', *Wartime*, no. 13, 2001
——*Australia's Boer War: The War in South Africa 1899–1902*, Melbourne, 2002
——'A different type of digger', *Wartime*, no. 23, 2003
Jeff Wilks and others, *Tourism in Turbulent Times: Towards Safe Experiences for Visitors*, Amsterdam, 2006
Peter Williams, *The Battle of Anzac Ridge: 25 April 1915*, Sydney, 2006
Shane Winser (ed.), *Royal Geographical Society Expedition Handbook*, London, 2004
Tony Wright, *Turn Right at Istanbul: A Walk on the Gallipoli Peninsula*, Sydney, 2003
Yap Siang Yong and others, *Fortress Singapore: The Battlefield Guide*, Singapore, 1992
R.A. Yates, *The Bulldog–Wau Road: A Bushwalking Guide,* Howtham, Vic., 1985

Index

Entries in italics refer to photo or illustration captions